P9-ASG-198

792.09418
H91a

126231

DATE DUE

WITHDRAWN
L. R. COLLEGE LIBRARY

THE ABBEY
IRELAND'S NATIONAL THEATRE
1904–1978

HUGH HUNT

THE ABBEY
Ireland's National Theatre
1904-1978

ERRATUM
The publishers regret the inconsistency in
dates between those shown on the title page
and jacket.
The correct title is

THE ABBEY
IRELAND'S NATIONAL THEATRE
1904–1979

CARL A. RUDISILL LIBRARY
LENOIR RHYNE COLLEGE

Columbia University Press
New York   1979

Copyright © 1979 Hugh Hunt
All rights reserved
Printed in Great Britain

Library of Congress Catalog Card Number: 79-53497
ISBN 0-231-04906-4

ACKNOWLEDGMENTS

Author and publishers wish to express their thanks for the lines from 'At the Abbey Theatre' reprinted with permission of Macmillan Publishing Co. Inc., from *Collected Poems* of William Butler Yeats. Copyright 1912 by Macmillan Publishing Co. Inc., renewed 1940 by Bertha Georgie Yeats.

792. 09418
H91a

126231
Sept, 1983

Contents

When we are high and airy hundreds say
That if we hold that flight they'll leave the place,
While those same hundreds mock another day
Because we have made our art of common things . . .
                              W. B. Yeats, 'At the Abbey Theatre'

List of Illustrations

Notes on the Illustrations

1 – 14: William Butler Yeats (1865–1939), Lady Gregory (1852–1932) and Edward Martyn (1859–1923), later joined by George Moore (1852–1933), founded the Irish Literary Theatre in 1898. This was the precursor of the National Theatre Society of which Yeats, Lady Gregory, and J. M. Synge (1871–1909) were the first Directors, while to the Fay brothers, William George Fay (1872–1937) and Francis John Fay (1870–1941), belongs the credit for forming the first company of Irish players in 1902. The plays were presented in various halls until they acquired, through the generosity of Miss Horniman, a permanent home in the Abbey Theatre in 1904.

1. Photo taken in the thirties. *(G. A. Duncan Collection)*
2. Bust by Jacob Epstein. *(Municipal Gallery of Modern Art, Dublin, Photograph Rex Roberts Studios)*
3. Portrait by Norman McLachlann. *(National Gallery, Dublin)*
4. Portrait by J. B. Yeats *(National Gallery, Dublin)*
5 and 6. Portraits by J. B. Yeats. *(Courtesy of the Abey Theatre)*
7. Drawing by J. B. Yeats. *(Courtesy of the Abbey Theatre, photograph Rex Roberts Studios)*
8. Drawing by Sarah Purser. *(Courtesy of Anne Yeats)*
9. First production of Cathleen Ni Houlihan, St Teresa's Hall, 1902. L to R, W. G. Fay, Maire T. Quinn, Dudley Digges, Maud Gonne. *(The Mander and Mitchenson Collection)*
10. First production of *The Hour Glass*, Molesworth Hall. *(The Mander and Mitchenson Collection)*

11. 'I can afford a very little theatre and it must be simple,' Miss Horniman wrote to Yeats in April 1904. *(G. A. Duncan Collection)*
12. Brid Lynch and M. J. Dolan seated by the fire; F. J. McCormick standing centre; Eileen Crowe seated R of couch. *(G. A. Duncan Collection)*
13. Costume design for Cuchulain. *(Courtesy of Anne Yeats)*
14. Hildo Krop designed masks for an Amsterdam production of Yeats's play, *The Only Jealousy of Emer* in 1922. These were lent to Yeats for the 1929 production of *Fighting the Waves,* choreographed by Ninette de Valois. *(Stedelijk Museum, Amsterdam)*

15 – 19: In the twenties the Abbey gained fresh lustre from the plays of Sean O'Casey (1880–1964) whose trilogy of Dublin plays was matched by a company of players that might have been hand-picked to perform them.

15. Barry Fitzgerald (1886–1961), the Abbey's greatest comedian. *(Courtesy of the Abbey Theatre)*
16. F. J. McCormick (1884–1947), the most versatile of all Abbey actors. *(Courtesy of the Abbey Theatre)*
17. Maureen Delaney (d. 1961), a great personality actress. *(Courtesy of the Abbey Theatre)*
18. Sarah Allgood (1883–1950), the Abbey's greatest tragedienne; like Barry Fitzgerald she eventually emigrated to America. *(Courtesy of the Abbey Theatre)*
19. Photo taken at the dress rehearsal, 7 February 1926, inscribed by Sean O'Casey, 'Be clever, Maid, and let who will be good.' *(G. A. Duncan Collection)*

20 – 4: The thirties saw an infusion of new blood into the administration of the theatre. Links with the past were maintained through Lennox Robinson whose first play was produced at the Abbey in 1908. From then on until his death he was associated with the theatre as playwright, manager and director.

20. Lennox Robinson (1880–1958). *(G. A. Duncan Collection)*

21. Frank Dermody (1910–78). He was associated with the theatre as director of the school of acting and director of plays from 1939 to 1971. *(Courtesy of the Abbey Theatre)*

22. Seaghan Barlow joined the Fays in 1904 and remained with the theatre until his death in 1970. *(Courtesy of the Abbey Theatre)*

23. Hugh Hunt, director of plays 1934–8, artistic director 1969–71. *(Courtesy of the Abbey Theatre)*

24. Tanya Moseiwitsch, resident designer 1934–9. *(Courtesy of the Abbey Theatre)*

25 – 41: In 1951 the Abbey was destroyed by fire. For fifteen years the company performed at the Queen's Theatre before entering its present home. The new Abbey is built on the same site as the old and consists of two theatres, the Abbey itself and the highly adaptable Peacock Theatre.

25. The burning of the Abbey, Wednesday, 18 July 1951. A sad remnant salvaged from the fire was the frame of the pram used in Act 2 of *The Plough and the Stars*. *(G. A. Duncan Collection)*

26. Ria Mooney (1903–71), joined the theatre in 1924 as an actress; director of plays 1948–63. *(G. A. Duncan Collection)*

27. The Queen's Theatre, traditional home of melodrama, demolished 1968. *(Courtesy of the Abbey Theatre)*

28. Tomás Mac Anna, designer and director of plays in Irish and English, including pantomimes, 1947–66; artistic adviser 1966–8, artistic director 1973–8. *(Courtesy of the Abbey Theatre)*

29. Ernest Blythe (1889–1975), managing director 1946–72. 'Once he had made a decision he allowed no public outcry to change his mind.' *(G. A. Duncan Collection)*

30. President de Valera laid the foundation stone of the new theatre in 1963 and officially declared the theatre open on 18 July 1966. *(G. A. Duncan Collection)*

31. In 1965 twenty-five new shareholders were appointed. *(Cartoon by G. Kelly,* Dublin Opinion, *photograph Rod Tuach)*

32 and 33. The new Abbey and Peacock theatres were designed by Michael Scott and Partners. The distinguished French architect, Pierre Sonrel acted as consultant. *(John Donat Photography, London)*

34. L to R, John Richardson, Desmond Perry, Frank Grimes (the young Behan), Philip O'Flynn. *(Courtesy of the Abbey Theatre)*

35. The production was designed by Alan Barlow and visited Helsinki and Brussels in May 1973. *(Courtesy of the Abbey Theatre)*

36. The revue, *A State of Chassis,* raised strong objections from visitors from the North of Ireland. *(Irish Times)*

37. Tom Kilroy's play was presented at the Royal Court Theatre, London after a successful run at the Abbey in 1977. *(Courtesy of the Abbey Theatre, photograph Fergus Bourke)*

38. Bronwen Casson, a grand-daughter of Dame Sybil Thorndyke and Sir Lewis Casson joined the Abbey as a resident designer in 1970. *(Courtesy of the Abbey Theatre, photograph Charlie Collins)*

39. After a distinguished career as a designer for Irish TV and for theatres in Britain, Wendy Shea joined the Abbey as a resident designer in 1975. *(Courtesy of the Abbey Theatre, photograph Charlie Collins)*

40. The Golden Jubilee production of O'Casey's play visited New York, Boston, Philadelphia and Washington as the Abbey's contribution to the American Bicentennial Celebrations. *(Courtesy of the Abbey Theatre, photograph Fergus Bourke)*

41. Chekhov's play was directed by V. B. Monakhov of the Maly Theatre, Moscow, and designed by Bronwen Casson. *(Courtesy of the Abbey Theatre, photograph Fergus Bourke)*

Preface

When I was asked by the Directors of the National Theatre Society to write an up-to-date history of the Abbey Theatre to celebrate its seventy-fifth anniversary, it was rightly decided that this should not be an official publication. At the same time I was granted the unique privilege of access to the minute books and other records of the Society at present retained in the theatre's archives, as well as first call on the material recently handed over to the safe keeping of the National Library of Ireland. I wish to acknowledge the help given to me by the staff of both institutions.

In particular I thank Micheál Ó hAodha, Chairman of the Directors of the National Theatre, and Tomás Mac Anna for the loan of books and for reading and commenting on my manuscript, Deirdre McQuillan for researching and advising on illustrations, Mairin MacCormac for help in compiling the list of plays, Sally Sweeney, Martin Fahy and Tadhg Crowley for their ever willing assistance, while not least I am indebted to the forbearance of Susan Horsey, Elizabeth Grzelinska in typing the manuscript and, of course, my wife.

For what is included in this book, and for what is omitted, I take full responsibility. Inevitably limitation of space has prevented me from doing justice to many who have contributed to the long and eventful history of the Abbey; I can only seek to make amends by dedicating it to

All who serve, and have served,
Ireland's National Theatre

Hugh Hunt
January 1979

Prologue

What is an Irishman?

> When I say I am an Irishman I mean that I was born in Ireland, and that my native language is the English of Swift and not the unspeakable jargon of the mid-XIX century London newspapers . . . I am a genuine typical Irishman of the Danish, Norman, Cromwellian, and (of course) Scotch invasions. I am violently and arrogantly Protestant by family tradition; but let no English government therefore count on my allegiance; I am English enough to be an inveterate Republican and Home Ruler. It is true that one of my ancestors was an Orangeman; but then his sister was an abbess; and his uncle, I am proud to say, was hanged as a rebel.[1]

A national drama expresses through the personal vision of the playwright the consciousness of a nation. No single ethos pervades this consciousness. The many cultures that compose and divide a nation — wealth, class, religion, the accidents of birth and brains — are bound together by a common historical process; a process that is constantly evolving. The manifold expressions of a nation's consciousness are not to be equated with the nationalist rantings of its political hustings, still less with provincialism. The former idealises, selecting half truths for a purely transitory purpose. The latter cultivates insularity at the expense of the universal.

Aeschylus, Shakespeare, Molière, Goethe, Ibsen, Chekhov and Lorca not only enlarged the consciousness of their nations, but also the consciousness of mankind. If a nation is a house of many mansions, so too is the world we live in.

Look here, comrade, there's no such thing as an Irishman,
or a German or a Turk; we're all only human bein's. Scientifically speakin', it's all a question of the accidental gather-
in' together of mollycewels and atoms . . . that, accordin'
to the way they're mixed, make a flower, a fish, a star
that you see shinin' in the sky, or a man with a big brain
like me, or a man with a little brain like you.[2]

It is not only 'mollycewels and atoms', nor only the accidents
of birth and religion, that create an Irishman, but the colours
of his countryside, the life of his cities, the smell of a turf
fire, the talk in the pubs, the screech of a rabbit in the furze,
the roar of the sea, together with a myriad of memories and
symbols, conscious and subconscious, public and private.

The expatriates

'This race and this country and this life produced me', wrote
James Joyce in *A Portrait of the Artist as a Young Man*. Like
Samuel Beckett, Joyce belonged to those expatriate writers
who, without sacrificing their Irishness, have merged their
national heritage with the literary heritage of Europe; not
only enriching and enlarging that heritage but paradoxically,
as Kevin Sullivan has pointed out, 'to the extent that their
work has become European it has become more distinctively
Irish'.[3] It is within a European context that the Irish genius
can escape from provincialism on the one hand, and the per-
vasive influence of its powerful neighbour on the other. It
was within a European context that the birth of the Irish
national theatre took place. Yeats, Martyn, Moore, Synge,
W. G. Fay and his brother, Frank, were all, in their different
and often opposing ways, part of the literary and dramatic
movements that swept through Europe in the second half of
the nineteenth century and by a strange paradox — for paradox lies at the heart of Irish affairs — they restored to the
English theatre, on which they had turned their backs, a
sense of the high purpose of theatrical art which years of
material interest mixed with Puritan distrust had robbed of
its poetry and power.

For centuries Ireland had exported its playwrights and
actors, as in earlier centuries it exported its saints and schol-

ars, but it was not until the nation had regained its cultural and political consciousness that Irish theatre took its place among the theatres of the world. Farquhar, Congreve, Sheridan, Goldsmith and Wilde were among those who were drawn by the gravitational pull of London, they brought with them something of the vitality and satiric wit of their native country, but their success depended upon their ability to adopt the idioms and attitudes of an alien society. Shaw, alone, amongst the expatriate writers of the nineteenth century, retained something of his Irish attitude to his adopted country, as he somewhat ostentatiously retained his Dublin accent, but Ireland for Shaw was less of a theme than a target — 'one of the many on which he drew his own bull's-eye and then scored with a palpable hit'.

Adoption of a foreign culture can result in a work of genius. No one can deny the debt that English drama owes to Ireland's expatriate writers; but the expatriate remains at heart an observer of the life of his adopted country. The race consciousness bred in the bones, blood and guts of a Shakespeare can never be his. He can hold the mirror up to nature, but it is not his nature, nor that of his people, that the mirror reflects.

The stage Irishman

> Man alive, don't you know that all this top-o-the morning and broth-of-a boy and more power-to-your-elbow business is got up in England to fool you, like the Albert Hall concerts of Irish music? No Irishman talks like that in Ireland, or ever did, or ever will. But when a thoroughly worthless Irishman comes to England, and finds the whole place full of romantic duffers like you, who will let him loaf and drink and sponge and brag as long as he flatters your sense of moral superiority by playing the fool and degrading himself and his country, he soon learns the antics that take you in. He picks them up in the theatre and music hall.[4]

The earliest form of the stage Irishman was the pugnacious braggart with a mouth full of oaths who appears in Shakespeare's *Henry the Fifth* in the person of Captain Macmorris. During the eighteenth century he reappears as Captain. O'Blunder in Thomas Sheridan's *Captain O'Blunder or The Brave Irishman* (1738), Sir Lucius O'Trigger in Richard Brinsley Sheridan's *The Rivals* (1775), Sir Callaghan O'Bralligan in Charles Macklin's *Love à la Mode* (1760), and Major O'Flaherty in Richard Cumberland's *The West Indian* (1771). The braggart soldier — the 'Miles Gloriosus' of Plautus, Terence and the Italian Comedy — is a familiar figure in world drama. This form of stage Irishman was equally fair game for the eighteenth-century satirists as were the oafish English squires and London fops for the Irish expatriate playwrights. But the gross portrayal of the Irish peasant in the music halls of the nineteenth century was an invidious form of propaganda; not only flattering British audiences with a sense of their superiority to their second-class neighbours, but blinding them to the very real suffering of Ireland's peasants from famine and eviction.

If the clod-hopping Irish peasant was invented for the amusement of British audiences, the patriotic melodrama was invented mainly for the popular audiences that flocked to Dublin's Queen's Theatre during the second half of the nineteenth century. J. W. Whitbread, Fred Cooke, John Baldwin Buckstone and others, whose names and plays are best forgotten, presented a mythical land of blarney and blather, peopled by patriotic heroes of exclusively aristocratic descent, betrayed by villainous informers and mourned by impossibly innocent colleens. Dion Boucicault alone among the hack writers of Irish melodrama can claim a place, if not as a major dramatist, at least as a highly competent one. While his three major Irish melodramas — *The Colleen Bawn; or, The Brides of Garryowen* (1860), *Arrah-Na-Pogue; or, The Wicklow Wedding* (1864) and *The Shaughraun* (1875) — relied on the current taste for spectacle and sentiment, he possessed a genuine Irish humour and a master craftsman's skill in creating excitement and suspense. His plays, if performed with conviction, can still delight a modern audience. The Abbey Theatre's production of *The Shaughraun*, with Cyril Cusack in the part of Conn, drew enthusiastic audiences to the Aldwych Theatre during the 1968 World Theatre

Season. The success of more recent revivals of this play, and of *Arrah-Na-Pogue,* at the Abbey Theatre are further testimonies of his enduring theatrical skill. But the sheer badness of the majority of Irish melodramas resulted in the boorishness of Dublin audiences in the latter years of the century, from which not even Boucicault's plays were exempt. Frank Fay wrote in the *United Irishman* (2 July 1899) of a performance of *The Colleen Bawn* at the Theatre Royal,

> A very large audience assembled in the popular portions of the house to witness the performance, but with regret, I feel myself compelled to say that the majority of them seemed to be of the intensely uncritical and ignorant type, only too common in Dublin ... That they were noisy and ill-behaved is nothing, because one does not expect much from such people; but that they should scream with boorish laughter, when one of the characters in the play spoke a few words of Irish, will scarcely be credited by anyone who was not present, or who, not frequently attending public entertainments in Dublin, is not aware of the terrible lack of artistic feeling and refinement that is rapidly growing up in our midst.

But if the audience behaved badly, so, often, did the actors. Joseph Holloway, later to become the indefatigable diarist of the Abbey, wrote of a production by Fred Cooke's company of *On Shannon's Shore, or The Blackthorn,* at the Queen's in 1895,

> Oh my! it was shockingly bad! Too absurd for anything! Mr. Fred Cooke, the author, behaved in the character of 'Barney Shanaghan' as a blithering idiot right through and nearly made me ill by his exaggerated tomfoolery.[5]

The English theatre

If stage-Irish drama and its players offered no firm basis upon which the founders of the national theatre could build, the English theatre of the eighties and nineties seemed equally barren. Burlesque, operetta, musical comedy, melodrama, frivolous comedy and farce occupied most of the London theatres. From 1878 to 1899 Henry Irving reigned supreme at the Lyceum with spectacular productions of romantic drama and 'bowdlerised' Shakespeare. In 1899 Tree succeeded him at Her Majesty's. Apart from the flamboyance of the melodramatic stage and the banality of London's star-conscious theatre, the predominant acting style was that of the fashionable 'drawing-room' school of Sir George Alexander at the St James' Theatre, in which lack of vocal variety, restless movement and 'business' went under the guise of 'natural' acting.

Frank Fay, who was later to play so large a part in evolving the Irish acting style, was particularly aware of the tendency of English actors to rely on movement and 'business' at the expense of the spoken word.

Rifts in the clouds that enveloped the English theatre had, indeed, begun to appear during the nineties. A handful of critics, managers and playwrights were becoming aware of the new drama of the European Continent. Shaw, as dramatic critic of the *Saturday Review* from 1895 to 1898, William Archer and Edmund Gosse as critics and translators, were ardent champions of Ibsen. Janet Achurch, Elizabeth Robins and Florence Farr were giving performances of his plays, more often than not in matinéé performance only. In 1891 J. T. Grein followed the example of André Antoine's Théâtre Libre by establishing the Independent Theatre of London, whose object was 'to give special performances of plays which have a literary and artistic, rather than a commercial value'. In the following year Grein presented the first performance of a play by Shaw — *Widowers' Houses;* but Shaw preferred to publish his plays rather than submit them to the uncertain treatment of the commercial managers. In 1894 William Poel formed the Elizabethan Stage Society to restore the simplicity of the Shakespearean stage and the musical utterance of verse.

However, by 1898 hopes for a radical reformation of the English stage were rapidly fading. The Independent Theatre collapsed for want of sponsors, and the reformers themselves were split into their separate literary factions. If Irving's Shakespearean spectacles at the Lyceum earned the censure of the literary purists, Tree's mammoth vulgarisations at Her Majesty's were worse.

However degraded the London theatres, Dublin could offer nothing better. There was melodrama at the Queen's; the Theatre Royal and the Gaiety depended for the greater part of their livelihood upon touring companies presenting the more successful productions from the English metropolis. It would have been hard to find a less propitious climate in which to found a literary theatre.

The French connection

Frank Fay was a fervent admirer of the French traditions of training actors. In an article published 1 July 1894 he wrote:

> Thanks to the Conservatoire which, since 1784 has supplied and trained French actors, a company of thoroughly competent players, with a uniform mode and perfectly familiar with the traditional method of interpreting the classics on the stage, can easily be obtained in Paris, and such a company M. Coquelin brought with him. The result was an example of life-like playing which it would be almost impossible to get on the English stage.

Again in September 1900 he referred to Coquelin's visit: 'Those of my readers who were fortunate enough to see M. Coquelin in the comedies mentioned above (*Tartuffe* and *Les Précieuses Ridicules*) will remember the simplicity of the stage appointments and the care taken to centre the attention of the audience on what was being *said* and not on what was being done.' The training of 'a company of thoroughly competent players with a uniform mode' and the need 'to centre the attention of the audience on what was being *said* and not on what was being done' were to become basic principles of the Fay brothers' approach to acting.

Gabriel Fallon maintains that the acting style of the Abbey 'appears to consist of an amalgam of methods — the unrestrained "naturalism" of Antoine, the controller "creation" of Coquelin, the mixture of passion and self-possession advocated by Yeats'.[6] From 1887 onwards the example of Antoine's Théâtre Libre began to erode the out-worn traditions of theatrical presentation. Otto Brahm in Berlin,

Stanislavsky in Moscow and Grein in London were inspired by Antoine's challenge to the Parisian 'boulevard' theatre. His 'facsimile' stage replaced the pictorial stage with its painted backcloths, borders and wings. Real doors, ceilings, furniture and properties — on one occasion real meat — exemplified Zola's exhortation to 'put a man of flesh and bones on the stage, taken from reality, scientifically analysed without one lie'. 'Naturalistic' movement replaced the stage 'strut'; 'naturalistic' gesture replaced histrionic posturing; 'naturalistic' speech replaced stage declamation. But while the example of Antoine's theatre which, like the early National Theatre Society, arose from the enthusiasm of a group of amateur players who possessed neither the training nor the experience to emulate the professionals, was an inspiration to the Irish players, it would seem unlikely that their acting style which was distinctly stylistic, if not static, bore much resemblance to the real life naturalism of Antoine's players. So far as Yeats was concerned naturalism was 'like telling a good Catholic to take his theology from Luther'. 'Be just to Antoine's genius', he wrote in a letter to Frank Fay on 26 August 1904, 'but show the defects of his movement. Art is art because it is not nature, and he tried to make it nature. A realist he cared nothing for poetry which is founded on convention.'

It was among the French Symbolists that Yeats first found a sympathetic climate for his early thoughts on acting, scenery and dramatic theory. In 1894 he visited Paris for the first time. Through his close friend and mentor, the poet and critic Arthur Symons, whose translations introduced the Symbolist movement to England, Yeats became acquainted with the poets Paul Verlaine, Stéphane Mallarmé and Villiers de l'Isle Adam. Despite a limited knowledge of French, he was profoundly impressed by the latter's symphonic drama, *Axël,* with its theme of renunciation of all worldly things in the search for the infinite.

Professor Flannery and others have pointed out that although Yeats had a similar theme in *The Shadowy Waters* as early as 1893, he did not put it into writing until 1894.[7] It was, however, from a man of the theatre that Yeats began his lifelong search for an acting style.

In 1893 Aurélien Lugné-Poe, a young actor who had triumphantly directed Maeterlinck's Symbolist master-work, *Pelléas et Mélisande,* founded the Théâtre de l'Oeuvre which, like its predecessor the Théâtre d'Art, was dedicated to the Symbolist cause. To it came not only Yeats but his co-founders of the Irish Literary Theatre, George Moore and Edward Martyn. Yeats's ideas of chanted verse and symbolic decorative scenery were at least confirmed, if not inspired, by the measured speech, ritualistic movement and simplistic scenery that characterised Lugné-Poe's theatre, which Yeats declared 'would rid the stage of everything that is restless, everything that draws the attention away from the sound of the human voice'.

With the exception of Maeterlinck, however, the French Symbolists produced little that could be called valid drama. The paramount genius of the movement was Richard Wagner. Yeats never visited Bayreuth, but Martyn and Moore as well as Arthur Symons were among the stream of pilgrims who, encouraged by Shaw's eulogies, flocked to the temple of the high priest of German cultural nationalism. For Yeats Wagner's music-dramas represented 'the most passionate in the arts of Europe'. His great cycle of *The Ring of the Nibelungen,* his passionate music-dramas *Lohengrin* and *Tristan und Iseult,* reached down to the deep subconscious of the German soul. Might not the sacred myths of Ireland be the means whereby an Irish theatre could do the same?

The Norwegian connection

The Norwegian national revival and the birth of its theatre, to which Ibsen was a major contributor, undoubtedly occupied the thoughts of those who founded the Irish theatre.

The political history of Norway bears many similarities to that of Ireland. Both countries possess an ancient cultural heritage in their pre-Christian sagas. Both became vassals of powerful neighbours whose governments had suppressed their native languages and cultures. Norwegian poets and playwrights of the eighteenth and early nineteenth centuries wrote for a Danish market, as Irish playwrights did for an English one. Both had preserved their vital folk-lore through their peasant populations. In Christiania (Oslo) the actors and repertoire of the theatres were predominantly Danish, but in 1850 Olë Bull had established a theatre in Bergen with Norwegian actors and producers. Both Ibsen and Björnson held appointments in the Bergen theatre, and it was here that the early plays of Ibsen, celebrating the past glories of Norway, were produced. In 1899 — the same year that saw the first productions of the Irish Literary Theatre — the National-teater was opened in Christiania, and Norwegian theatre became firmly established in its own right.

It is clear that Norway's example, as well as the examples of Antoine in Paris and Grein in London, was much in the thoughts of the founders of the Irish Literary Theatre. In the first number of *Beltaine,* the occasional magazine that was published in conjunction with the Literary Theatre's productions, Yeats, as editor wrote,

> Norway has a great and successful school of contemporary drama, which grew out of a literary movement very similar to that now going on in Ireland. Everywhere critics and writers, who wish for something better than the ordinary play of commerce, turn to Norway for an example and an inspiration.[8]

The same number included an article entitled 'The Scandinavian Dramatists' by C. H. Herford, reprinted from the *Daily Express.* In this the writer referred to Ibsen's early political nationalism and his later development.

> Ibsen was too solitary and self-centred a nature to comply submissively with the Nationalist formula when it had ceased to be a battle-cry. The battle won, it was inevitable that he who held that 'no one is so strong as the man who stands alone' should go his own way and work out his own ideal. An artist of the first rank can, indeed, rarely take any other course. Nationalism in art is an inspiring power in the early stages of artistic growth; it rallies the scattered forces of imagination, disciplines vagrant and chaotic enthusiasms, brings the neglected ore of tradition under an eager scrutiny which detects and disengages its hidden gold. But when all this is done, the artist who has an in-

dividual message will impress his own meaning and his own *cachet* upon the instruments of expression which the fire of national enthusiasm has forged ready to his hand.

This could well stand as a prophetic utterance for the future development of the Irish theatre.

The Celtic revival

Ireland's national theatre was born of a short-lived marriage between political and cultural nationalism in the form of the Celtic, or in Ireland's case the Gaelic, revival. Political nationalism and art make uneasy bedfellows. The child of that marriage might well have proved sterile if its outlook had been purely parochial. But this revival was not confined to Ireland; it was part of a European movement with roots in Brittany, Scotland, Wales and, through the Arthurian legends, in Germany and France, as well as in England. It was itself part of a general cultural movement which ever since the latter years of the eighteenth century had been increasingly turning away from classicism to discover new literary inspiration in the sagas and legends of the pre-Christian and medieval civilisations of northern Europe. In many countries, not only in northern Europe but also in Greece, Hungary and the Balkans, the literary revival was backed by a linguistic revival and by the study of folk-lore and archaeology. In many cases this movement was linked to national aspirations for independence; for, as Thomas Davis said, 'There is a close connection between National Art and National Independence. Art is the born foe of slavery — of ignorance, or sensuality and of cowardice.'[9]

The fact that the cultural revival in Ireland was more strongly linked to national independence than in other countries was due to a combination of political, social and economic circumstances that arose in the later years of the century.

By 1891 aspirations for Home Rule had reached a point at which nationalists could no longer rely on the manoeuvering of the Irish Parliamentary Party. A constitutional solution through the Westminster parliament seemed impossible.

Nationalist Ireland had to find new outlets. Some, like Sir Horace Plunkett and Lord Dunraven, sought to build bridges between Irishmen of different creeds, classes and origins. Their efforts were doomed to failure since their hopes were founded on the false assumption that economic and social amelioration would bring an end to the desire for political independence. Others, like Arthur Griffith, sought separatism under a dual monarchy in the Austro-Hungarian pattern. Some, like Maud Gonne and the Irish Republican Brotherhood, threw themselves whole-heartedly into the cause of open rebellion. A few sought an outlet for Ireland's frustrated nationalism in a cultural and linguistic revival.

Between 1878 and 1880 Standish O'Grady published his *History of Ireland* (the so-called 'Bardic History') and 'found the Gaelic tradition, like a neglected antique *dún* with its doors barred . . . Listening, he heard from within the hum of an immense chivalry, and he opened the doors and the wild riders went forth to work their will.'[10] Douglas Hyde's *Love Songs of Connacht* (1893) in Irish and English, which Yeats declared 'were the coming of a new power into literature', opened up the world of folk-lore. These two sources — the ancient Gaelic literature and the living folk-lore of the country people — were to provide the material from which the literary and dramatic movement arose; while the Irish language in its Anglo-Irish translation was to inspire its expression.

The Celtic revival did not end with its literary manifestation, for it was the poets and playwrights of that movement whose words did much to foster and inspire the political revolution from 1916 onwards. Many years later, remembering his play *Cathleen Ni Houlihan* and the fiery speeches of Maud Gonne who first played the leading part in it — the spirit of Ireland calling on her sons to sacrifice their lives for her sake, Yeats wrote,

> I lie awake night after night
> And never get the answers right.
> Did that play of mine send out
> Certain men the English shot?
> Did words of mine put too great strain
> On that woman's reeling brain?[11]

In his study of the Irish revolution in literature Peter Costello points out that the roots of the Celtic revival and the revolution were inextricably tangled together.

> The ideal of Ireland which motivated the very small group of men who plotted the Easter Rising had its origins in the materials which had been recovered by Irish scholars and recreated by Irish poets. That ideal, rather than any realistic political considerations, brought about those men the English shot.[12]

Just as Yeats and his fellow playwrights found in the ancient heroes and in the fiery and tender imagination of the people of the remote parts of Ireland the symbols of cultural nationalism — 'Dream of the noble and the beggar-man'[13] — so, too, did Padraig Pearse and the leaders of the 1916 Rising find in the Celtic warrior, Cuchulain, and in the old language the symbols of political nationalism. In addressing his pupils of St Enda's school, some of whom were to follow him into the General Post Office on that fateful Easter Monday 1916, Pearse declared,

> We must recreate and perpetuate in Ireland the knightly tradition of Cuchulain, the noble tradition of the Fianna . . .[14]

Yeats, too, was aware of the potent influence of that primitive hero who became a central figure in his plays and poems upon the romantic idealism of the Rising.

> When Pearse summoned Cuchulain to his side,
> What stalked through the Post Office? What intellect,
> What calculation, number, measurement, replied?[15]

For some today the shade of 'the Hound of Ulster', who slew his own son and his foster-brother, still darkens that unhappy province.

National sensitivity

In 1891 Yeats, together with T. W. Rolleston, founded the Irish Literary Society in London, and in the following year the National Literary Society in Dublin. 'No political purpose informed our meetings,'[16] Yeats was later to declare but, in fact, the National Literary Society — not least through its association with Young Ireland Societies — raised the expectations of those nationalists whose main interest in Irish literature and language was centred upon its political purpose.

Despite the disillusionment that followed the split in the Parliamentary Party, and the attempts at conciliation made by successive British governments, young patriots did not cease to debate the best way to achieve political and economic independence. Clubs and societies, dedicated to a variety of ways and means of resurrecting a sense of nationhood, multiplied throughout the country. In such circumstances the literary and linguistic revivals were inevitably regarded by many patriots as weapons to achieve their political aspirations. In the final years of the century two events were to inflame national feelings and to provide a popular basis for nationalist sentiments.

The year 1898 was the centenary of Wolfe Tone's insurrection which had sought the establishment of an Irish republic. Every kind of nationalist paid homage to the memory of the United Irishmen. '98 clubs sprang up all over the country; supplements on '98 appeared in the national newspapers; fife and drum bands played 'A Nation Once Again' and 'Who Fears to Speak of '98' at meetings and demonstrations. In Dublin Maud Gonne, accompanied by Yeats, headed a procession to lay the foundation stone of a statue to Tone which, however, failed to materialise for another sixty-two years.

In the following year passions were further inflamed by the recruitment of Irishmen for the Boer War, a war that seemed to some a ruthless suppression of a nation's independence. From these two events a new national newspaper arose, the *United Irishman* whose editor, Arthur Griffith, was to become the founder of Sinn Féin and one of the principal architects of the Irish Free State; he was also to become a formidable critic of Yeats and Synge.

During these early years, and until some years after the foundation of the new state, national feelings were highly sensitive. To some extent this was a reaction against the gross misrepresentation of Ireland and Irishmen in the British press, as well as in the music-halls and variety theatres; to some extent it stemmed from the disunity, political and religious, that made Ireland vulnerable, both at home and abroad, to those who maintained that she was incapable of self-government. Ireland's credibility as an independent nation was at stake, and to the more fiery nationalists any portrayal of their country that was not entirely favourable, was placing more ammunition in the hands of the opponents of Home Rule. Irish men and women must be depicted as morally unblemished, true patriots and happy and virtuous wives. In this the political nationalists had the full support of the Irish Catholic Church with its strongly Jansenist, or puritan, outlook. The combination of political nationalism and religious puritanism was to prove a formidable opposition to the 'intellectual freedom' that Yeats claimed for the creative artist.

Indeed, the founders of the Irish theatre were particularly vulnerable to the distrust of those mistaken nationalists who held that the only true hallmarks of an Irishman were Gaelic ancestry and the Catholic faith. Yeats, Lady Gregory, Edward Martyn, George Moore, George Russell and Synge were all of Anglo-Irish descent; Martyn was an ardent Catholic, but Moore was decidedly a lapsed one; the others were either Protestants, atheists, agnostics, or — worse still — dabblers in the occult sciences. As for Annie Horniman, she was not only English, but never tired of declaring her opposition to Irish nationalism and to 'those wicked politics which teach you to hate each other so intensely'.[17]

Yeats and his fellow playwrights were nationalists in a wider sense. Although he, himself, was for a short time a member of the Irish Republican Brotherhood, this was motivated by his devotion to Maud Gonne rather than to political militancy. 'I am no Nationalist,' he wrote in 1937, 'except in Ireland for passing reasons.' However, if, in their different ways, the early playwrights of the dramatic movement refused to accept the function of literature as propaganda for the national cause, they were profoundly concerned with nationality in literature. In this the creative artist follows his own genius which is seldom that of the crowd; and, being of necessity a destroyer of clichés, his creations will inevitably challenge and offend the political nationalists in their attempt to build the nation itself.

The linguistic revival

Just as the literary revival and dramatic movement were regarded by some as potential instruments of national propaganda, so too were the efforts to revive the old language. In 1893 Douglas Hyde founded the Gaelic League, together with Father Eugene O'Growney and Eoin MacNeill. Its original aims were the preservation of Irish as the national language and the study and publication of Gaelic literature. Like the National Literary Society, Hyde intended the League to be non-political, but his intentions were overtaken by the pressures of the nationalist movement.

In 1900 Griffith founded Cumann na nGaedheal to link up all national societies and to advance the cause of independence. Its aims also included the study of Irish literature and language. Griffith's campaign to discourage enlistment in the British army during the Boer War inspired Maud Gonne to form a patriotic women's society, Inghinidhe na hEireann (Daughters of Ireland). Apart from urging Irish women to refrain from consorting with soldiers, this militant organisation held classes in Irish history, literature and language. Thus the literary and linguistic revival became increasingly linked with what were, as yet, conflicting political views on what separatism involved, and how it was to be achieved.

For a time the founders of the dramatic movement held strongly to the principle that their repertoire should include plays in the Irish language. In the second number of *Beltaine* Yeats wrote:

> We are anxious to get plays in Irish, and can [sic] we do so will very possibly push our work into the western counties, where it would be an important help to that movement for the revival of the Irish language on which the life of the nation may depend.[18]

But despite the enthusiasm engendered by Hyde's *Casadh an tSúgáin* (*The Twisting of the Rope*) when it was first performed by the Literary Theatre in 1901, it was not until the

1940s that a sufficient flow of plays in the Irish language —
mostly translations — made it possible for the Abbey to include them as a regular feature of its repertoire. Those playwrights who spoke Irish were understandably unwilling to
commit themselves to writing plays in a language that only a
small minority of Dublin playgoers understood. Even today,
after over fifty years of an Irish-controlled educational system, productions of plays in Irish are, for financial reasons,
largely confined to one-act plays, pantomines and revues.
But, if the initiative of the Gaelic League and subsequent
educational efforts have failed to revive Irish as the spoken
language of most Irishmen, it is nevertheless its imagery, syn-
tax and metaphor that are the basis of Anglo-Irish, which,
though differing from county to county and heightened by
poets and playwrights, has provided the Irish theatre with its
distinctive form of expression.

Among the other activities of Inghinidhe na hEireann was
a dramatic class which included Máire T. Quinn, Sara Allgood
and Máire Nic Shiubhlaigh[19] — all three to become leading
players in the future Irish theatre. Frank and his brother, W.
G. Fay, whose Ormonde Dramatic Society was the leading
amateur society of the time, were invited to coach this class.

In 1901 W. G. Fay directed the first performance of a play
in the Irish language to be seen in Dublin, *Tobar Draoidheacta,*
by Father Dinneen. This was presented, together with Alice
Milligan's one-act melodrama, *Red Hugh,* for an autumn *feis*
(festival) organised by Cumann na nGaedheal in which members of the Ormonde Dramatic Society and the ladies of Inghinidhe na hEireann took part. Both Yeats and Russell, who
were present at this performance, were moved by the dedication of these amateur players. Russell had already agreed to
allow the Fays to produce his as yet unfinished play, *Deirdre;*
he now persuaded Yeats to offer them his one-act patriotic
play, *Cathleen Ni Houlihan.* This union of Irish playwrights
and players set the stage for a truly native theatre. Without it
the Literary Theatre would have been a short-lived appendage
of the literary revival, provided by courtesy of English actors.

1

The Irish Literary Theatre

1899–1901[1]

A manifesto, 1898

We propose to have performed in Dublin in the Spring of
every year certain Celtic and Irish plays, which whatever
their degree of excellence, will be written with a high
ambition, and so to build up a Celtic and Irish school of
dramatic literature. We hope to find in Ireland an un-
corrupted and imaginative audience trained to listen by its
passion for oratory, and believe that our desire to bring
upon the stage the deeper thoughts and emotions of Ireland will ensure for us a tolerant welcome, and that freedom of experiment which is not found in theatres in England, and without which no new movement in art and
literature can succeed. We will show that Ireland is not the
home of buffoonery and of easy sentiment, as it has been
represented, but the home of an ancient idealism. We are
confident of the support of all Irish people, who are weary
of misrepresentation, in carrying out a work that is outside
all the political questions that divide us.[2]

Thus Yeats, Lady Gregory and Edward Martyn declared their
intention to found a literary theatre. Lady Gregory in *Our
Irish Theatre* says, 'I think the word "Celtic" was put in for
the sake of Fiona Macleod whose plays however we never
acted, though we used to amuse ourselves by thinking of the
call for "author" that might follow one, and the possible appearance of William Sharp in the place of the beautiful
woman he had given out to be . . .'[3]

The Literary Theatre was formally founded at a meeting of the Council of the National Literary Society on 16 January 1899 at which Yeats stated that he wished the project developed and carried out under the Society's auspices.

The title 'Irish Literary Theatre' confirms that the founders' original intention was not only to create a theatre directly opposed to the non-literary, commercial, London theatre, but a theatre firmly anchored to the national literary revival. It was, therefore, under the auspices of the National Literary Society that the first performance took place in May 1899. In the first number of *Beltaine* Yeats emphasised this close connection with literature: 'In all or almost all cases the plays must be published before they are acted, and no play will be produced which could not hope to succeed as a book.'[4]

When Lady Gregory, Mr. Edward Martyn, and myself planned the Irish Literary Theatre, we decided that it should be carried on in the form we have projected for three years. We thought three years would show whether the country desired to take up the project, and make it part of the national life, and that we, at any rate, could return to our proper work, in which we did not include theatrical management, at the end of that time.[5]

What they planned was a somewhat exclusive literary theatre playing to 'that limited public which gives understanding and not to that unlimited public which gives wealth'. As yet they could not look far enough into the future to see that their venture might be a theatre for the general public.

We must make a theatre for ourselves and our friends, and for a few simple people who understand from sheer simplicity what we understand from scholarship and thought. We have planned the Irish Literary Theatre with this hospitable emotion, and that the right people may find out about us, we hope to act a play or two in the spring of each year; and that the right people may escape the stupefying memory of the theatre of commerce which clings even to them, our plans will be for the most part remote, spiritual and ideal.[6]

'The right people'

Following a meeting between Yeats, Lady Gregory and Edward Martyn in Duras House, Kinvara, the summer home of Count Florimond de Basterot, an appeal was sent to a number of friends for a guarantee fund of £300 to launch the experiment. In *Our Irish Theatre* Lady Gregory dates this meeting in 1898, but her biographer, Elizabeth Coxhead, suggests that this must have taken place a month or two after July 1897.[7]

The list of guarantors covered a wide selection of 'the right people': politicians such as Tim Healy, John Redmond, John Dillon, W. E. H. Lecky and William O'Brien M.P.; a fair number of the peerage, including the Marquis of Dufferin and Ava, the Duchess of St Albans, the Earl of Westmeath, Viscount Gough and the Viscountess de Vesci, the Lords Castletown, Ardilaun and Morris, as well as three knights, a Papal count, the Provost of Trinity College and a judge. To these were added the veteran Fenian leader, John O'Leary, Maud Gonne and the future 'Red Countess', Constance Gore-Booth, together with Douglas Hyde, George Russell, Sara Purser, George Moore and others of the literary set. One cannot help wondering if all these had turned up on the opening night what reactions there might have been; or indeed if all would have continued their support in the light of future events. Fortunately Edward Martyn forestalled this situation by underwriting their financial guarantee himself, not only for the first season but almost certainly for the three following seasons as well.

Edward Martyn

Amongst the founders of the Literary Theatre Edward Martyn was the most paradoxical. He was descended from Anglo-Norman invaders, his ancestors amongst the few Catholic landowners exempted from the confiscation of their estates; his father a leading member of society in County Galway, the owner of Tulira Castle, an eighteenth-century mansion which Martyn gothicised at a cost of £20,000; his mother belonging to humble stock and having a large fortune amassed by buying up properties that came on the market through the opera-, tion of the Encumbered Estates Act. Educated by the Jesuits at colleges in Ireland and England, and subsequently at Christ Church, Oxford, he remained an ardent Catholic in the European tradition throughout his life. A misogynist with a pathological dislike of women; preferring to sleep in monk-like austerity on an iron bedstead in his damp Norman keep; a gourmet who consumed vast quantities of caviare and enjoyed the finest French wines; his interests including the sartorial reform of clerical dress, the cause of the Gaelic League to which he was a generous subscriber, and Arthur Griffith's Sinn Féin to which he gave considerable financial support as well as being its first president. At the same time he was a member of the almost exclusively Protestant Kildare Street Club. Next to the theatre, his greatest passion was music. By endowing the Catholic Pro-Cathedral of Dublin with the means to introduce the Palestrina choir he was amongst those who influenced the Church to restore the plain chant as an integral part of its liturgy, discovering in the process the future John MacCormack amongst the choir boys.

'Few men of his generation could claim to have achieved as much by individual effort in assisting movements which have all made a profound mark on modern times,' wrote his biographer, Denis Gwynn,[8] to whom I am indebted for the above summary of Martyn's achievements. Yet this complex personality, without whose generosity the Literary Theatre might never have succeeded, is chiefly remembered by the malicious, though undoubtedly witty and sometimes lovable, caricature of 'dead Edward' in the three volumes of his cousin, George Moore's, *Hail and Farewell.*[9]

Amongst the founders of the Irish Literary Theatre Martyn was alone in his awareness of the poetic vision and symbolism of Ibsen's plays. In 1899 after witnessing a performance of *Little Eyolf* he wrote,

After the performance of this play in the Little Theatre, I went away with its exquisite music still trembling in my heart; I wished to be alone so that the exaltation should not be interrupted. For the way with these wonderful plays, where subtle mental poetry finds expression in the most direct realism of speech, as here and in *Rosmersholm* and above all in *The Master Builder,* is to give the sensation of rare harmonies, to produce with their triumphant construction the effect of a symphony where idea grows naturally from idea, where dramatic effects are but the natural outcome of logical combinations of circumstances, where profound knowledge of the human heart and character is set down with such certainty of intellect as may be seen in the lines of a drawing by some great master.[10]

Unfortunately Martyn's attempts to infuse the spirit of Ibsen into his own plays were not matched by his dramatic ability. It was shortly after 1890 that he wrote *The Heather Field,* clearly influenced by Ibsen. After unsuccessful attempts, aided by Moore, to get it produced in London, Martyn published it together with a second play, *Maeve,* in 1897. Yeats was already familiar with his plays; thus it was decided that *The Heather Field* together with Yeats's play, *The Countess Cathleen,* should be the first plays to be presented by the Irish Literary Theatre.

William Butler Yeats

Yeats's immediate forebears were ship-owners, merchants and Church of Ireland clergymen. The poet's father, John Butler Yeats, broke away from the tradition to become at first a lawyer and then a distinguished portrait painter. His mother, Susan Yeats, came from a Sligo family, the Pollexfens. It was in Sligo in the far west of Ireland, 'Under bare Ben Bulben's head', that the young poet found his true spiritual home, and it was there he chose for his last resting place.

The family of John and Susan Yeats was uniquely talented; not only did it include Willie, the greatest of modern Irish poets, but his brother Jack, the most profoundly national of Irish painters, and their two sisters, Susan and Elizabeth, known to the family as 'Lilly' and 'Lolly' who established the Cuala Press in Dublin, famous for its beautifully illuminated and printed ballads and poems.

In 1887 the family settled in London where Yeats, who had previously studied at art school, became increasingly involved in the literary life of the capital; his first published book of verse, *The Wanderings of Oisin,* appearing in 1888.

At the same time he was heavily involved in occult studies which, next to poetry, were to provide the basis for his most important philosophy of life. 'If I had not made magic my constant study, I would not have written a single word of my Blake books, nor would *The Countess Cathleen* have ever come to exist,' he wrote to John O'Leary in July 1892, 'The mystical life is the centre of all that I do and all that I think and all that I write.'[11] In 1890 he joined the Order of the Golden Dawn, consisting of so-called Christian Cabalists and presided over by the baleful presence of MacGregor Mathers. Fellow-members for some time were Florence Farr and Annie Horniman, both of whom were to play a part in the early years of the Irish theatre.

At the same time, Yeats met and fell in love with Maud Gonne. It was her efforts to relieve the evicted peasants in Donegal at the cost of her health and much of her fortune that inspired the character of Countess Cathleen. But a far more practical help and inspiration came to him in his pursuit of the theatre from Lady Gregory.

Lady Gregory

'I doubt if I should have done much with my life, but for her firmness and care,' Yeats wrote in *Autobiographies.* Like Martyn and Yeats, Augusta Gregory had her roots firmly embedded in the west of Ireland. She was the youngest of the sixteen children of Dudley Persse, High Sheriff of Galway. At the age of twenty-eight she married Sir William Gregory, an ex-Governor of Ceylon, who was nearly three times her age. After his death in 1892 she spent the greater part of her time in maintaining and improving his estate, Coole Park, near Gort in County Galway. Here she provided Yeats with a permanent refuge in which to write, cossetted by her constant care for his welfare, sustained and helped by her womanly wisdom.

From 1894 onwards she set herself the task of learning Irish and, as her biographer, Elizabeth Coxhead, has pointed out, whilst she never mastered it sufficiently to write in the language, she learnt enough 'to follow a conversation, ask questions, read a modern text and translate accurately from it into English'.[12] It was her ability to communicate with her tenants and neighbouring country folk in their native language that evoked her interest in folk-lore, coupled with her discovery of Douglas Hyde's *Love Songs of Connacht*. Hyde's translations of these Irish poems taught her to appreciate the poetic values of the dialect of her native Kiltartan district, a dialect which she used in her plays and translations of Irish legends.

In her turn she herself was to become something of a legend, not only in her native district but amongst those connected with her work for the theatre. Her small, compact figure, dressed in sober black — in permanent mourning for her husband — heightened her resemblance to Queen Victoria for whom, however, she had no sympathy. Her slurred speech, which sounded as if she had a permanent cold in the head, was strangely reminiscent of another great lady of the Theatre, Lilian Baylis. Her indomitable courage in times of crisis, her outspoken criticism of those with whom she could not agree, her warmth to players and aspiring playwrights, not least her Gort cakes, regularly supplied to the green-room of the Abbey, created an aura of respect and affection that still lingers on today even among those who did not know her. 'The greatest living Irish woman' Shaw was to call her.

George Moore

Like his cousin Edward Martyn, Moore's ancestors were privileged Catholic landowners; but he himself had abandoned his faith and emigrated to Paris and London where he had already made a name for himself as a novelist. Now Ireland was to summon him back, but only for a time:

> As well as I can reckon, it was five years after my meditation in the Temple (where he had been visiting 'dear Edward') that W. B. Yeats, the Irish poet, came to see me in my flat in Victoria Street, followed by Edward. . . . My visitors appeared as a twain as fantastic as anything ever seen in Japanese prints — Edward great in girth as an owl

(he is nearly as neckless), blinking behind glasses, and Yeats lank as a rook, a-dream in black silhouette on the flowered wall-paper . . .

I waited for the servant to leave the room, and as soon as the door had closed they broke forth, telling me together they had decided to found a Literary Theatre in Dublin; so I sat like one confounded, saying to myself: Of course they know nothing of Independent Theatres, and in view of my own difficulties in gathering sufficient audience for two or three performances, pity began to stir in me for their forlorn project. A forlorn thing it was surely to bring literary plays to Dublin . . . Dublin of all cities in the world.[13]

Nevertheless Moore went to Dublin and for a time contributed to the venture as a playwright, as well as providing such knowledge as he had of rehearsals which, though it did not extend beyond his connection with the Independent Theatre, was still more than Yeats or Martyn possessed at that time.

Despite Moore's stipulation that he should not be involved in staging their plays, it was not long before Martyn came to beg him to attend a rehearsal of *The Heather Field* at a theatre in Notting Hill where things were going seriously wrong.

There is little doubt that Moore's humorous account is no exaggeration.[14] In her biography of her mother, Dame May Whitty, who eventually played the part of the Countess, Margaret Webster recalls her mother's description of these rehearsals more especially of Yeats's play:

He [Yeats] did little but wander about in a long, black cloak, accompanied by a drifting lady [Florence Farr] in a long, green one; he would discourse on the value of quarter tones in verse-speaking while she plucked at a psaltery throughout the "recitations", muttering, "Cover it up with a lonely tune." The lady's niece, aged fifteen [Dorothy Paget] was to act, or rather recite the long and difficult part of the Countess.[15]

Moore used draconian methods, sacking some actors and recasting others. Little Miss Paget was relegated to a non-speaking part of a fairy, though she was compensated by being allowed to speak Lionel Johnson's prologue. But Florence Farr was not to be dislodged from the part of the poet, Aleel, in keeping with the Victorian taste for male impersonations, as exampled by Sarah Bernhardt's performance as Hamlet and L'Aiglon and William Poel's casting of a woman for Romeo and Everyman. May Whitty and her husband, Ben Webster, were engaged, she to play the leading woman's part in both plays while Ben Webster consented to take over the direction on condition that Yeats ceased to interfere. In the event May Whitty was 'troubled by a dreadful cough, which made the speaking of verse in quarter, or any other, tones impossible.'[16]

Although Moore was never slow to overstate his part in the promotion of the Literary Theatre, there is little doubt that in this instance he may well have rescued the dramatic movement from instant death.

The first season – May 1899

The difficulty of obtaining a theatre at short notice, together with the costs involved, had apparently escaped the attention of the literary-minded promoters. Dublin theatres were all booked and, in any case, too expensive for the available funds, and public halls, under an act passed by Grattan's parliament in 1799, were not licensed for paid performances of plays. With her usual determination Lady Gregory managed to persuade W. E. H. Lecky, a member of parliament, to introduce a new clause into the Irish Local Government Act empowering the Municipality of Dublin to license public halls for theatrical performance. Martyn followed this up by obtaining a licence from the Municipality to present the plays in the Antient Concert Rooms in Great Brunswick Street (now the Academy Cinema in Pearse Street). But their troubles were not over.

The first version of *The Countess Cathleen* was published in 1892 along with *Various Legends and Lyrics*. The plot concerns a famine which laid waste the land. Countess Cathleen, returning to her estates with her lover, the poet Aleel, sacrifices her goods in order that her tenants may be spared from selling their souls to two demons, disguised as merchants, who offer them food in exchange. Faced with the moral decay of the starving peasants, the Countess sells them her own soul in order to provide enough money to save them from starvation, but as she dies an angel descends:

The Angel:
The light beats down; the gates of pearl are wide;
And she is passing to the floor of peace,
And Mary of the seven times wounded heart
Has kissed her lips, and the long blessed hair
Has fallen on her face; The Light of Lights
Looks always on the motive, not the deed;
The Shadow of Shadows on the deed alone.[17]

In the sensitive national and religious climate of the nineties, the play contained incidents that could well provoke angry reactions, such as the kicking of the crucifix by a starving peasant — an incident that was, in fact, omitted from the performance — as well as the theological question of whether a woman, who sells her soul to the devil, can be received into heaven.

Doubts about its orthodoxy were already circulating in Dublin. These troubled the Catholic conscience of Martyn. Yeats and Lady Gregory submitted the play to an Irish Jesuit, Father Finlay, and to an English priest, Father Barry. The former suggested cuts in the text, some of which Yeats accepted; the latter pronounced in its favour. This failed to satisfy Martyn who threatened to withdraw himself, his play and — importantly — his money from the Literary Theatre. The first performance was only a few weeks away. Yeats, ever a master at manipulating personalities, managed to dissuade him from an action that would undoubtedly have been the end of the whole enterprise.

Now new trouble was brewing. Frank Hugh O'Donnell, whom Parnell had expelled from the Irish Parliamentary Party, was determined to curry popular favour as well as to revenge himself upon Yeats and Maud Gonne, against both of whom he harboured a personal grudge. Shortly before the opening performance he sent a letter to the editor of *The Freeman's Journal,* containing a vicious attack on Yeats and his play. This he subsequently published under the title of

Souls for Gold. This hysterical pamphlet was eagerly discussed in leading articles and correspondence in the press.
Two days before the first performance an editorial in the
Daily Nation (6 May 1899) protested 'in the names of morality and religion and Irish nationality' against its performance.
The editorial concluded by trusting 'that those who are responsible for a gross breach of faith with the public of this
country, will receive their deserts on Monday night in the
practical evidence afforded to them that the people of the
Catholic capital of Catholic Ireland cannot be subjected to
affront with impunity'.

Yeats over-reacted to this incitement to riot by calling for
police protection on the first night — a tactical error he was
to repeat in the case of *The Playboy of the Western World.* In
the event no more than twenty students (some say a dozen)
from the Royal University expressed their disapproval by
hissing certain passages in the play. The whole affair appeared
to be a 'storm in a tea cup', but subsequent reactions brought
to the surface underlying religious and nationalist sensitivities.
Looking back on the criticisms — religious and nationalist —
that greeted Yeats's play, we can see that they were a mild
foretaste of the criticisms that were to accompany the
dramatic movement in its later years.

Martyn's play, which opened on 11 May, received a mainly
enthusiastic press — perhaps not uninfluenced by the criticisms
that greeted *The Countess Cathleen.* 'A fine wholesome
drama', declared the *Evening Herald.* Today we might consider the *Irish Times* to be nearer the mark: '*The Heather
Field* is wearisome because it has no action worthy of the
name; its dialogue is stilted; its characters are not very deftly
drawn; and its reflection of Irish life is not very convincing.'

The second season — February 1900

The interest created by the first season led to a more am-
bitious plan for the following year. Once again a company
was recruited from England; the Gaiety Theatre was hired
for the occasion, and Martyn's play, *Maeve,* was to be presented in harness with Alice Milligan's one-act play, *The Last
of the Fianna.* Yeats was reluctant to submit a play at this

stage; he had been disappointed in the verse speaking of the English players — with the exception of Florence Farr — in *The Countess Cathleen.* 'I rather shrink from producing another verse play, unless I get some opportunity for private experiment with my actors,' he wrote in the second number of *Beltaine.*[18] It was, however, necessary to have a second bill to draw a sufficient audience to the Gaiety season. Martyn submitted his new play, *The Tale of a Town,* an Ibsenesque drama reminiscent of *An Enemy of the People.* After reading it, Moore wrote to Martyn: 'There is not one act in the five you have sent me which in my opinion could interest any possible audience, English or Esquimaux!'[19]

According to Moore, Yeats's reaction was even more dismissive: 'No, no; it's entirely impossible. We couldn't have such a play performed.' Moore and Yeats then proceeded to re-plan the play in Martyn's house, while Martyn retired in high dudgeon to his Norman keep.

The play, rewritten under the title of *The Bending of the Bough,* is undoubtedly superior to Martyn's version. Its subject, a thinly disguised satire on the struggle between British commercial interests and Irish idealism, delighted a popular audience with its topicality when it opened on 20 February. On the previous evening (19 February) *Maeve* was presented, together with *The Last of the Fianna.* Martyn's play, an adaptation of his novel, concerns the daughter of an impoverished Irish landlord, torn between her filial duty to marry a wealthy Englishman and her vision of a dream-world in which she meets the legendary figure of Queen Maeve and an unnamed lover, into whose world of 'the ever-young' she eventually passes. According to Lady Gregory, there was 'such applause at the line "I am only an old woman, but I tell you that Erin will never be subdued" that Lady — , who was at a performance, reported to the Castle that they had better boycott it, which they have done.'[20]

The Last of the Fianna was perhaps the first play to treat a pre-Christian legend as its subject. The *Daily Express* critic commented, 'If the aim of the Irish Literary Theatre is to create a national drama it is obvious that the development of Miss Milligan's method is the proper road to reach ultimate success.'

The third season — October 1901

This thought was already in the minds of Moore and Yeats who had decided to collaborate in turning the legendary history of Diarmuid and Grania into a play against the advice of Lady Gregory who feared that a collaboration between her favourite poet and a realistic writer in a play of this kind would surely lead to strife — as it did.

Moore gives an amusing if much exaggerated version of their partnership in the final chapter of *Ave*. He tells how, unable to agree on the style to be adopted, Yeats hit upon the idea that Moore should write the play in French, this would then be translated into Irish, and re-translated by Lady Gregory into Kiltartan dialect, finally Yeats would 'put style upon it'. Of course this ludicrous procedure was not adopted.

Diarmuid and Grania was presented at the Gaiety Theatre by Frank Benson's Shakespearean Company on 21 October, Benson himself playing the part of Diarmuid and his wife that of Grania. The cast included the young Henry Ainley, Harcourt Williams and Matheson Lang. Great attention, we are told, was paid to historical authenticity, though Benson appeared in a pair of tartan trews. Edward Elgar composed some accompanying music, including a particularly fine funeral march. But despite all the efforts, including the introduction of a live goat, the reception was luke-warm, much of the press being openly hostile. Frank Fay wrote:

> To my mind, the greatest triumph of the authors lies in their having written in English a play in which English actors are intolerable. . . . All through the play the English voice grated on one's ear, and the stolid English temperament was equally at variance with what one wanted. The actors did not act the play as if they believed in it; the fact is they could not, for it is not in their nature.[21]

The criticisms Benson's company received were no doubt partly politically motivated. Nationalist feelings were increasingly aroused by press reports of the Boer War and the demand for Home Rule was becoming more persistent. However, the performance was not helped by the inability of the English actors to pronounce Irish names. No doubt Benson's feelings were hurt and this might explain the following fictitious account he gave of Yeats's curtain speech:

> The enthusiastic poet . . . seized the opportunity to indulge in invective against English actors and all their works. His eloquent periods were cut short by Mrs. Benson grasping his coat-tails and dragging him back to the stage. Three parts Irish herself, she volubly protested we were an English company, and that at his invitation we had crossed the stormy St George's Channel, and had done our best, according to our capacity for his play. We could not possibly allow him to step forward on our stage and insult us and our nation. Of course he saw he had made a mistake, and like the gentleman he is, reappeared with chastened brow to qualify his remarks and make the *amende honorable*.[22]

If Yeats had made such a speech it would certainly have been mentioned in the press and Joseph Holloway, the prolific diarist of the Irish theatre who was present on the first night, would not have failed to record it. However national pride is not confined to Irish theatre alone, and no doubt the Bensons felt particularly sore at the extravagant praise lavished on a group of amateur actors who appeared in the accompanying play. This was an event of far greater significance in the history of Irish theatre — a one-act play in the Irish language written by Douglas Hyde, the President of the Gaelic League. *Casadh an tSúgáin* (The Twisting of the Rope) was performed by members of the Keating branch of the Gaelic League with Hyde himself in the leading part. The play was directed by W. G. Fay. Holloway reported: 'Though their efforts were crude from an acting point of view, the "old tongue" flowed so expressively and musically from their lips as to send a thrill of pleasure through one's veins, and make one regret that most Irishmen (including myself) have been brought up in utter ignorance of their own language.'[23]

Hyde's play, laid in a cottage kitchen, complete with dresser, hearth and half-door, in which a group of country folk are celebrating a wedding, can justly be claimed as the forerunner of the peasant plays that were to follow, and for the first time in history a play in the Irish language was performed on the stage of a professional theatre.

2

Enter the Players,
1902–1904

The Fay brothers

Neither Frank, nor his brother, Willie (W. G. Fay), were great
actors. They did not possess the intellectual abilities or artistic judgment of Konstantin Stanislavky and Nemirovitch
Danchenko who, at much the same time, were founding the
Moscow Art Theatre. But between them they transformed
what, up to now, had been a predominantly literary movement into a living theatrical entity with its distinct national
flavour and stylistic form; distinguished, moreover, by the
team work of its players, the restraint of their acting, and the
emphasis they placed on the spoken word. Without the Fays
and their players the Abbey Theatre would never have existed,
nor would Yeats, Synge and Lady Gregory have devoted their
lives to its service.

It was Frank Fay who, as a contributor to the *United Irishman,* first called for a national theatre, employing Irish actors.

What I want to know is why the conductors of the Irish
Literary Theatre who pooh-pooh the ordinary English
commercial Theatre cannot entrust the performance of
their plays dealing with Irish subjects to a company of
Irish actors. I know, of course, that I shall be told there are
no Irish actors; that the Irishman who goes on the stage
must sink his individuality and his accent as much as it is
possible for him to do, otherwise he will not rise above the
class of stuff that Mr Whitbread is in the habit of presenting to his patrons. But Englishmen in Irish plays are as

absurd as the amateur singer of coster and Cockney music-hall ditties. The voice and temperament are wanting. It is manifestly the duty of those who will benefit by the Irish Literary Theatre plays to train up a company of Irish actors to do the work they want.[1]

Frank also advocated that a national theatre should present its plays in the Irish language, but practical considerations induced him to change his mind. Among the talented amateurs, trained under his brother's professional guidance, familiarity with the Irish language was either limited or non-existent; Willie himself admitted, 'My knowledge of Gaelic was not extensive, but my experience of producing amateurs was.'[2]

The Fay brothers came from country stock. Their grandparents, tailors from Galway on one side and farmers from the Midlands on the other, migrated to Dublin in the first quarter of the nineteenth century. Neither Frank, nor Willie, had much formal education. The elder of the two, Frank, became a clerk to a firm of accountants. Studious by nature, he acquired from an early age an extensive knowledge of the theatre, particularly the history of speech and acting, which he put to good use in his spare time as a teacher of elocution and as a dramatic critic. Together with his brother he took part in amateur theatricals and by dint of a systematic series of exercises succeeded in developing a fine resonant voice that was to be his chief asset as an actor. Willie, however, was determined to become a professional player. Leaving school at the age of sixteen, and having failed his examinations to enter the Civil Service, he worked for a time as a scene painter in the Gaiety Theatre. After a brief training under Miss Maud Randford, the actress wife of the actor-manager, J. W. Lacey, he managed to get a job with the latter's 'fit-up' company as advance agent. From then on he had a chequered career touring in England and Ireland, sometimes as an actor, sometimes as a song-and-dance man, and on one occasion as advance manager for a circus. It was above all as a comedian that Willie excelled, but opportunities for Irish actors were few and Willie was not destined for stardom. Economic circumstances eventually forced him to return to Dublin and accept work as an electrician. Here he devoted his time to working with the amateur societies he and his brother had founded, the Ormonde Dramatic Society and the W. G. Fay Comedy Combination.

In many ways the Fay brothers, so different in temperament, made an ideal partnership: Willie, eminently practical in all branches of theatre, a fine comedian and character actor, excelling in peasant parts; Frank, with an extensive knowledge of acting techniques, a much valued coach in speech, at his best in heroic parts, though he lacked physique and passion. 'I cannot take any interest in acting peasant parts,' he wrote to Yeats in 1903, 'first because I dislike dialect and secondly because I don't know the life or ways of the peasant.'[3] Both, however, had temperamental problems. Willie had a violent temper and Frank was subject to moods of arrogance that made it difficult for him to accept criticism. In the early years of the Irish theatre the qualities of the Fays were precisely what was needed to give practical expression to the literary gifts of the playwrights, but in the course of time this formidable partnership of theatre practitioners was bound to come into conflict with the literary aims of Yeats and his fellow dramatists over the inevitable question of who was to run the theatre. Willie as a thorough-going professional had little sympathy with plays, however artistic, that kept the customers out of the theatre, and although Frank was for a time Yeats's mentor in theatrical affairs, Yeats eventually realised his limitations as a classical actor. Inevitably, too, conflict was bound to arise between the Fays and those players who were drawn to the theatre as a form of dedication to the national cause, rather than as a profession.

A professional working with amateurs finds it hard to resist being dictatorial in his methods. Although Willie professed a belief in the participation of his fellow players in decision making, he was by nature a strict disciplinarian. Once his young and comparatively inexperienced players had been received with extravagant praise in the English press both his authority and Frank's influence as a teacher began to wane.

W. G. Fay's Irish National Dramatic Company

In 1902 however no such problems arose. The little band of his disciples who were gathered together to perform Yeats's play, *Cathleen Ni Houlihan* and Russell's *Deirdre,* were drawn from the dramatic class of Inginidhe na hEireann and the Ormonde Dramatic Society. They threw themselves whole-heartedly into rehearsals, more in the belief that they were serving the national movement than in any desire to become professional players. From this group of enthusiasts, which included Honor Lavelle (Helen Laird), Máire T. Quinn, Máire Nic Shiubhlaigh (Mary Walker), Padraic Colum, Brian Callender, Charles Caulfield, James H. Cousins, Dudley Digges, P 'J. Kelly, George Roberts, Frederick Ryan, and Frank Walker, the Fays formed what they called, somewhat ostentatiously, W. G. Fay's Irish National Dramatic Company, launched with a capital of ten pounds. They had, how-ever, a valuable box-office draw to hand, for Maud Gonne had consented to make her first and only stage appearance in Yeats's play.

It is important to remember that neither Yeats nor his co-founders of the Literary Theatre were instrumental in form-ing this so-called 'national' company; neither were Martyn and Moore. Yeats's decision to associate himself with the Fays led to a parting of the ways between him and his for-mer colleagues. The Fays and their Dublin amateurs might be capable of performing folk drama, but they possessed neither the background nor the technique to encompass the sophisti-cated social drama that Moore and Martyn wanted to pro-mote.

However, in Frank Fay, Yeats had found someone who not only shared his interest in verse speaking, but possessed a marked ability to teach others. This was to be the beginning of lengthy discussions and correspondence between the two on the theory and practice of stage-craft. Yeats was quick to learn and eager to contribute the results of his research. Their discussions eventually led to his abandoning some of his more extravagant ideas of verse speaking; though it would seem, from Holloway's comment on the speaking of verse in the first performance by the new company, that the players were still required to 'cantilate': 'Most of the performers chanted their lines after the monotonous method of the "Ghost" in *Hamlet,* and a few having very marked accents, the effect produced at times was not impressive, to put it mildly.'[4]

Later in the year Frank wrote to Yeats advocating Coquelin's theory of speaking verse 'not singing or chanting it'.[5]

The two plays by Russell and Yeats were presented in St Teresa's Hall, Clarendon Street, for three performances commencing on 2 April under the auspices of Inghinidhe na hEireann. The hall had no dressing rooms and Maud Gonne arrived late on the first night, causing 'a minor sensation by sweeping through the auditorium in the ghostly robes of the Old Woman in *Cathleen Ni Houlihan* ten minutes before we were due to begin'.[6]

Yeats's play with its intensely patriotic theme was clearly the highlight of the evening. *Deirdre,* for which Russell himself designed the costumes as well as appearing as a Druid, won somewhat grudging approval.

George W. Russell (AE)

Essayist, poet, theosophist, visionary painter, and editor of *The Irish Homestead* — the journal of Sir Horace Plunkett's Irish Agricultural Organisation Society — Russell, whose pseudonym was AE, the first two letters of the word 'aeon', was one of the warmest and most selfless of the founders of the dramatic movement. He had none of Moore's vindictiveness, nor Yeats's aloofness, nor Martyn's 'touchiness', nor Lady Gregory's aristocratic aura. 'To live with him always seemed to us an unreasonable share of human happiness,' George Moore, generous for once, wrote in *Vale.* By Russell's fireside successful literary figures mingled with young and aspiring writers. His counsel on literature and art was eagerly sought, and his advice and help always available. In the few years during which he was connected with the embryo National Theatre, he contributed much to its organisation and administration. Many of the actors regarded him as the real leader of their movement. Undoubtedly this was resented by Yeats and Lady Gregory. His eventual withdrawal from active participation was, to them, a relief. 'I know you will be considerably relieved by my taking this step and that you have wished it for some time,'[7] he wrote to Yeats; but this was in the future.

The Irish National Dramatic Company

The loss of 'several hundred letters' addressed to the Fays, which Gerard Fay tells us[8] was due to a Black-and-Tan raid on his family's house, has made it difficult for historians of the Abbey Theatre to follow the sequence of events between W. G. Fay's Irish National Dramatic Company (1902) and the emergence of the Irish National Theatre Society (1903)

The Fays used a number of titles for the dramatic enterprises in which they were engaged. The first one to be registered under the Companies Act was the Irish National Theatre Society with its offices at 34 Camden Street of which Yeats was invited to become the President. This society did not come into existence until February 1903; in the meantime it was under the title of the Irish National Dramatic Company that the plays were presented, Fay's name having been omitted after the first productions. In a letter to Yeats, dated 14 August 1902, Frederick Ryan, acting as secretary of the Company, thanked Yeats for accepting the presidency of the new Society, and outlined the plans for the autumn season.[9] These included the production of two plays by Seamus Ó Cuisin (James H. Cousins), *The Sleep of Kings* and *The Racing Lug*, and a play by Ryan, himself, suitably named *Laying the Foundations*. It is noteworthy that these plays were written by members of the Irish National Dramatic Company themselves. Yeats offered them *A Pot of Broth*, a one-act farce in which he and Lady Gregory had collaborated.

In relating the events of this crucial year, in which the foundations of the future National Theatre were being laid, it might seem that Lady Gregory played no part. In fact she not only collaborated with Yeats in writing this one-act farce — a form of theatre in which she was to excel — but she had also written much of the dialogue of *Cathleen Ni Houlihan*. In September 1902 she submitted the first play wholly written by herself, *Twenty-Five*. This sentimental little play was turned down by the Fays on the surprising grounds that 'Willie does not approve of card playing as a means of getting money, and he thinks the play in country districts might incite to Emigration, on account of the glowing terms in which America is spoken of.'[10] Shortly after her far more brilliant one-act play, *The Rising of the Moon*, was rejected by the

Fays on the grounds that the character of a sympathetic police sergeant might upset nationalist feeling. Yeats's play, *The Land of Heart's Desire,* was also rejected, this time on religious grounds. The Fays feared that the reference to a crucifix, bearing the figure of Christ, as a 'tortured thing', might lead to the resignation of one of their most valued actors, Dudley Digges.

On another occasion Padraic Colum's patriotic play, *The Saxon Shillin'* was withdrawn from rehearsal by Willie Fay ostensibly on the grounds of a weak ending. Colum, however, later declared that Fay did not wish to incur the hostility of the 'garrison'.

Looking back on the events of these early years, it is plain that the Fays' judgment of plays was weak and that they lacked Yeats's fearless and combative approach in confronting the hostility of nationalist and religious criticism.

The Fays now found a base for their work in 34 Lower Camden Street. These premises they transformed into a minute theatre and workshop. As such it became a meeting-place for playwrights and actors, where ideas were eagerly exchanged and methods debated.

While the new premises were being made ready the Irish National Dramatic Company gave its first performance in the Antient Concert Rooms on 28 to 31 October 1902.[11] Father P. T. MacGinley's play, *Eilís agus an Bhean Déirce* was added to the plays already mentioned, as well as revivals of *Deirdre* and *Cathleen Ni Houlihan.*

On 4 December 1902 the Camden Street Theatre was opened with repeat performances of the season's repertoire. This proved a sad disappointment: 'The hall was cold and so was the audience. The roof leaked. The stage was so small you couldn't swing a kitten, let alone a cat.'[12]

However, Holloway, who attended a performance on 6 December, recorded his pleasure at the performances of the company in spite of the cold.

In fact the all-round acting of this little company is so effective and unconventionally realistic, as to be startling in result. The effects are all gained without the slightest effort at 'point making,' and the amount of business introduced unaccompanied by speech is very great and always effective. This habit, perhaps, at times makes the progress appear slow, but the general result makes for completeness of effect and illusion, so that each little piece becomes a perfect minature of unblemished realisation of the moving scenes enacted therein.[13]

The Irish National Theatre Society

The first meeting of the new society was held on 1 February 1903. Yeats was formally elected President, with Russell, Douglas Hyde and Maud Gonne as Vice-Presidents of the Society, the objects of which were set out in the following terms:

> ... to create an Irish National Theatre, to act and produce plays in Irish or English, written by Irish writers, or on Irish subjects; and such dramatic works by foreign authors as would tend to educate and interest the public of this country in the higher aspects of dramatic art.[14]

These objects were almost identical with those to be later stated as the objects of the Society when the patent for the use of the Abbey Theatre was granted in 1904. The most important rules were those concerning the Management and Reading committees. The former was confined to the seven signatories to the rules who were at the same time the first members of the Society; these were: the two Fay brothers, Patrick J. Kelly, Frederick Ryan, Helen S. Laird (Honor Lavelle), Máire Walker (Máire Ni Shiubhlaigh), James Starkey, with George Roberts as Secretary of the Society. The selection of plays was the duty of the Reading Committee — consisting of six members — in the first instance, but final acceptance was by majority vote of all the members.[15]

This rule was eventually to lead to the dissolution of the Society; it was inevitable that Yeats would never submit to placing power to accept or reject the plays of Synge, Lady Gregory and himself with a meeting of players whose artistic judgment he already had reason to distrust.

Rifts in the Society already began to appear later in the year when Maud Gonne and Arthur Griffith resigned in October 1903, ostensibly on grounds of heavy political work, though a deeper reason was the lack of political commitment shown by the Fays, and the feeble excuse Willie made for rejecting Colum's play *The Saxon Shillin'*. With their departure the last links were severed with the political organisations, Inghinidhe na Eireann and Cumman na Gaedheal.

For the time being, however, the little group of ardent amateurs were fired with enthusiasm for the new ideas of theatrical art that the Fays were preaching and what they believed to be a major contribution to the national revival. Willie Fay was appointed stage manager, his duties to include management of the Society and the direction of the plays;[16] as such he had the 'sole right', together with the author, 'to decide on questions as to how a scene shall be acted', and the choice of actors was left to 'the decision of the stage manager in consultation with the author'.

The Management Committee had the power 'to remunerate any official of the Society for his work', but it was not until Willie left his job as an electrician to supervise the reconstruction of the building that was to become the Abbey Theatre that he received a salary. From the time of the opening of the theatre this amounted to two pounds a week. The Society was unique at the time in that it was organised as a co-operative with equal voting rights and shares allotted to its members, an arrangement that was certainly due to George Russell who with Sir Horace Plunkett was largely responsible for organising agricultural co-operatives throughout the country. In the election of new members the Management Committee was expected to defer to the votes of all the members; among those who were elected in 1904 were Lady Gregory, Stephen Gwynn and Udolphus Wright, familiarly known as 'Dossie'. Among the new acting recruits was Sara Allgood who was elected in 1903.

Sara (Sally) Allgood had been coached by Willie Fay as a member of Inginidhe na hEireann and with Frank's aid had succeeded in eliminating a pronounced Dublin accent, acquiring in the course of time a fine resonant contralto voice. Both she and her younger sister Máire O'Neill (Molly) who joined the players in 1906 were to become popular favourites and considerable box-office attractions. More than any other players in the theatre's history the Allgood sisters possessed 'star quality' — a quality that is seldom concordant with the type of ensemble acting that the Fays were to develop. Sadly enough when they left the company their talents were to wither away in comparatively poor plays and too frequent repetitions of their Abbey successes. Sara Allgood made her first appearance as a 'walk on' in Lady Gregory's play, *Twenty-Five,* which, despite the Fays' objections, was presented together with Yeats's one-act morality, *The Hour Glass,* on 14 March in the Molesworth Hall. This stood in Molesworth Street between Kildare Street and Dawson Street and was considerably more commodious than the Camden Street premises.

Yeats and 'The Reform of the Theatre'

Between the plays Yeats lectured on 'The Reform of the Theatre' providing Holloway with an opportunity to exercise that particular brand of sarcasm that he reserved for his observations of the poet's mannerisms and utterances.

> Mr. Yeats said little to my mind of any value, and retired dreamily without reference to the little stage perched on the impromptu table awaiting the explaining that never came. Shortly after, Mr. Yeats mingled among the audience, and evidently someone asked him "What about the model?" for he got on the platform again and apologised for his completely forgetting to tell them about the little stage. 'But dreamers must be forgiven a little thing like that!'[17]

The 'little stage' that Yeats forgot to mention was a model that Gordon Craig had made for Yeats.

Craig's inspirational revolt against the elaborate illusionary scenery of Irving and Tree was little heeded in Britain though widely influential on the Continent. In March 1901 Yeats saw Craig's production of Purcell's opera, *Dido and Aeneas* and *The Masque of Love* at the Coronet Theatre in London. In his feverish pursuit of new ways for theatrical expression he was quick to realise that what Craig had to offer in terms of the play of light on his bold, stylised settings was precisely what he was seeking in his desire to place the actor and the words he had to speak firmly in the centre of the stage picture. In 1902 he wrote in a letter to the *Saturday Review* (5 March 1902),

> Last year I saw *Dido and Aeneas* and *The Masque of Love* ... they gave me more perfect pleasure than I have met with in any theatre this ten years. I saw the only admirable stage scenery of our time, for Mr Gordon Craig has discovered how to decorate a play with severe, beautiful, simple effects of colour, that leaves the imagination free to follow all the suggestions of the play. Realistic scenery takes the imagination captive and is at its best but bad landscape painting, but Mr Gordon Craig's scenery is a new and distinct art.

As Katherine Worth has said, 'There is no more impressive demonstration of Yeats's almost demonic intellectual energy than the speed and thoroughness of his assimilation of Craig's ideas.'[18] While the close association between the two did not begin until 1910, when Yeats commissioned a set of Craig's screens for the Abbey, yet in this 1903 production of *The Hour Glass* in the Molesworth Hall the influence of Craig's ideas was already apparent. Willie Fay constructed the set according to an overall design by T. Sturge Moore and Robert Gregory designed the costumes, but both artists were given precise instructions by Yeats: the background olive green, the costumes of the Wise Man and the Fool in various shades of purple. 'It was', wrote Máire Nic Shiubhlaigh, 'an outstanding example of that classic simplicity of decor which is so often sought on a stage, but seldom achieved.'

As the son of a painter, and himself for a short time a student in an art school, Yeats was a perceptive and keen observer of stage design, in many ways a pioneer of the modern stage with his 'driving originality' (as Katherine Worth calls it) and 'his extraordinary capacity for picking up hints and assimiliating them and for allowing one part of his mind to fertilise another'.[19]

In his 1903 lecture on *The Reform of the Theatre*, as revised and published in *Samhain* (October 1903), he was clearly thinking on what were at the time revolutionary lines of staging: 'I think the theatre must be reformed in its plays, its speaking, its acting and its scenery. That is to say, I think there is nothing good about it at present.' He called for plays that 'will make the theatre a place of intellectual excitement'. But first there must be 'in writers and audiences a stronger feeling for beautiful and appropriate language and gesture . . . if we are to restore words to their sovereignty we must make speech even more important than gesture upon the stage.' He denied that he desired 'a monotonous chant' in stage speech, but 'an actor should understand how to discriminate cadence from cadence, and so to cherish the musical lineaments of verse or prose that he delights the ear with a continually varied music'.

Unfortunately Yeats was tone deaf and whilst he knew when an actor was speaking his lines as he wanted them spoken, he was incapable of demonstrating other than in a vague — too easily ridiculed — manner. On the question of scenic art he was on firmer ground:

> As a rule the background should be but a single colour, so that the persons in the play wherever they stand, may harmonize with it, and preoccupy our attention. In other words it should be thought out not as one thinks out a landscape, but as if it were the background of a portrait, and this is especially necessary on a small stage where the moment the stage is filled the painted forms of the background are broken up and lost. Even when one has to represent trees or hills they should be treated in most cases decoratively, they should be little more than an unobtrusive pattern. There must be nothing unnecessary, nothing that will distract the attention from speech and movement. An art is always at its greatest when it is most human. Greek acting was great because it did everything with the voice, and modern acting may be great when it does everything with voice and movement. But an art which smothers these things with bad painting, with innumerable garish colours, with continual restless mimicries of the surface of life, is an art of fading humanity, a decaying art.[20]

Despite Holloway's dismissal of Yeats's views on the reform of the theatre, he concluded his diary entry for Saturday 14 March, 'I think the evening was the turning point in the career of the Irish National Theatre Company, and has placed them on the wave of success. May the tide be taken at the flood is my wish!' His wish was to be granted a few weeks later.

The first London visit

Stephen Gwynn, the Secretary of the London branch of the Irish Literary Society, had seen the performances in the Antient Concert Rooms in November 1902. Greatly impressed, he negotiated with Yeats for the Society to appear for two performances at the Queen's Gate Hall, South Kensington.

Since most of the players were working during the week, the visit had to take place at the weekend. On Saturday, 2 May 1903, the little band of Fay's disciples presented a matinee performance of *The Hour Glass, Twenty-Five* and *Cathleen Ni Houlihan,* and on the same evening *A Pot of Broth, Cathleen Ni Houlihan* and *Laying the Foundations.* Gwynn had conducted the advance publicity with considerable skill. The audience included many of the leaders of the literary set as well as the leading dramatic critics.

The genuine Irish voices, the sincerity of these young amateurs, their simple scenery and restrained acting accounted for much of the enthusiasm with which the London critics greeted the event. It was a welcome change from the wary praise and open hostility of the Dublin press. A. B. Walkley in the *Times Literary Supplement* (8 May) described the style of the acting:

> First and foremost, there is the pleasure of the ear. This, of course, is an accidental pleasure; we mean that it has nothing to do with the aesthetic aims of the Society, nothing to do with the dramatic theories or poetic gifts of its President, Mr. W. B. Yeats, nothing to do with art at all; it results from the nature of things, from the simple fact that Irish speakers are addressing English listeners. It is none the less a very exquisite pleasure. We had never realised the musical possibilities of our language until we had heard this Irish people speak it. Most Englishmen, we fancy, get

their notions of Irish pronunciation from Thackeray, and though, no doubt, Thackeray's version was always good-natured enough, yet the talk of Costigan and the Mulligan and the O'Dowd tends to burlesque the truth. The association is always one of drollery, whereas the English of these Irish players gives us an impression, not of drollery at all, but of elegance . . .

We are listening to English spoken with watchful care and slightly timorous hesitation, as though it were a learned language. That at once ennobles our mother-tongue, brings it into relief, gives it a daintiness and distinction of which, in our rough workaday use of it, we had never dreamed. But the charm does not stop there. These Irish people *sing* our language – and always in a minor key. It becomes in very fact "most musical, most melancholy". Rarely, very rarely, the chant degenerates into a whine. But, for the most part, the English ear is mildly surprised and entirely charmed. Talk of *lingua Toscana in bocca Romana!* The English tongue on Irish lips is every whit as melodious.

The next pleasure is for the eye. These Irish gentlemen and ladies are good to look at; the men are lithe, graceful, bright-eyed, and one at least of the maidens, with the stage name of Maire Nic Shiubhlaigh, is of a strange, wan, "disquieting" beauty. But we are not thinking so much of what Elia's Scotch friend would call their "pairsonal pretensions" as of their postures and movements. As a rule they stand stock-still. The speaker of the moment is the only one who is allowed a little gesture – just as in the familiar convention of the Italian marionette theatre the figure supposed to be speaking is distinguished from the others by a slight vibration. The listeners do not distract one's attention by fussy 'stage business', they just stay where they are and listen. When they do move it is without premeditation, at haphazard, even with a little natural clumsiness, as of people who are not conscious of being stared at in public. Hence a delightful effect of spontaneity. And in their demeanours generally they have the artless impulsiveness of children – the very thing which one found so enjoyable in another exotic affair, the performance of Sada Yacco and her Japanese company. Add that the scenery is of Elizabethan simplicity — performance is a sight good for sore eyes — eyes made sore by the perpetual movement and glitter of the ordinary stage.

For Willie Fay, upon whose shoulders had fallen the tasks of organising the travel arrangements, stage managing the plays and playing three important parts in one day, the visit was a triumph. His performance in *A Pot of Broth* was unanimously acclaimed. The critic of the *Morning Leader* (4 May) wrote, 'The gem of the evening, however, was W. G. Fay's performance of the beggar man . . . no professional actor could have played the genial scamp with greater humour as Mr. Fay puts into the part, and few certainly would have shown so much artistic moderation and sincerity.'

'Moderation' and 'sincerity' together with an emphasis on what was being *said,* rather than what was being *done,* were in the year 1903 part of the wind of change that was to sweep away the mannerisms of the Victorian stage tradition. The new 'naturalism' of Granville Barker's Court Theatre season was about to be born. In their simple and naïve way these Irish players had anticipated it.

They returned with the applause of the London audiences ringing in their ears. From now on the Dublin press could no longer refer to their work as 'amateur dramatics', but the applause of an English audience, which included the Chief Secretary for Ireland, was hardly likely to win favour in extreme nationalist circles. The hostility that greeted Yeats's *The Countess Cathleen* was now directed at the first play of John Millington Synge.

John Millington Synge

The story has frequently been told of how Yeats encountered Synge in Paris in 1896 and urged him to go to the Aran Islands, 'there to express a life that has never found expression'. Whether this advice led directly to Synge's discovery of his latent powers as a dramatist is open to question. Synge visited the Islands on five successive occasions between 1898 and 1902, but his purpose was to collect material for his book, *The Aran Islands.* During this period he completed a play, *The Moon Has Set,* a poor piece of autobiographical playwriting that showed few signs of the qualities that suddenly burst forth in 1902. It was in this year that he completed two plays, *In the Shadow of the Glen* and *Riders to the Sea;* the former laid in the Wicklow Mountains where from early childhood he frequently wandered, discovering his love of nature and listening to the talk of the people of the roads. The latter was laid in the Aran Islands and rightly acclaimed a dramatic masterpiece.

From 1898 onwards Synge visited Coole Park on his way to and from the Aran Islands, sharing with Lady Gregory his interest in the lives and lore of the country people, and following with interest the plans and developments of the Literary Theatre. In 1901 he witnessed Douglas Hyde's *Casadh an tSúgáin* at the Gaiety Theatre, and recorded that it was this play that awoke him to the possibilities of the peasant life as a matter of drama. Meanwhile he had read and admired Hyde's translations of the *Love Songs of Connacht* and Lady Gregory's *Cuchulain of Muirthemne.* In these he discovered the elements of the poetic language he was to fashion in his plays. Thus by 1902 Synge had found an environment and a linguistic form. Subject matter and a wealth of incident were to hand in the tales he had read and recorded in the Islands. His love of nature and of wild and passionate life could now find an outlet in the portrayal of the people of the remote Wicklow glens and of the desolate places of the far west — an outlet that was denied him as a writer of Petrarchian sonnets and literary criticism. There were, too, the encouragement of Lady Gregory and the challenge of a theatrical organisation anxious to obtain new forms of dramatic work. But above all Synge had discovered himself.

He was a silent man, in many ways an enigma. John Masefield who knew him better than most wrote, 'I do not know what Synge thought, I don't believe anybody knew, or thinks he knows.'[21] There were two sides to his nature: on the one hand the introspective personality, morbidly concerned with death and violence, romantically attracted to women but obsessed by his failure as a lover; a writer of introspective verse and *fin-de-siècle* fragments, such as *Etude Morbide* and *Vita Vecchia.* On the other hand there was the keen observer

and recorder of nature and human character. He was a physically powerful man who, despite his asthmatic condition and
the illness that was eventually to strike him down, could
tramp for miles over rough roads or ride a bicycle sixty miles
in a day, demanding no comfort except a good turf fire. Once
released from the gentility of his middle-class Ascendancy
background and the literary circles of Paris and London, he
found in the wild and primitive life of the Islanders a parable
of the universal human condition stripped of all surface values.
In the stories of Pat Dirrane he found parallels with Greek
myths and European folk-tales. He rejoiced in the wildness
and humour of the Island men and the frankness and beauty
of the girls, performing conjuring and gymnastic tricks for
their entertainment or accompanying their dancing on his
violin — for he was a talented musician.

It was this observer, this poet with the eye of a naturalist
and the ear of a musician who wrote, not only one of the
finest tragedies, but also one of the finest comedies in the
English language. It was because he was both subjective and
objective in the portrayal of the characters in his plays, able
to identify with their passion and their joy, as well as observ-
ing them as an outsider that he, more than any of his contemporaries, expressed the ethos of the primitive peasant
world in whose 'fiery, magnificent and tender' imagination
lay the roots of the nation's consciousness.

Synge's critics, however, were not concerned with national
consciousness; they were concerned with the national image
at a particularly sensitive period of the country's struggle for
independence and international recognition. To Arthur
Griffith and his fellow nationalists the presentation of an
adulterous Irish woman on the stage was a libel on the character of the Irish peasant.

Synge was concerned with underlying truths rather than
surface appearances and, as Seán Ó Tuama has said, 'Synge,
intuitively and by observation, felt that the pre-Christian sub-
stratum of the Irish mind was still the most important factor
in the conduct of daily life.'[22] While this was true of the remote and primitive people from whom his characters were
drawn, it was totally unacceptable to the respectable Catholic
outlook of the urban population. His plays were more vulner-

able than the legendary drama of Yeats since, with the exception of *Deirdre of the Sorrows,* produced after his death, they purported to depict contemporary — or nearly contemporary — Irish men and women speaking in what Synge inadvisedly claimed to be the authentic language of the countryside. Synge's language, that Griffith was to call 'Whitechapel Cockney', was fashioned partly from the Cromwellian English that still lingered in the Aran Islands, and partly from direct translation of Gaelic. Like all stage speech it was heightened and selective, and sometimes purely poetic, in his search for a stage language in which 'every speech should be as fully flavoured as a nut or apple.' This, of course, does not make it less 'real' than the language of Shakespeare or Shaw.

To the ear of a Dubliner in the early years of the century a language based on that of native speakers in the Aran Islands or the more remote areas of the 'Gaeltacht' inevitably seemed unreal. 'At first I found Synge's lines almost impossible to learn and deliver,' wrote Máire Nic Shiubhlaigh who played the part of Nora Burke in the first production of *In the Shadow of the Glen.* 'Every passage brought some new difficulty, and we would stumble through the speeches until the tempo in which they were written was finally discovered.[23]

'In the Shadow of the Glen'

It was however on moral and nationalist grounds that Synge's critics developed their attack on *In the Shadow of the Glen,* first presented in the Molesworth Hall on 8 October 1903. Before the play opened Arthur Griffith obtained a copy, by what means it is best not to enquire, and condemned it in the *United Irishman* as 'a crude version, pretending to be Irish, of the famous, or infamous, story of the Widow of Ephesus'. Dudley Digges, probably the best of Fay's actors, and Maire T. Quinn, whom he later married, resigned from the company in protest against its production, marking their disapproval by walking out on the opening night accompanied by Maud Gonne. Their action was, in fact, prompted by a more fundamental question that troubled many of the early players, namely what policy should the theatre adopt in relation to the national movement? The story of the Abbey Theatre might well have have been different had it not adopted the emotive word 'national' in the title of its organisation. The controversy that followed the production of Synge's play was continued for some weeks in the columns of the *United Irishman* in which Yeats skilfully diverted Griffith's criticism of Synge to himself, thereby gaining a valuable opportunity for defending and expounding his case for artistic and intellectual freedom. To Griffith's credit it must be said that, despite his attacks on Synge, he gave generous space in his publications to Synge's defenders, and did much to foster the early writers of the dramatic movement.

Enter Miss Horniman (Annie Elizabeth Fredericka Horniman)

Yeats's play, *The King's Threshold,* that accompanied *In the Shadow of the Glen* in the Molesworth Hall, while not exactly overshadowed by it, received less attention than it deserved, for it marked a considerable advance in the poet's mastery of stage technique. But the story of a legendary poet who chooses to go on hunger-strike because he is denied the prestige of sitting at the king's council table was unlikely to stir the emotions of an audience concerned with more vital political questions. Micheál Ó hAodha has pointed out that it was not until seventeen years later when Terence MacSwiney, a minor poet, playwright and Lord Mayor of Cork, died in Brixton Prison after a seventy-four-day hunger-strike as a protest against his arrest by the British Forces, that Yeats's play became something more than a matter of the prestige of a poet.[24]

Of more immediate importance was the fact that *The King's Threshold* brought Miss Horniman on her first visit to Dublin into direct relationship with the Society for which she was to provide a permanent home. Consciously or unconsciously, Yeats drew forth the protective instinct in women of a certain age. Both Lady Gregory and Miss Horniman considered it was their special responsibility to protect him in the mundane problems of his daily life, and preserve him from those who might try to divert his genius to an alien cause. Predictably this was to lead to rivalry as to which of these two formidable ladies should assume the exclusive guardianship of the poet.

Annie Horniman came from a middle-class commercial family whose fortunes were derived from Horniman's Tea. To the Irish temperament she was hardly an ingratiating character with her outspoken way of expressing her views, more especially when these were committed to the bilious yellow notepaper that caused Synge to have a lasting dislike of daffodils. There was in her nature a strange combination of a shrewd and prudent business woman, a rebel against conventional social values, a generous — if prejudiced — patron of the arts and a would-be artist. 'Do you realise you have given me the right to call myself "artist"', she wrote to Yeats for whom she designed and made the costumes for *The King's Threshold*, as well as financing the production.[25] Lennox Robinson described her costumes as 'incredibly graceless and ugly, clumsy material cut skimpily and often bordered with mock fur which would not tempt a puppy'.[26] On the other hand the critic of the *Daily Express* (9 October) wrote: 'In the matter of staging, nothing could be better. The colour scheme was conceived with great taste and the individual dresses were well designed — especially attractive were the costumes worn by the two princesses.'

Robinson had good reason to dislike Miss Horniman, as future events were to prove.

Yeats and Miss Horniman had met in London where both were members of the Order of the Golden Dawn. For several years she acted as his secretary and amanuensis when he was suffering from eye trouble. In 1894 she financed, at some personal loss, the production of his first play *The Land of Heart's Desire* at the Avenue Theatre, London. This was presented in harness with Dr John Todhunter's play, *The Comedy of Sighs* and subsequently with *Arms and The Man*, one of Shaw's first plays to be staged in the capital.

The British repertory movement owes her a lasting debt as the founder and manager of the Gaiety Theatre, Manchester, and as a generous subscriber to the Old Vic. Yet she denied that she was a philanthropist, believing the theatre must eventually pay its own way. 'It falls dead unless the public give it their aid.'

Her habits and dress expressed her unconventional and independent spirit – an ardent feminist who enjoyed smoking from the age of seventeen; an enthusiastic cyclist, wearing 'bloomers', astride a man's bicycle on which she rode across the Alps unaccompanied. Her interests included the study of astrology, and it was her favourable reading of the Tarot cards that persuaded her that the right moment had come to provide Yeats with a theatre in which his genius could flower. But whether it was the Tarot cards, or Yeats's lecture on *The Reform of the Theatre* as she herself declared, or his skilful 'softening up' of his wealthy patron that first put the idea into her head is of little consequence; what is certain is that the Abbey Theatre was not her gift to the national movement, it was an expression of her belief in Yeats's genius. It remains a paradox that the Irish National Theatre should have been provided by an English woman who strongly disapproved of the cause of Irish nationalism. Inevitably that paradox resulted in resentment and misunderstanding.

As early as April 1902 Frank Fay received a letter from Yeats containing the following:

> . . . Now as to the future of the National Theatre Company. I read your letter to a wealthy friend who said something like this. 'Work on as best you can for a year, let us say, you should be able to persuade people during that time that you are something of a dramatist and Mr. Fay should be able to have got a little practice for his company. At the year's end do what Wagner did and write a "letter to my Friends" asking for the capital to carry out your idea.' Now I could not get from this friend of mine whether he himself would give any large sum, but I imagine he would do something. I think we must work in some such way, getting all the good plays we can from Cousins and Russell and anybody else, but carrying out our theories of the stage as rigorously as possible. The friend I have quoted is interested in me . . . and I think it likely that we will ultimately get a certain amount of money . . .[27]

Despite the male sex of this 'wealthy friend' there is little doubt of 'his' identity, for it was Miss Horniman herself who wrote the letter to Yeats's dictation.

On her second visit to Dublin in January 1904 she confided to Willie Fay that should her investment in the Hudson Bay Company 'do anything exciting, I shall have enough money to buy the Society a little theatre in Dublin'.[28] From then on he scanned the financial columns with feverish excitment.

Padraic Colum
(Padraic Mac Cormac Colm)

Meanwhile a new dramatist had been discovered in Padraic Colum (in the early years he spelt his name in a variety of ways). He was a railway clerk who had been a member of the acting company from its inception.

Colum wrote three plays for the Society,[29] *Broken Soil* (3 September 1903) later revised and renamed *The Fiddler's House* (19 August 1919), *The Land* (9 June 1905) and *Thomas Muskerry* (5 May 1910). At the time it seemed he might become the most influential playwright of the Irish theatre. Sadly enough he was to emigrate to America in 1914, severing his connection with the stage. His plays differ radically from Synge's, and indeed from those of the founders of the Theatre. He made no attempt to 'poetise'. His dialogue is far closer to the actual speech of the greater part of Ireland than is the dialogue of his predecessors. The plots of his plays concern relevant and vital situations: the desire of a peasant musician to escape from the humdrum life of a small farmer (*The Fiddler's House*); the conflict between the older generation which had fought for its share of Irish earth and the young who seek the bright lights of the city (*The Land*). As a play *Thomas Muskerry* is reminiscent of Strindberg in its grim portrayal of how Muskerry from being Master of the workhouse is driven by the pressure and greed of his petty bourgeois family to his death as a pauper in the institution he once ruled.

Colum was in many ways the first of the Irish 'realists', if that ambiguous term is used in its more 'naturalist' connotation as laid down by Zola in presenting 'a man of flesh and blood on the stage, taken from reality, scientifically analysed without one lie'. 'The great merit of the play', declared the critic of *The Leader* in his review of *Broken Soil*, 'is that it deals with ordinary persons, and with the typical problems of Irish country life.' The distinction between 'realism' and 'naturalism' is hard to define, sufficient to say that Colum's plays ushered in a new trend in Irish theatre that was very different from Yeats's poetic theatre — 'remote, spiritual and ideal' — a trend that was to be developed in the plays of Lennox Robinson, T. C. Murray, St John Ervine, and many others. Unlike Synge, whose second play *Riders to the Sea* was to be presented early in 1904, Colum's plays were generally praised by the nationalist critics.

'Riders to the Sea'

Although Synge's critics could find little to offend nationalist sentiments in his one-act play, *Riders to the Sea* (25 January 1904), there was a general feeling that it was too gruesome and morbid for an audience. The *Irish Times*, in a criticism consisting of a bare ten lines, dismissed the play as 'unfit for presentation on the stage . . . the long exposure of the dead body before an audience may be realistic, but it certainly is not artistic'. *The Leader* described it as 'the most ghastly production I have ever seen on the stage'. The acting, however, was generally praised, especially Sara Allgood's performance as Cathleen, 'acted with a simplicity that resembled nature so closely that it ceased to be acting,' wrote Holloway. The Society was badly in need of a new impetus if it was to survive the attacks of its critics and the indifference of its home public. This impetus came once more from recognition overseas.

London or America?

In the spring of 1904 the Irish Literary Society again invited the Society to play in London. This time it was to be in the Royalty Theatre, the company's first appearance on a legitimate stage. In the audience were the Lord Lieutenant of Ireland, the Chief Secretary for Ireland, J. M. Barrie and Bernard Shaw.

At the matinee performance on 26 March, Synge's two plays, *In the Shadow of the Glen* and *Riders to the Sea* were presented with *The King's Threshold;* in the evening *The King's Threshold, A Pot of Broth* and Colum's *Broken Soil.* The press was generally enthusiastic, more especially for the plays of Synge and Colum. Both C. E. Montague of *The Manchester Guardian* and Max Beerbohm in *The Saturday Review* (9 April) recognised *Riders to the Sea* as a masterpiece. Beerbohm, however, had some shrewd remarks to make about the acting:

> As for the acting, I am not sure that so much simplicity as the players exemplified was quite artistically right. Mr. Yeats's poetry, doubtless — or any other man's poetry — gains by simple recitation. Dramatic inflexions of the voice, dramatic gestures and so forth, do, of course, detract from sheer melody; but, equally, their absence detracts from drama. For dramatic poetry, therefore, the right treatment is a compromise. And when these players, trained to heed Mr. Yeats's poetry, and untrained to express anything dramatically, came to interpret Mr. Synge's modern realistic prose, they did seem decidedly amiss. They, with their blank faces and their stiff movement, taking up their cues so abruptly, and seeming not to hear anything said by their interlocutors, certainly did impede the right effect of the play. For all that, I would not they had been otherwise. One could not object to them as to the ordinary amateur. They were not floundering in the effort to do something beyond their powers. With perfect simplicity, perfect dignity and composure, they were just themselves, speaking a task that they had well by heart.

Meanwhile Yeats had set out on a lecture tour of the United States and Canada, organised by the wealthy New York lawyer, John Quinn, who was to prove a stalwart champion of Irish theatre in America as he was of Irish art and literature.

Yeats realised that the praise of literary and critical circles in London was unlikely to be of use in achieving recognition in Dublin; indeed it was counter-productive in converting his nationalist critics, whereas recognition by the politically

powerful Irish-Americans might well induce them to alter
their attitudes. Moreover, there were valuable financial ad-
vantages to be reaped in the American market, and Yeats was
a keen, if unconventional, salesman.

During his visit to St Louis T. P. Gill made a generous offer
through the organisers of the Irish section of the 1904 International Exposition to sponsor a visit by the Society. The
Fays were sorely tempted, but since their players' livelihoods
depended on employment outside the theatre, the offer had
to be turned down. Dudley Digges and Maire T. Quinn
accepted the offer and with them went P. J. Kelly who was
still a member of the Society. Dudley Digges and Maire
Quinn were later married, and Digges became a successful
actor in New York and Hollywood. This break-away movement, that was later repeated by other members of the
Society, emphasised the problem that faced the Fays of how
to hold together an amateur society consisting partly of
members whose main interest was to serve the nationalist
cause, and partly of those who might be tempted to accept
offers of professional work overseas. Inevitably much depended on providing an economically viable theatre in Dublin
and an adequate livelihood for those members who wished to
become professional actors. The first of these needs was already on the way to fulfilment. The second was a more complex problem.

3
The Abbey Theatre
1904–1908

Premises

Miss Horniman's Hudson Bay shares had risen spectacularly before the London visit, and Willie Fay had drawn her attention to premises on the corner of Lower Abbey Street and Marlborough Street that could be acquired on a ninety-nine year lease. These consisted of a small music-hall theatre within the Mechanics Institute, condemned under new fire regulations, and adjacent premises in Marlborough Street. The latter had served as a bank, the home of a nationalist debating society, a recruiting centre for the Fenian movement, and the City Morgue: thus providing ample opportunity for future witticisms.

Miss Horniman acted swiftly. The lease was acquired at the cost of £170 a year; Joseph Holloway was appointed as the architect; his estimate of £1,300 for the alterations was accepted; Willie Fay abandoned a fairly lucrative job as an electrician to act as a consultant to the architect at the lordly salary of thirty shillings a week. In April 1904 Miss Horniman wrote to Yeats as President of the Society with copies to the Vice-Presidents and Willie Fay as stage-manager offering them the cost-free use of the theatre. Since the Society could only mount their productions for one week in each month, Miss Horniman proposed to let it for lectures and entertainments at 'a rental proportionate to seating capacity'.[1] The greenroom, however, was to be kept for the sole use of the Society; thus the tradition of a meeting-place for players, playwrights, stage-hands and friends — a feature that had distinguished the Camden Street premises — was continued at the Abbey. Here plays were read to the company, discussions were held and visitors entertained. Here, too, Lady Gregory provided sustenance for the players after dress rehearsals; tea was brewed and her vast Gort cakes — two feet in diameter and eight inches thick — were avidly consumed. At first this hub of the Society's life was located off the vestibule. Later this area was incorporated into the vestibule itself to make room for a coffee bar, and the green-room was moved backstage.

The vestibule was adorned with portraits by John Butler Yeats of Miss Horniman, Máire Nic Shiubhlaigh and the Fay brothers. As the years passed others were added to form what is today a unique gallery of the leading figures of the theatre's history. The vestibule was lit by three stained-glass windows, fashioned in the image of a tree in leaf, the work of Sara Purser. Steps led down to the stalls and up to the horse-shoe balcony. Beyond the installation of new seating, the auditorium itself was unchanged from its original form, but a new stage was provided with a proscenium opening of twenty-one feet and a depth of only sixteen. This was a serious defect, entailing the necessity for players, who left the stage on one side and were required to enter from the other, to use the public lane at the rear of the building whenever the full stage depth was required for scenic purposes.

Despite all its shortcomings, the old Abbey had about it the feeling of a family theatre with its close relationship between players and public. Modest and unpretentious, it could hardly be equated with the technical wonders and palatial edifices of more wealthy European national theatres. It was a beginning; a first bold gesture of Ireland's cultural identity. 'I can only afford to make a very little theatre and it must be simple,' Miss Horniman wrote to Yeats in April 1904, 'You all must do the rest to make a powerful and prosperous theatre with a high artistic ideal.'[2] Her letter was received with some reserve by the more nationalist orientated members of the Society who foresaw a danger of their plays and policies being vetoed if an English woman, known to be antagonistic to politics of any sort and particularly to Irish nationalism, was to gain control of their activities. However, her offer could hardly be refused, and a letter undertaking to abide by her conditions was duly dispatched.

At first there was no scene dock, workshop, paint-frame or wardrobe; scenery had to be made and painted on the stage, inevitably interfering with rehearsals. In 1905 Miss Horniman was able to acquire some old stables adjacent to the stage which were converted into a scene dock, workshop and paint room. In 1906 additional premises were purchased to house the wardrobe, green-room and six dressing rooms. The refusal to grant the theatre an excise licence for the sale of alcohol was of considerable benefit to the adjacent pub, but a serious disadvantage to the economics of the Abbey. More serious was Miss Horniman's embargo on cheap seats. This, she explained in her letter offering the theatre to Yeats, was 'to prevent cheap entertainment from being given that would lower the letting value of the hall'.[3] Apart from depriving the box-office of revenue, her decision gave rise to nationalist criticism. The *United Irishman* declared her action to be 'undemocratic' and 'unpatriotic', accusing her of depriving Dublin artisans from participating in their national theatre, while *The Leader* attacked the embargo on sixpenny seats that were available at other Dublin theatres, as placing 'the Theatre outside the sphere of utility of the Gaelic League'. In a letter to Holloway in August 1905 Miss Horniman wrote, 'An old friend has just arrived from Ireland. She says I am accused of religious, or political motives, of a wish to make a large fortune! No one seems to grasp the simple fact that I care for Dramatic Art.'

In the strained relations that were to ensue between herself and the Society it should be remembered that her generosity received scant acknowledgment from the national press, and was too often forgotten by the members themselves. For this, her lack of tact was largely to blame. There was, too, a lack of clarity from the beginning in the role she expected to play in the running of the theatre; more particularly when, at a later date, she was financing the Abbey company's tours in Britain. Understandably, Willie Fay resented her interference in the management and artistic work of the company, while she complained of his failure to render box-office returns and of his dilatory payment of accounts. Had she been willing to live in Dublin, the considerable business abilities which she was to use later in her management of the Manchester Gaiety Theatre might have been of considerable value during these early years of the theatre's development. But this would have required a change of heart in her attitude to national aspirations, and a greater understanding of the national temperament. As it was, her maniacal hatred of Irish politics, her resentment of Lady Gregory's influence with Yeats, and her feeling that she was merely being used as a bank, were to lead to the bitter quarrels, the vitriolic letters and eventually to the severance of her connection with the theatre.

> You are ceaselessly victimised by Lady Gregory on the score of your gratitude for her kindness. You are being made a slave, your genius is put under a net in that precious 'garden' and you are only let out when you are wanted to get something out of *me*.[4]

But this was in the future. Her present concern was to ensure the Abbey would open on time.

The patent

There remained the problem of obtaining a patent. Under Irish law application for a patent had to be made to the Lord Lieutenant and referred by him to an enquiry held by the Solicitor General at which objections could be lodged. The Gaiety, the Royal and the Queen's theatres, fearing competition of any kind, opposed the application. After lengthy consultations between the respective lawyers a formula was agreed which would permit the theatre to operate without threatening the livelihood of the other houses. The clause contained in the Society's rules relating to the plays to be performed by the Society was retained in the terms under which the patent was granted. As Miss Horniman was not resident in Ireland the patent had to be applied for in Lady Gregory's name, and she was duly 'enjoined and commanded by His Excellency not to put on the stage any exhibition of wild beasts or dangerous performances. No women or children were to be hung from the flies nor fixed in positions from which they cannot release themselves'.

More seriously, the Solicitor General in his summing up reminded the applicants that 'some questions had been asked in cross-examination of the witnesses ... that in previous productions of the Society there had been an attempt to run upon lines ... of a somewhat immoral, anti-religious and highly political character'. In view of these suggestions he advised the Lord Lieutenant that the patent should be restricted to six years, instead of the usual twenty-one and reminded the Society that it was 'on its trial'.

Curtain Up

On Tuesday 27 December 1904 the Abbey Theatre opened its doors for the first time to an audience, only a week or two later than the scheduled date. Unfortunately this delay prevented Miss Horniman from being present, but the week before she had given a large tea-party in the theatre for her friends and proudly shown them over the premises. It was indeed a triumph for her, as well as for the tireless Willie Fay. Throughout negotiations with contractors and city authorities she had displayed her keen business sense, acting promptly in making decisions, and generously providing what she could afford to create a theatre worthy of Yeats's genius.

The opening programme consisted of three one-act plays: Yeats's *On Baile's Strand* for which Miss Horniman had designed (and paid for) the costumes; Lady Gregory's farcical comedy, *Spreading the News;* and a revival of *Cathleen Ni Houlihan.* On the following evening Synge's one-act play, *In the Shadow of the Glen* was included. Máire Nic Shiubhlaigh, who played the part of 'The Old Woman' in Yeats's patriotic play, records the scene:

As was only to be expected on such an occasion we had a full house. It was the most fashionable event of the year. Distinguished-looking visitors kept drifting into the tiny vestibule, scrutinising the fittings and discussing the history of the Society, standing in little knots on the stairs. Yeats was impressive in evening dress, and kept coming

behind the scenes to see how things were getting along.
Back stage, Willie Fay, dressed for his part in one of the
new plays, a wild wig slipping sideways over his elfin face,
swung unexpectedly from a baton high in the flies, arranging the lighting. Beneath passed an endless procession of
figures carrying ladders, tools, canvas screens, draperies.
Idlers at the back of the drawn hessian curtain eyed the
swelling audience; a muffled mumble of voices rose from
the auditorium . . .[5]

On Baile's Strand with its skilful and ironic weaving of tragic
plot — Cuchulain's slaying of his unrecognised son — and
comic sub-plot — the chatter and knavery of the Blind Man
and the Fool — is one of Yeats's most successful dramas.
Frank Fay, despite his lack of inches, made a noble Cuchulain,
and Willie was at his best in the part of Barach, the Fool. His
simple setting of hessian curtains was greatly admired, so too
was his amber lighting. Amber, indeed, was the *sine qua non*
of the Abbey's lighting arrangements from now on.

In *Spreading the News* Lady Gregory displayed her skill as
a writer of high comedy, and Sara Allgood displayed an un-
suspected talent as a comedienne in the part of Mrs Fallon.
Finally Yeats, who seldom missed an opportunity to appear
on the stage, thanked Miss Horniman for the home she had
given and for the freedom that went with it enabling the
Society to ask, before putting on a play, 'Does it please *us?*
and not, until this was answered, the more usual question
'Does it please *you?*' In conclusion he declared, 'We will be
able to be courageous, and can take as our mottoes those
written over the three gates of the City of Love by Edmund
Spenser — over the first gate was "Be Bold", over the second
"Be Bold! Be Bold! and Evermore Be Bold", and over the
third "Be Bold! And Yet Be Not Too Bold".'[6]

The problem of an audience

This was a fine motto for a theatre, but its interpretation was
subject to differences of opinion between the theatre and its
audience.

Visiting the theatre two nights after its opening performance Holloway wrote, 'Oh, what a falling off this was in the audience at the Abbey tonight . . . Is it possible that there is not an audience with a love for the beautiful in Dublin sufficient to fill the little theatre for more than one night at a time?'[7] The attendance was even worse when Synge's three-act play, *The Well of the Saints,* entered the repertoire on 4 February 1905. On the third night Holloway found no more than fifty people in the house.

The rehearsals for Synge's play showed signs of the rifts amongst the players that were to be part of future troubles. Objections were made to the language, frequent reference to the Deity being particularly disliked. Máire Garvey, a member of the Society, objected to a line of Timmy, the Smith: 'And she after going by him with her head turned the way you'd see a priest going where there'd be a drunken man in the side ditch talking with a girl.'

'Tell Miss G—, or whoever it may be — that what I write of Irish country life I know to be true, and I most emphatically will not change a syllable of it,'[8] retorted Synge in a letter to Willie Fay. Yet Miss Garvey, under the existing rules of the Society, had the right to object to any passage or play whether she was in it or not.

Once again a play by Synge was attacked by the nationalist press. 'The point of view is not that of a writer in sympathetic touch with the people from whom he purports to draw his characters', wrote the critic of *The Freeman's Journal,* while Griffith made his much quoted remark about Synge's language being 'less Irish than Whitechapel Cockney'.

Lady Gregory's folk-history play, *Kincora,* based on the semi-legendary story of King Brian and his queen, Gormlaeth, was presented on 25 March. Once again Holloway remarked on the thinness of the audience: 'It is very evident that the general public has scarcely begun to nibble, much less bite with relish, at the wares presented by the Irish National Theatre Society.'[9]

It was not until William Boyle's play, *The Building Fund,* entered the repertory on 25 April 1905 that the theatre was able to display a 'House Full' notice. Laid in the midland counties, the play had neither the rich language nor the extravagant metaphors of the plays of Yeats, Synge and Lady

Gregory. It was in fact a thoroughly prosaic, well-made play of country life, providing easily acceptable entertainment. Its success, however, emphasised the problems of an amateur society whose playing time was restricted to one week in each month, making it impossible to exploit a success to set against the losses of less profitable productions.

The Spring season ended with the production of Colum's play *The Land,* which opened on 9 June 1905, written to celebrate the emancipation of the small farmer by the Irish Land Act of 1903. The critic of the *Irish Times* wrote:

> *The Land* is the work of an artist, but of an artist who loves the smell of ploughed earth and the falling rain, and balances his love exquisitely with the love of spiritual things . . . There is tragedy here, the bitter tragedy of the conflicts of ideals, and Mr. Colum has used his materials with knowledge and sympathy, with great technical skill, and with that hint of poetic exuberance which is the breath of true art.

But popular audiences in these early days were not interested in 'the breath of true art'. Even a revival of Boyle's popular comedy, *The Building Fund,* drew thin houses; for this the embargo on cheap seats was probably to blame, while the location of the theatre on the unfashionable side of the city discouraged a large stalls audience. 'I'm beginning to wonder if the Dublin playgoing public will ever find out about the National Theatre,' wrote Holloway.[10] By the end of the 1905 season it was evident that a drastic revision of the Society was necessary.

The National Theatre Society Limited

Basically the problem was economic and the fact that the players, being amateurs, could only provide one week's entertainment in each month. If larger audiences were to be encouraged, there had to be continuity of performance which in turn entailed the abandonment of the players' amateur status and the provision of a subsidy to cover their salaries until such time as the theatre could become self-supporting.

If the players could be induced to become professionals a

valuable source of revenue might be obtained by touring, for which the success of the London seasons and the offer made to Yeats of an American visit gave reason for optimism. For many of the players the prospect of relinquishing their amateur status not only entailed leaving secure jobs for an uncertain future, but seemed a betrayal of their ideals of serving the national cause. Their apprehensions were further increased by Miss Horniman's offer to guarantee their salaries up to a maximum of £400 a year. If such a subsidy was accepted from an Englishwoman, known to be hostile to Home Rule, it was feared the Society's independence would be threatened. Meanwhile Miss Horniman was negotiating a brief exploratory tour of Oxford, Cambridge and London for the end of November. Willie Fay was adamant that if a longer and more lucrative tour was to be negotiated the players must be placed under contract. Yeats, Lady Gregory and Synge were equally adamant that the power to accept or reject plays must no longer be entrusted to the uncertain judgment of the acting members.

A general meeting of the Society was called for 22 September 1906, and Yeats had written to John Quinn in New York on 16 September, 'I think we have seen the end of democracy in the theatre, which was Russell's doing, for I go to Dublin at the end of this week to preside at a meeting summoned to abolish it. If all goes well Synge and Lady Gregory and I will have everything in our hands.'[11] Yeats was ever a master tactician in dealing with committees. He was now careful to arrange that Russell — more popular with the players than he was — should move the resolution for the formation of a new society whose control would be vested in a Board of Directors consisting of himself, Lady Gregory and Synge. This meant the end of Russell's co-operative in which all members had an equal share in decision making. By fourteen votes to one Russell's reluctant motion was carried. Yeats, Synge and the Secretary, Frederick Ryan, were empowered to draw up the rules and articles of association. Yeats, again with his usual skill, delegated his share of the process to Russell. On 24 October the National Theatre Society Limited was registered under the Friendly and Industrial Societies Act.

Before the players left for their brief British tour a further meeting was held to approve the rules. By now the mood of the players had drastically changed, and the resolution that some of the members should become professionals, their salaries to be guaranteed by Miss Horniman, met with strong resistance.

> Yeats was adamant . . . 'Miss Horniman offers to subsidise us; we will accept her offer.' . . . There was some fiery talk; a number of opinions were aired. The meeting split into two factions — the Directorate and some of the members on one side strongly advocated acceptance; over two-thirds of the original Irish National Theatre Society members on the other. Eventually on the strength of shares the motion was carried in favour of the Directorate.[12]

The inevitable happened: Russell resigned and with him went most of the founding members of the old Society; they agreed, however, to stand by their decision to undertake the brief tour that was scheduled to commence on 27 November. On this occasion the London press reception was slightly less enthusiastic than on previous visits, but the success of the visits to Oxford and Cambridge encouraged Miss Horniman to start planning an extensive tour of provincial cities for the following spring. When the company returned, managerial control was firmly in the hands of Yeats, Lady Gregory and Synge with power to engage the players and arrange the repertoire. The Abbey had become a playwrights' theatre; Willie Fay continued as manager at the same salary of two pounds a week, and Frank gave up his employment as a clerk to receive thirty shillings a week. Neither were offered a place on the Board of Directors. Among those who left was Máire Nic Shiubhlaigh, although she consented to remain until 15 December in order to play in Lady Gregory's new play, *The White Cockade,* which was to open on 9 December. Her departure was a severe loss; not only was she one of the finest actresses but an idealist whose faith in the theatre as an integral part of the national movement never wavered. In 1916 she was to play her part in the Easter Rising.

For some time the situation looked critical since the seceding players announced their intention of reviving Colum's play, *The Land,* under the aegis of the old Society. This had been kept in existence in order to avoid making any change in the conditions of the patent. Since the seceding players were still members, they could theoretically swamp the voting powers of Yeats and his colleagues, and present this and other plays in the Abbey itself. The key to the situation lay in Miss Horniman's hands, and when Colum duly applied to Miss Horniman for the use of the theatre, she indignantly refused, declaring that 'the theatre was given for the carrying out of Mr Yeats's artistic dramatic schemes and for no other reasons'.[13]

For a time 'the enemy', as Willie Fay called them, was held at bay, but in May 1906 Edward Martyn and Stephen Gwynn called a meeting of the seceding members and other politico-cultural groups to discuss the formation of a new society. On 6 June The Theatre of Ireland was formed as an amateur organisation with similar aims to those of the National Theatre Society. Martyn became President and Colum its first Secretary; the members were all amateur and dedicated to the nationalist cause. Among the plays presented were Colum's *The Fiddler's House* and Seamus O'Kelly's *The Shuiler's Child,* both of which were later presented at the Abbey. In the latter play Máire Nic Shiubhlaigh returned as a guest artist in 1910 and subsequently joined the company for its first American tour.

Despite the new professional status of the players and the loss of so many who had pioneered under the Fays, the family feeling that had characterised the early years was preserved. This was partly due to Lady Gregory's matriarchal role, but in no small measure to the loyalty of those members who, unacclaimed by the public, served the theatre in the front of the house and backstage: Barney Murphy, the prompter, who had no belief in actors' pauses, Mick Judge, who served the theatre backstage for over forty years, as did Lady Gregory's close friend, Mrs Martin, who superintended the cleaning of the theatre and dispensed tea from a vast black teapot in the green-room. Udolphus ('Dossie') Wright remained with the theatre until the fifties serving as a small-part player, sometimes as a manager, at others as stage manager, occasionally as play director, more often as chief electrician, in which capacity he indulged his passion for flooding the stage with amber light and was undoubtedly more at home. An even longer record of service was that of Seaghan Barlow, master carpenter, scenic painter, impromptu designer, a student of Greek and an occasional actor, a veritable dragon in guarding his stock of scenery. Lennox Robinson rightly described him as 'sullen over his cocoa and his Greek, he states he can do nothing. An hour later, everything is done to perfection'.[14]

'Dissension is truly the curse of this country', wrote Holloway in his diary for 12 January 1906. The years 1906—7 were to bring no end to the dissensions that surrounded the newly constituted Society. For the Fays they were to bring an end to their association with the theatre; for the Directors they were to signal their eventual break with Miss Horniman; for the theatre they were to witness the greatest riot in its history. In November 1905 Yeats had noted in *Samhain* that 'Mr. Synge has practically finished a longer and more elaborate comedy than his last.'

The year 1906 opened successfully with William Boyle's comedy *The Eloquent Dempsey* (20 January). Yeats found Boyle's previous play, *The Building Fund,* 'impossibly vulgar', and his new comedy was equally far removed from Yeats's 'theatre of beauty'. Boyle's plays were the forerunners of a school of country town comedies later developed by Lennox Robinson, St John Ervine, Edward McNulty, Brinsley Macnamara and George Shiels.

Lady Gregory's satirical comedy of country town life, *Hyacinth Halvey,* which opened on 19 February, displays the influence of classical comedy in its construction; it was followed by *The Doctor in Spite of himself* (16 April), the first of her translations of Molière into her native Kiltartan dialect. In this, as in her Irish farcical comedies, Willie Fay found a perfect vehicle for his talents as a comedy actor.

The acting members of the Society were now receiving regular weekly salaries; where necessary their numbers were supplemented by part-time actors — actors who were employed elsewhere during the daytime — paid on a performance basis. This custom of drawing on semi-professional talent continued until the middle of the century, involving con-

siderable problems in scheduling rehearsals, since these had to
be held during the lunch break or in the evenings, often without the full-time players being present.

Dissension on tour

In the spring of 1906 Miss Horniman arranged a brief tour of
two night stands in Manchester, Liverpool and Leeds, inter-
spersed with visits to Irish country towns. In the summer a
more extensive tour was arranged including Glasgow, Edinburgh, Aberdeen, Newcastle-on-Tyne and Hull. Synge accompanied the players as advance manager. The spring tour had
resulted in heavy losses, and no doubt Miss Horniman feared
this tour might do the same. Willie Fay became the main target of her attacks which took the form of a veritable bom-
bardment of letters to Yeats accusing Willie of every form
of negligence, financial and artistic, as well as discourtesy to
herself. Willie was no stranger to the problems of touring. He
also possessed a hot temper and not unnaturally resented her
interference, not least her appointment of a much disliked
English manager who, she proposed, should 'make up' the
players. But her strictures were not confined to Willie. Synge
was accused of being 'under the Fays' thumb'. The girls came
under fire for leaning out of the carriage windows and talking
to men on the station platforms. One can, however, sympa-
thise with her objections to the younger members of the
troupe playing a toy trumpet in the early hours of the morning.

In an attempt to meet her objections to Willie's management, the Directors met in July at Coole Park and appointed
W. A. Henderson as Secretary with managerial duties. Now
that the theatre was operating full time, additional administrative help was essential; Willie was undoubtedly overworked;
the repertoire was small; so too was the regular public, many
of whom had deserted out of sympathy with those who had
seceded from the company. Henderson proved to be a wise
choice. On 20 October Lady Gregory's moving one-act play,
The Gaol Gate, entered the repertoire together with *The
Mineral Workers,* a new play by William Boyle. Henderson
managed to overcome Miss Horniman's refusal to allow the

sale of sixpenny seats and the theatre was crowded to over-flowing, but it was Boyle's play that drew the popular audience.

Meanwhile Yeats had been persuaded by Miss Horniman that he needed a more experienced actress than Sara Allgood to play the leading roles in his plays. Accordingly Florence Darragh, a successful London actress, was engaged at a salary far higher than the Abbey players, a fact that not unnaturally caused strong resentment. On 24 November she appeared in the leading part in Yeats's *Deirdre*.

Rehearsals for his new play were conducted by Yeats himself, which drew forth the following malicious comment from Holloway in his diary entry for 16 November, 'Yeats' attitudes during rehearsal would have made a fortune for a comic artist had he been there to note them down. He is a strange odd fish with little or no idea of acting, and the way he stares at the players from within a yard or two of them, as they act, would distract most people. You would think he had a subject under a microscope he stares so intently at them.'[15]

Another distracting habit of Yeats's was pacing up and down the auditorium during performances — 'the perpetual-motion poet' Holloway called him.

Deirdre, accompanied by Lady Gregory's play, *The Cana-vans*, was generally praised by the press, as was Miss Darragh's performance though, as Willie Fay pointed out, her highly professional technique 'was like putting a Rolls Royce to run in a race with a lot of hill ponies up the Mountains of Mourne, bogs and all. The ponies knowing every inch of the way could outpace the Rolls every time.'[16]

Yeats's *Deirdre* was to have a more distinguished revival from 9 to 11 November 1908 when Mrs Patrick Campbell, then at the height of her career, accepted Yeats's invitation to play the leading part. This time it seems that the 'Rolls Royce' and the 'hill ponies' ran smoothly side by side. 'Perhaps the most striking feature of this production,' wrote the critic of the *Daily Mail* on 10 November 1908, 'is the wonderful combination of voices, Mrs Campbell's rich, subtle, stealthy, sense-enthralling, Miss Allgood's high and sad, stimulating as strong wine, and Mr Sinclair's (as Concobar) heavy with the seven years frustrated passion.'

After appearing in a revised version of Yeats's *The Shadowy Waters,* Florence Darragh, disliked by both Synge and Lady Gregory, returned to England. But Miss Horniman was not to be deterred from her attempts to change the acting style of the Abbey. Willie Fay must be replaced by an English play director. To Synge fell the unenviable task of negotiating the situation. A compromise was reached by which Willie was to direct the peasant plays and the new play director and manager, Ben Iden Payne, was to direct all the others at a salary of £500 a year. Willie, at Synge's insistence, was to receive an extra two pounds a week; such authority as he possessed was now totally undermined. Iden Payne arrived in January 1907, aged twenty-six, unaware that he was walking into a hornet's nest. His encounter with the Abbey was brief and unhappy. Even before he arrived the players' resentment was aroused by rumours of his salary. Lady Gregory and Synge were apprehensive. What effect would this Englishman whose experience had been largely confined to Shakespearean production (he had been a member of Benson's company) have on the Abbey's style? Would the new manager have equal rights with the three Directors in the choice of plays? Yeats's insistence on Payne's engagement was the nearest thing to a rift in their relationship. It would seem that the overriding reason Lady Gregory and Synge reluctantly consented was the fear that refusal would jeopardise Miss Horniman's subsidy. In the event Payne had little chance to effect any changes. His only productions were a translation of Maeterlinck's *L'Intérieur* (the first foreign play to be produced by the Abbey) which opened on 16 March 1907, W. S. Blunt's *Fand* (20 April) and a revival of Yeats's *Deirdre* (1 April) in which he unwisely cast his wife, Mona Limerick, in the title role to the fury of Sara Allgood. When Fay was given the task of directing a revival of *The King's Threshold* Miss Horniman claimed that this was a breach of the arrangement. In fact, the division of responsibilities for directing the plays between Fay and Payne was by no means clear. When Lady Gregory asked if her Kiltartan translations of Molière were considered to be peasant plays Miss Horniman scornfully replied, 'I've made my protest against *adapting* Molière instead of using a good translation, so I have no more to say on the matter.'[17]

Meanwhile a more serious dissension was to shake the foundations of the theatre. On 26 January 1907 Synge's new comedy, *The Playboy of the Western World,* was first presented to the public.

The Playboy riots

Visitors to Dublin applying for seats for the performance on Tuesday night might well have been surprised by the following printed note in reply to their application.

> National Theatre Society,
> Abbey Theatre,
> Lower Abbey Street,
> Dublin.
> Dear Sir,
> In response to your application, we enclose Voucher to be exchanged at Booking Office at Theatre, or at Messers Cramer's, Westmoreland Street for Numbered Ticket. Should it be impossible to hear the play the night you select we will send you another Voucher on receiving your application.
> Yours faithfully,
> W. A. Henderson,
> *Secretary.*

The events of the momentous week that followed the opening night have been adequately recorded. It is, however, worth summarising the reasons why a play, intended as a comedy and subsequently acclaimed as a masterpiece, aroused such a storm of anger.

Nationalist resentment against the policy pursued by Yeats in his demand for the intellectual freedom of the artist had, as we have seen, been present from the birth of the Literary Theatre. The adoption of the name 'National Theatre' by a society subsidised and, as some believed, controlled by an Englishwoman known to be hostile to Irish nationalism was a further cause for offence, added to which was a feeling of sympathy for those players who had left the theatre for idealistic reasons. While the plays of Lady Gregory and Yeats gave little cause for offence — *Cathleen Ni Houlihan* had largely assuaged the anger aroused by *The Countess Cathleen* — Synge's plays were a very different matter. With the exception of *Riders to the Sea* they had been a constant irritant to his nationalist critics, portraying, as their author claimed, actual incidents from peasant life in the West of Ireland and couched in language that seemed to many to be not only unreal, but often offensive if not blasphemous. Stung by the ignorance and, what seemed to him, malevolence of his critics, Synge had remarked to Willie Fay, 'The next play I write I will make sure I will annoy them.'[18] It is unlikely that in writing *The Playboy* Synge set out to provoke the anger of his critics, but it contains more violence and what was considered at the time 'bad language' than his earlier plays. When the play was submitted to the Lord Chamberlain for production in England many of the references to the Deity as well as other offending passages were removed. It was to be another five years before Shaw's 'Eliza Doolittle' shocked the London public with her 'Not bloody likely!'

From the beginning of rehearsals Willie Fay had seen trouble ahead.

> As soon as I cast my eyes over the script of *The Playboy of the Western World* I knew we were in for serious trouble unless he would consent to alter it drastically. . . . We might as well have tried to move the Hill of Howth as move Synge. That was his play, he said, and barring one or two jots and tittles of 'bad language' that he grudgingly consented to excise, it was the play that with great screwing up of courage we produced.[19]

Yeats and Lady Gregory, too, had asked for cuts without avail. Holloway records that one of the actors had heard that 'there was organised opposition to hiss the play', and Mary Colum recalls 'reports spread through Dublin that there were improprieties in the play and that the womanhood of Ireland was being slandered . . . At the opening night there was tenseness and expectation in the air.'[20] It was in an atmosphere of considerable apprehension that the actors faced the public on Saturday 26 January.

Whether the apprehensions of the actors and the tense feeling in the auditorium accounted for the fact that much of the comedy appears to have been lost and the play seemed too close to reality, lacking the 'joy' that Synge demanded in his preface, it is impossible to judge. When 'Old Mahon' made his surprise appearance in Michael James's 'shebeen' — a *coup de théâtre* that normally produces a gale of laughter — Padraic Colum recorded, 'There stood a man with horribly-bloodied bandage about his head, making a figure that took the whole thing out of the atmosphere of high comedy.'[21] Máire Nic Shiubhlaigh who believed that Synge's irritation at the reception of his earlier plays accounted for the 'nasty streak' in his characterisation wrote, 'Imaginative production on the first night, however, less emphasis on tragedy, more on comedy, would have hidden this . . . when it was given on the first night it was played seriously, almost sombrely, as though each character had been studied and its nastiness made apparent.'[22]

C. P. Curran, who was also present on the first night, declared, 'I was and am satisfied that it was the unrelenting realism of the production in its last scene, a realism never again attempted in any of the later performances I have seen, that threw the audience into final revolt . . . We were living, it should be remembered, in 1907, unconditioned to excess in speech and action.'[23]

Certainly Willie Fay, who carried the greatest burden on that fatal first night, seems to have failed to present the more attractive side of Christy's character. The critic of *The Leader* described him as 'a broken down evil-looking tramp', and Holloway, recording a conversation with James Joyce in which the latter referred to Fred O'Donovan who later played the part, stated, 'He [Joyce] thought O'Donovan's 'Christy Mahon' the true type intended by the author, but I told him W. G. Fay's was a much more repulsive and realistic type, and the latter was rehearsed under the dramatist's own direction and, therefore, his idea of the part.'[24]

Synge, it must be remembered, was not only under considerable pressure from his actors and fellow Directors to cut and alter lines, but was also far from well during rehearsals, and this too may account for the lack of comedy in his direction of the play. Finally these criticisms refer to the opening night when all too often performances suffer from first night nerves – surely never more so than on this occasion.

Word of mouth spreads quickly in Dublin. The reactions of the first night audience and the violent press criticisms were quite sufficient, given the sensitive political climate and the hostility felt towards Synge himself, to draw an angry crowd – whether organised or not – to the theatre on the following Monday. The presence of the Dublin Metropolitan Police lining the walls of the auditorium, the subsequent arrests and court proceedings, and – worst of all – Yeats's agreement to introduce a gang of toughs from Trinity College who, besides being drunk, chose to sing the British National Anthem, added fuel to a highly inflammatory situation; but what angered the opponents of the play most was the refusal of Yeats and his fellow Directors to bow to popular demand for the withdrawal of the play. Yeats's determination to stand firm was both courageous and justified, though for many months the theatre was to suffer a serious financial loss. William Boyle, the Abbey's most popular playwright, withdrew his comedies from the repertoire 'as a protest against your [Yeats's] action in attempting to force a play – at the risk of a riot – upon the Dublin public contrary to their protests of its being a gross misrepresentation of the character of our Western peasantry'.[25] Boyle had neither read nor seen the play.

Undoubtedly mistakes were made by Synge and Yeats in dealing with public reactions. It may also be true that the production was lacking in balance, but the reactions of a large section of the audiences on subsequent nights were totally unjustified, since not a word was heard of the play until the end of the week by which time severe cuts had been made and passions were exhausted.

Yeats's courageous challenge to meet Synge's opponents in open debate on the following Monday provided a further opportunity for a demonstration of mindless antagonism and did nothing to convert the opponents. It did, however, give Yeats a chance of restating his unwavering belief in the freedom of the artist – a chance he was never slow to seize. Ever at his best when facing opposition, and fearless in the face of insults and abuse, he showed once again that, while he might have 'little or no idea of acting', he was a splendid performer when it came to a public debate. 'I never witnessed a human being fight as Yeats fought that night,' wrote Mary Colum, 'nor knew another with so many weapons in his armory.'[26] Synge himself was too ill to attend the meeting. To Miss Horniman's credit she wrote to Synge, 'I feel myself a worm not to have come over, but the Directors took no notice of my offers to come and join the fray.' Meanwhile *The Playboy* was published and sold two hundred copies in the first week.

Whatever damage the riots did to the finances of the theatre they focused international attention upon it, and upon Synge himself. As Yeats was to declare when facing the riots that accompanied *The Plough and the Stars,* 'From such a scene in this theatre went forth the fame of Synge.'

'The Playboy' vindicated

The Abbey now faced a largely hostile audience; its future existence was in jeopardy. The productions that followed *The Playboy,* including Lady Gregory's plays *The Jackdaw* (23 February), *The Rising of the Moon* (9 March), the revival of Yeats's *Deirdre* with Mona Limerick and *Fand* (20 April), averaged thirty pounds a week as compared with the average takings in the latter months of 1906 of two hundred and forty pounds a week. The future now depended on the Abbey's chances of recuperating its losses on tour.

In May the company set forth on an itinerary that again included Oxford, Cambridge and London. Yeats and Lady Gregory were determined, despite the fears of the company, to submit *The Playboy* to the reactions of the London critics, though omitting it from the repertoire in Glasgow and Birmingham where large Irish audiences might be expected to repeat the Dublin disturbances. In Oxford the play was well received, and on 6 June 1907 the play opened at the Great Queen Street Theatre in London. Yeats's belief in Synge was confirmed. The press reactions were almost unanimous in their praise, and Synge became a literary lion overnight. When *The Playboy* was revived at the Abbey in 1909, except for a few hisses on the first night, it was applauded by the audience, though the press maintained its hostility. It says much for Yeats's generosity, against those who accused him of jealousy of the success of other playwrights, that he, whose dream of a 'theatre of beauty' had found no support, selflessly fought the battle for Synge. In 1911 Lady Gregory fought that battle again in America.

Miss Horniman withdraws

When the tour ended Iden Payne, feeling he could not find a way of working with the Abbey, left the company. His departure was a further blow to Miss Horniman's attempts to change the character of the theatre. She now informed Yeats that she would withdraw from active participation in its affairs, and provide no more money for further ventures, though her annual subsidy was to continue for the next three years. Her interests were transferred to the Gaiety Theatre, Manchester, after a fruitless appeal to Yeats to join her and bring his plays with him.

A lost playwright

Back in Dublin a new playwright appeared on the horizon, George Fitzmaurice. *The Country Dressmaker* was presented on 3 October 1907. Despite Yeats's fear of another riot, the play was well received, and frequently revived. Holloway found the playwright 'a nice unassuming fellow with, I am sorry to say, a hankering after Synge and his methods of presenting the Irish character on the boards . . . I like Fitzmaurice and hope he won't be spoiled by the cult.'[27] Yeats, however, never liked Fitzmaurice's plays. Writing to John Quinn, his American agent, he called *The Country Dressmaker* 'a harsh strong, ugly comedy. It really gives a worse view of the people than *The Playboy*. Even I rather dislike it, though I admire its sincerity.'[28] Fitzmaurice's subsequent dramatic fantasies with their rich Kerry dialect were too far removed from the mood of Dublin audiences of the time. The literary critic, W. J. Lawrence, dismissed his powerful one-act morality *The Pie-Dish* (1908) as 'a studied insult to play-goers' 'a lot of gabble strung together'.[29]

In his introduction to Fitzmaurice's published plays (Vol. 1, *Fantasies*) Austin Clarke expressed the view that Yeats and

Lady Gregory kept the plays out of the theatre's repertoire
through jealousy stemming from the favourable criticisms
The Magic Glasses received from the London critics.[30] For
this there is no real evidence. There were many plays that the
two Directors disliked, notably those of William Boyle, that
were both performed and revived, but like all managers — and
dramatic critics — their judgments were not infallible. The
rejection of Fitzmaurice's delightful fantasy, *The Dandy Dolls,*
undoubtedly came as a bitter blow to the highly sensitive and
reserved character of the playwright. Whether or not this was
the reason for his loss of interest in having his plays performed, Fitzmaurice became a recluse, secretly writing plays
for publication in the *Dublin Magazine,* and refusing to discuss his work or allow it to be performed. In recent years the
publication of his plays and their revival by the Abbey has
brought about a re-appraisal of a forgotten dramatist who,
had he received greater encouragement, might have proved a
worthy successor to Synge. A theatre run by playwrights will
always be open to the charge that its directorate favour their
own plays at the expense of others. The Abbey has been no
exception; even Synge believed his plays took second place to
those of Yeats and Lady Gregory.

The Fays depart

When the players returned from London in June 1906 Willie
Fay was reinstated as manager. His position, however, had
been severely undermined, not only by Iden Payne's appointment but also by the players' realisation that he no longer enjoyed the full confidence of the Directors. Moreover the
praise that the English critics had lavished on the players,
both in London and in other cities, put them in no mood to
submit to his authoritarian methods.

Two new plays, Lady Gregory's *Dervorgilla* (31 October)
and a play written by herself and Yeats, *The Unicorn from
the Stars* (21 November), entered the repertory before the
company set out again on tour at the end of November.
Willie Fay complained bitterly of slackness and lack of punctuality at rehearsals — the high-spirited Molly O'Neill being
particularly difficult, 'using her influence with Mr. Synge to

do as she likes,' as Willie wrote to Lady Gregory. J. M. Kerrigan and Sara Allgood were threatening to resign, and Willie, too, was reaching a point when he could no longer work as the hireling of the literary-minded directorate. In November he confessed to Holloway that he and Frank were 'quite sick of the Yeats-Gregory management'.[31] Clearly a storm was brewing.

On 4 December the Directors met to consider a memorandum from Willie containing the following proposals:

1. That the Directors put up a notice shortly that all contracts within the National Theatre Society terminate on such a day. That people wishing to re-engage write to W. G. Fay.

2. That all engagements be for a season only and terminable by a fortnight's notice on either side.

3. That where the Directors require special actors or actresses for their performances I should engage them on terms to be decided between the Directors and myself and for such parts or performances as the Directors shall decide.

4. That the power of dismissing those under my contracts shall rest with me after due consultation with the Directors in the case of principals.

5. There shall be no appeal to any other authority than mine by the people engaged by me on all matters dealt with in their contracts.[32]

This last proposal referred to that habit of players of appealing to the Directors whenever they disagreed with Fay's rulings. Basically what Fay was seeking was the right of an artistic director to control his own company, a right which today would be unquestioned, but there was clearly more to it than that. Willie's authority had been effectively undermined by the appointment of Payne, as well as by Miss Horniman's endless complaints, some of which may well have been justified. There is no doubt that discipline was slack. On 17 December Willie wrote to Yeats,

I wish to bring to your notice that out of seven rehearsals on tour, Miss M. Allgood [Molly O'Neill] was only in time for one and on one occasion was an hour late. A rehearsal is called for this evening and her sister Miss Sara Allgood told me that she . . . could not come to rehearsal as she had an appointment. I asked her what the appointment was and she said it didn't matter. Owing to the fact that I have no direct control over these people, and consequently have no power to make them obey my orders, I must refuse to carry any responsibility as to the date of productions arranged . . .[33]

Willie was playing directly into Yeats's hands; for some time he had been seeking an opportunity to curb the Fays' independent attitude. Now that Willie had lost the confidence of his players, the last vestiges of W. G. Fay's National Dramatic Company could be removed. 'We must have a change somehow, or we shall all be worn out, and that change must be more than good resolutions on everybody's part,'[34] Yeats wrote to Synge on 18 December. In the meantime the Directors had decided to turn down Willie's proposals. Their reply, dated 4 December, was duly recorded in the minutes:

1. That we could not agree to his proposal about dismissal of the Company and re-engagement by him personally.

2. That we cannot enlarge the powers already given under contract.

3. We cannot abrogate the right of appeal to the Directors already possessed by the Company.

4. That an improvement in discipline is necessary, and that rules with this object be drawn up in consultation with the Company. That the Company be asked to elect, say three members to consult with the Stage Manager and Directors as to the rules of discipline. That the rules so drawn up be put to the Company as a whole for their decision.

5. That it be explained to the Company that this Theatre must go on as a theatre for intellectual drama, whatever unpopularity that may involve. That no compromise can be accepted on this subject, but that if any member find himself unable to go on with us under the circumstances, we will not look upon it as unfriendly on his part if he go

elsewhere, on the contrary we will help him all we can.

    6. That henceforth a Director must always go with the Company upon the more important tours.[35]

As the company was still on tour, it was not until the beginning of January that Lady Gregory explained to Willie that the Directors could not accept his proposals. On 13 January Willie wrote to Yeats,

> Dear Mr Yeats,
> I regret that under present circumstances I do not see my way to continue my engagement with the National Theatre Society. I herewith give one month's notice. My engagement will terminate on Thursday 13th February 1908.
> I am, faithfully yours,
> William G. Fay.[36]

On the same day Frank also resigned, making it clear that he did not resign his membership of the National Theatre Society. With them went Willie's wife, Brigit O'Dempsey.

    Their departure caused almost as much clamour as *The Playboy*, though Yeats tried to gloss it over with a suitable valedictory paragraph in the press which he later repeated in *Samhain*.[37] For Willie the break may not have been unwelcome. It was clear that he was fundamentally out of sympathy with the literary policy of the directorate, as exemplified in paragraph five of their reply to his proposals. He had in any case been shockingly rewarded for his work as he bitterly complained to Holloway: 'he had trained several companies and had arrived at the age of thirty-five and had made nothing. Had he worked fourteen hours [a day] for over five years in America he would have been a rich man today and not a poor fellow without a copper.'[38]

    The opportunity to seek 'a world elsewhere' was probably already in Willie's mind. In March 1907 the American impresario, Charles Frohman, had visited the Abbey and there was talk of an American tour. Now Frohman was to invite him to go to New York to play in a one-act Irish play as a curtain-raiser to a play he was currently presenting at the Savoy Theatre in 34th Street. Willie hastily summoned his brother from Dublin and on the 18 February they appeared

together with Brigit O'Dempsey in *A Pot of Broth,* followed
shortly after by *The Rising of the Moon* in which they were
joined by Dudley Digges. Unfortunately word reached Dublin
that they were being billed as 'The Irish National Theatre
Company' and Yeats's name was being freely used in connection with the production. Yeats was furious and John Quinn
in New York, acting on his instructions, threatened an in-
junction. On 18 March at a meeting of the Society the Fay
brothers were suspended from membership of the organisation whose existence was largely due to their selfless devotion. Worse was to follow when they were publicly repudi-
ated by four of their leading players, Sara Allgood, Arthur
Sinclair, J. M. Kerrigan and Máire O'Neill, in a letter to the
editor of the *Evening Mail* (21 May 1908) in which they
stated that 'the acceptance of the proposals of Mr W. G. Fay
by the Directors would have led to the dissolution of the
company, and we, the undersigned, take this opportunity to
say that we certainly would not have rejoined under Mr Fay's
proposed conditions'.

'The end of the story was', as Gerard Fay wrote, 'a dismal
one with recriminations flying both ways and generosity out
of the question.'[39] It was ten years before Frank appeared
again at the Abbey, and then only in short-lived revivals of
The Hour Glass and *The King's Threshold.* After leaving Dublin he spent some years touring England with Shakespearean
companies, returning to Dublin in 1921 where his major
occupation was teaching acting and elocution. He died in
1931. Willie was never invited to return. In England he pursued a comparatively satisfactory career as an actor and play
director until his death in 1947.

The Fays were not destined to become great actors, but
what they contributed to the Abbey Theatre was unique;
without them the Irish National Theatre might never have
been born. Now their work was done; had they stayed longer
their reputation would have been overtaken by members of
the company they themselves had trained, a company that
was to develop into the most powerful group of players in
the theatre's history. Sara Allgood was on her way to gaining
an international reputation; Arthur Sinclair was coming to
the height of his career as a comedian; Máire O'Neill possessed

the power to rivet attention upon herself from the moment she walked on the stage; in Fred O'Donovan there was a fine romantic actor in the making; and to support these were Sydney Morgan, Ambrose Power, J. A. O'Rourke and J. M. Kerrigan.

With the Fays' departure much of the particular acting style that had characterised the early years of the Society began to change. Comedy was played more broadly, acting generally was treated with greater naturalism; simplicity gave way to technique. In brief, the days of the gifted amateur were over and a new professionalism was being born to meet the needs of a new generation of audience and playwrights.

4
The Professional Theatre
1908–1914

Plays and controversies

The strength of the Abbey is its ability to recover from the mistakes and misfortunes that would have overwhelmed a less resilient organisation. Not the hostility of its critics, the departure of its players, the withdrawal of its playwrights, not financial disaster, nor incompetent management, not even fire itself, have succeeded in destroying it. Decade after decade it has been declared moribund, written off as the relic of departed greatness, and yet the supply of new plays has never dried up, and, though its actors have been wasted and dispersed, new talent has never been lacking to take their place. The fact is that Ireland needs the Abbey, if only as a cockpit to fight out her own internal conflicts, but more importantly, as Yeats above all realised, as the eyes and voice of the nation, its memories and its dreams.

The clamour and excitement about the Fays' departure from the Abbey had scarcely died down, the leading articles, the letters and the interviews in the newspapers had scarcely ceased, when the players were again facing a hostile audience, though this time less persistent than the riots that had greeted *The Playboy* a little more than a year earlier. *The Piper,* by Norreys Connell (Conal O'Riordan) who for a short time was manager of the theatre, was produced on 13 February 1908. The play — a satire on the garrulousness of a group of Irish patriots involved in the 1798 Wexford rising — was booed and hissed on the grounds that it was a slander on Irish patriots.

Later in the same year the vitality of the Abbey as the keeper of the nation's conscience was again demonstrated by the anger and dislike aroused by Lennox Robinson's *The Clancy Name*, the first play from the so-called school of 'Cork Realists'.

But the playwright against whom the patriotic zealots chiefly vented their spleen was now to pass beyond the reach of the slings and arrows of criticism. On 24 March 1909 Synge died.

His death robbed the Abbey of a playwright who might have provided a valid artistic alternative to the wave of prosaic realism that was approaching. 'My next play must be quite different from *The Playboy*,' he wrote to his fiancée, Molly O'Neill in December 1906. 'I want to do something quiet and stately and restrained and I want you to act in it.' Synge completed the first draft of *Deirdre of the Sorrows* in November 1907, but he was still working on it when he died. In it he was searching for a new language, abandoning the exuberance of *The Playboy* in favour of a tauter and more muted effect while still capable of rising to the higher flights of poetic expression. By re-telling a story that had inspired Yeats and George Russell in those early days of the Celtic renaissance, Synge was building a bridge between the poetic movement and the character realism and language of his peasant plays. On 13 January 1910 *Deirdre of the Sorrows*, edited by Lady Gregory, Yeats and Molly O'Neill, was performed for the first time. Molly directed it as well as playing the leading part. For the first time, now that he was dead, his critics had no reason to attack.

Draw a little back with the squabbling of fools when I am broken up with misery. I see the flames of Emain starting upward in the dark night; and because of me there will be weasels and wild cats crying on a lonely wall where there were queens and armies and red gold, the way there will be a story told of a ruined city and a raving king and a woman will be young for ever. I see the trees naked and bare, and the moon shining. Little moon, little moon of Alba, it's lonesome you'll be this night, and tomorrow night, and long nights after, and you pacing the woods beyond Glen

Laoi, looking every place for Deirdre and Naisi, the two lovers who slept so sweetly with each other.[1]

It was Lady Gregory more than any other playwright who came nearest to Synge's last play in fusing together the legendary world with a language based on the Anglo-Irish language of the west of Ireland, though she lacked his genius. Her output of plays, mostly in the Kiltartan dialect, was truly remarkable. Between 1902 and 1912 — her most productive period — she wrote no less than nineteen plays, albeit some of them in one act, made four translations, or rather adaptations, in addition to her collaborations with Yeats and Douglas Hyde.

Among the new dramatists whose work was encouraged by Lady Gregory was W. F. Casey who for a time acted as Secretary to the Society, and later was to become editor of *The Times*. His two plays, *The Man who Missed the Tide* (1 February 1908) and *The Suburban Groove* (1 October 1908) illustrate the new trend towards realism, the former treating middle-class country-town society, the latter the pretensions of Rathmines suburban life.

The first night of *The Suburban Groove* was also memorable as the debut of a new musical director, Dr J. F. Larchet. Music was introduced during the intervals shortly after the opening of the theatre. For a time Arthur Darley, a distinguished violinist, was engaged to play traditional Irish airs in front of the curtain; later a small orchestra was installed in front of the stage. When Larchet took over the musical direction he established a tradition of fine music that seldom failed to please the critics no matter how harshly they might judge the play. Larchet was to remain with the Abbey for twenty-six years, becoming in the course of time as well loved by the regular patrons as the most popular players. Indeed a popular myth records that there were those who would leave the theatre during the acts and return to enjoy Jack Larchet's music during the intervals.

The Cork realists — Esmé Stuart, Lennox Robinson and Thomas Cornelius Murray

Lennox Robinson, as he later styled himself, was the son of a

Protestant clergyman from County Cork, a county that has given Ireland many fine writers. As a young man his experience of the theatre was limited to the touring companies – mostly English – that visited the Cork Opera House; his favourite actor being Martin Harvey. In 1907 he witnessed a performance of the Abbey company.

> Here on the Cork stage was life, real Irish life. . . . It came on me in a flash, as a revelation, that play-material could be found outside one's own door, at one's own fireside. . . . If the plays seemed real, so did the players. I had been accustomed to players who moved somewhere, anywhere, at the end of almost every speech, who never made a direct exit, but always turned half-way and again at the door to deliver their penultimate and ultimate speeches. But these players behaved on the stage like human beings. . . . Gone now for ever were plays for Martin Harvey and his like, gone for ever novels about dukes – even Irish ones. In the future, in the words of William Allingham, I must 'sing of what I know'.[2]

His first play, *The Clancy Name,* the plot of which concerns a murder story laid in West Cork, was produced at the Abbey on 8 October 1908. It drew forth from the critic of *The Freeman's Journal* a notice so preposterous that even his fellow critics were moved to remonstrate. Briefly, he claimed that a libel had been perpetrated on all who owned the name of Clancy, and that the fate of the author be 'referred in the usual way to the acting sub-sheriff of the city'.

Lennox was later to become attached to the Abbey for the greater part of his life as manager, director of plays and eventually as a member of the directorate.

It was after the success of his second play, *The Cross Roads* (19 April 1909) that Yeats summoned him to Dublin to meet Lady Gregory and himself who 'were considering new arrangements at the Abbey Theatre'. He was offered the post of manager and director of plays, but before this totally inexperienced young man took up his post, he was sent for a six weeks attachment to Charles Frohman's repertory season at the Duke of York's Theatre, London, to observe the directing methods of Dion Boucicault (the son of the playwright),

George Bernard Shaw and Harley Granville Barker. How much he learned from so short an apprenticeship is doubtful. As a play director Lennox had a fine feeling for dialogue and character, but little visual sense, but the Abbey's financial resources were limited and its predominantly naturalistic plays made small demands on the scenic artist. When he returned to Dublin the play director's name was, at Granville Barker's suggestion, henceforth included in the programmes of all new productions.

As a dramatist Lennox's plays were amongst the most popular in the theatre's repertoire. His early work was marked by the disenchantment and didacticism of a frustrated idealist, but he was soon to discover in his comedies of suburban and country town life a gay and gentle wit slightly marred by sentimentality. Many of his plays were seen in London and New York: *The Whiteheaded Boy* (1916) in particular proved to be one of the longest running comedies in wartime London. But success at the Abbey brought meagre financial rewards and, despite his overseas productions, Lennox was never a rich man. It is worth remembering that until 1910 Abbey dramatists received no royalties for their plays.

Like Lennox Robinson, T. C. Murray, a schoolmaster from Macroom, West Cork, had his interest in the stage awakened by visits to the Cork Opera House, and he, too, was inspired to write plays by the establishment of the Abbey Theatre.

In his four major plays, *Birthright, Maurice Harte, Autumn Fire* and *Michaelmas Eve,* he used as his materials the characters and themes of his native county — the frustration of the loveless marriage, the tragedy of exile, the slavery of the hired farm hand, the problem of the spoiled priest and the bleak years of the old; yet so basic is his creation of human character and so elemental his themes that these plays have a universality that reaches out far beyond their provincial background. Micheál Ó hAodha has pointed out that Murray was the first realistic playwright to write tragedies of rural life from the inside. As a son of the soil himself he seems at times inhibited from adopting a critical attitude to the frustrations and unhappiness that he depicts with such heart-rending accuracy. Unlike Synge's treatment of peasant life, Murray's characters are neither flamboyant nor brutal, restraint being the keynote of his approach to character. When in later life Murray moved to Dublin he attempted to emulate the dramatists of the twenties in their portrayal of city and suburban life. As a result his plays, though always the work of a craftsman, lack the insight and truth of his rural tragedies. Nevertheless Murray must be counted amongst the great playwrights of the Irish dramatic movement.

'The Shewing-Up of Blanco Posnet'

While Lennox was learning his trade in London, the Abbey once again found itself involved in conflict. This time the trouble arose, not with the nationalists, but with Dublin Castle in the persons of the Lord Lieutenant and his officials. Shaw's 'Sermon in Crude Melodrama', *The Shewing-Up of Blanco Posnet,* had fallen foul of the English censorship on grounds of blasphemy.

With his usual adroitness Shaw promptly offered it to the Abbey for production in Ireland where the Lord Chamberlain's writ did not run. The Abbey had turned down his Irish play, *John Bull's Other Island,* in 1905 on the grounds that they had no actor capable of playing an English character. These grounds seem in hindsight to be rather strange, since the Abbey now saw no problem in presenting a play the entire cast of which was American. Whether it was to atone for this error or because Yeats — who, like Shaw, was ever quick to seize a propaganda point — saw an opportunity to confound his nationalist critics by demonstrating his theatre's independence of English opinion, is hard to say.

The theatre's decision to produce a play considered by the Lord Chamberlain to be blasphemous, presented the Castle with a serious dilemma. The Lord Lieutenant had no power to censor the play, but he could withdraw the theatre's patent which disallowed 'any representation which should be deemed or construed immoral'. If, on the other hand, he took no action he could be accused of defying the Crown of which he was the representative. To Lady Gregory fell the task of arguing the case for the theatre's right to present the play, a task that she undertook with considerable tact and determination in the face of the threats of the Castle officials on the one hand, and the pleading of Lord Aberdeen on the other. The play was presented on 25 August 1909. The theatre was crammed to the roof and Lady Gregory recorded that, 'guineas were offered for standing room in the wings'.[3] Everything depended on whether objections were lodged on the grounds of blasphemy. There were none: the 'blasphemies' were uttered by an American horse-thief, not by an Irish peasant.

The end of the subsidy

For some months the Directors had been negotiating with Miss Horniman for the purchase of her lease of the Abbey. An agreement was eventually reached on 20 February 1910 by which she would continue to pay the subsidy until the end of the year and would sell the lease of the premises, on the purchase and adaptation of which she had spent over £10,000, to the Directors for £1,000. This was a generous offer, bearing in mind that Miss Horniman was not a rich woman and at this time was heavily committed to financing her Manchester repertory theatre. Had this been the end of the affair the story of her relationship with the theatre might have ended happily. Events were to prove otherwise.

On Friday 6 May 1910 King Edward VII died. The Abbey was currently performing Padraic Colum's play, *Thomas Muskerry*, under Lennox Robinson's direction. There was to be a matinée as usual on the Saturday. In the event all the Dublin theatres closed down out of respect, except the Abbey. Lennox, young and inexperienced, learnt the news at eleven fifteen that morning. Yeats was in Paris, Lady Gregory in Gort.

> I knew that the Abbey Theatre had been carried on from the beginning as a purely artistic venture. I knew that its policy was to ignore politics, and I thought if we closed we would be throwing ourselves definitely on one side and that we should remain open taking no notice of a circumstance that had no significance to the arts. However I decided to leave the matter to Lady Gregory and wired her as follows: 'Theatres closing here. What am I to do? I think we should remain open but leave decision to you.'[4]

Lady Gregory promptly cabled, 'Should close through courtesy.' It seems, however, that the telegraph boy had more important things to do than the menial task of delivering telegrams. It was not until the matinée performance was almost over that Lady Gregory's instructions reached the Abbey. This does not of course exonerate Lennox from continuing with the evening performance. Miss Horniman was furious. Here was another example of her theatre being used for those 'wicked politics'. She demanded that a public expression of regret be made, claiming that the failure to close was a breach of her agreement with the Directors (Miss Horniman claimed she had stipulated that the theatre should not be used for political purposes). A somewhat half-hearted regret was published in the press, attached to the announcement of the following production. This failed to satisfy Miss Horniman and at the same time drew down upon the Directors the scorn of the nationalist press for acceding to the demands of an Englishwoman. Arthur Griffith, now editor of *Sinn Fein,* labelled them 'Bootlickers'. Miss Horniman demanded the dismissal of Lennox and the manager, Norreys Connell. The latter resigned, fed up with the whole business of coping with this difficult lady. Yeats indignantly refused to dismiss Lennox, upon which Miss Horniman announced that she would withhold the remaining half-yearly portion of the subsidy, amounting to £400. The Directors countered this by withholding the money due for the purchase of the theatre.

To C. P. Scott, editor of the *Manchester Guardian,* fell the unenviable task of arbitration. The case was argued interminably and bitterly. It was not until a year later that Scott found in favour of the Abbey. Miss Horniman's solicitors accepted the decision, but argued on her behalf that the agreement had been broken by Lennox's action; to which the Directors replied that, if she could not accept the integrity of their explanation, they could not accept the remaining portion of the subsidy.

This was the sad end to this fundamentally well-meaning woman's connection with the theatre she had generously provided. Was it her hatred of Ireland and its national aspirations that was the true cause of this unhappy relationship, or was it jealousy – the 'green-eyed monster'? Miss Horniman's favourite brooch was a silver dragon with an emerald eye which she used to say was a likeness of herself.

Poverty and survival

It was above all due to the indomitable spirit of the woman of whom Miss Horniman had written to Yeats, 'you are ceaselessly victimised by Lady Gregory,' that the Abbey survived the financial crisis that followed the withdrawal of the subsidy. Lady Gregory set forth for London determined to raise £5,000 for the purchase of the theatre and to provide a capital sum to keep it alive. Appeals were made to her wealthy English friends, a task not made easier by the damaging effect of the quarrel with Miss Horniman which made the Abbey appear to be a hot-bed of disloyalty to the English Crown. Yeats delivered a series of subscription lectures and the Abbey visited Oxford and the Court Theatre, London in June 1910 where Mrs Patrick Campbell repeated her performance in Yeats's *Deirdre*.

Another task that faced Lady Gregory and Yeats was to obtain a renewal of the patent which, like the subsidy, expired in 1910. The new patent was granted for a further twenty-one years in November, and a new limited liability company was formed with a fixed capital of £1,000. This was divided into one pound shares of which 376 were held by the two Directors — Lady Gregory and Yeats. No shares were issued to the public. Thus the Abbey became virtually the private property of the two Directors until 1923, when Lennox became a share-holder and a member of the directorate.

By July 1911 Lady Gregory had raised £3,500 towards her target of £5,000, and the survival of the Abbey was for the time being assured by a three months guaranteed tour of America.

First American tour

On 23 September 1911 the Abbey Company appeared for the first time on the American stage at the Plymouth Theatre, Boston. Yeats and Lennox Robinson accompanied the players. Yeats left shortly after for New York, handing over the management to Lady Gregory who arrived a week later.

The opening performance included T. C. Murray's starkly realistic play, *Birthright,* of which Holloway had reported, 'of late the Abbey has earned for itself [the title of] "the house of drama of bad language", and *Birthright* caps all previous efforts in this direction'.[5]

There were rumours of trouble even before the company arrived. In *The Gaelic American* John Devoy, the formidable champion of Irish-American nationalism, had worked hard to stir up hatred of Synge as being unchristian and unpatriotic. Opposition to the Abbey's plays was, so it was said, being organised from Dublin. Although the initial reception from American audiences was friendly enough, many of the Irish-Americans were deeply shocked by Murray's play.

In a letter to the editor of the *Boston Post* (4 October) a certain Dr J. T. Gallagher wrote, 'I never saw anything so vulgar, vile, beastly, and unnatural, so calculated to calumniate, degrade, and defame a people and all they hold sacred and dear.'

The Ireland the Irish-Americans dreamed of in this their first encounter with the new Irish drama was very different from the stark tragedy of Murray's play and the 'libel perpetrated on the Irish character' by Synge's *Playboy* Lennox Robinson wrote,

Only two generations before, the fathers and mothers of the people who threw brickbats had been forced to emigrate from Ireland ... They crossed to America, almost illiterate, with hardly a penny in their pockets ... But there is a memory behind, a memory of Ireland that has come down from a silver-haired grandmother. She came out on the emigrant ship and she remembers the lovely Irish scenery, the winding lane, the turf fire. She has forgotten after sixty years (and small blame to her), the poverty, the hunger and the cold. She sees Ireland, and so does her man, through a mist of sentiment. Her children, if they go to a play by Dion Boucicault, see Chauncey Alcott playing a broth of a boy, swaggering round the stage in immaculate white breeches; the colleen, Mollie

O'Flynn, looks lovely in a little plaid shawl ... and the old white-haired mother crouches over the fire and some old song is sung and there is The Wicked Landlord in the background and always the Informer.

This was the Ireland that the Irish-Americans dreamed of till 1911, and then smashing their dream, came T. C. Murray's *Birthright*. Here is no cottage with roses round the door, no Wicked Landlord, no loving old mother, just a stark, ugly tragedy played between father, mother, and two sons. There is not even a love-affair in the play.[6]

The Playboy was announced for 16 October. Two days before the opening, *The Gaelic American* published a resolution of the United Irish Societies of New York in which the members pledged themselves 'to drive the vile thing from the stage'. However, Boston audiences failed to respond to the challenge, apart from some hissing and booing which, Lady Gregory states, was noisily drowned by the cheering and applause of the Harvard students.[7] But some newspapers were loud in their denunciations; it was clear trouble lay ahead. In Providence a petition was laid with the Police Commissioners demanding the banning of the play. In New Haven the Mayor was asked by a deputation of Irish-American citizens to forbid the performance. In Washington a pamphlet issued by the Aloysius Truth Society quoted a passage from another of Dr Gallagher's letters, 'Nothing but hell-inspired ingenuity and a satanic hatred of the Irish people and their religion could suggest, construct, and influence the production of such plays. On God's earth the beastly people of the plays never existed. . . . Will Washington tolerate the lie?'

Not only did Washington tolerate *The Playboy,* but the audiences applauded it. However, when the play reached the Maxine Elliott Theatre, New York, on 27 November the attempts to stop it, which had so far proved unsuccessful, broke out into open rioting. 'Potatoes, an old watch, a tin box with a cigar in it and a cigarette box' were hurled at the stage, accompanied by stink bombs in the auditorium. Ten arrests were made. Lady Gregory knelt behind 'the opening of the hearth, calling to every actor who came within earshot that they must not stop for a moment, but must spare their voices, as they could not be heard'.[8]

On the following night the play was performed with the house lights up. Theodore Roosevelt gallantly responded to Lady Gregory's invitation to attend the performance and followed this up with an appreciative article in *The Outlook*. During the rest of the week the houses were packed; tickets were sold on the 'black market'; opposition petered out. 'Last week was a real triumph', wrote Lady Gregory on 2 January 1912. The players left New York having accepted an offer from the Liebler agency to extend the tour by a further three weeks. 'So I shall most likely stay with them till then,' wrote Lady Gregory. 'The only thing I am at all afraid of is want of sleep. I don't get much.'[9]

Philadelphia – Adelphi Theatre, 16 January 1912

ANCIENT EGGS HURLED AT ACTORS
RIOT STARTS WHEN PLAYBOY APPEARS
TWELVE HELD FOR THEATRE RIOT
PLAYBOY CAST WILL FACE CHARGES OF IMMORALITY

Not only were the protestors arrested but so was the company; charged with presenting plays likely to corrupt the morals of the good citizens of Philadelphia. On 18 January Lennox Robinson posted the following unusual notice on the theatre call board:

The Cast of the Playboy are to appear before Magistrate A. Carey at 633 Walnut Street at nine o'clock.

Bail was granted for $5,000 and the case referred to Quarter Sessions under Judge Carey on the following afternoon. Meantime John Quinn was hurrying from New York, arriving in time to make a dramatic appearance in court and, brilliant lawyer that he was, to confound the prosecution witnesses. Shaw, interviewed in London on 18 January said, 'All decent people are arrested in the United States. That is the reason why we refused all invitations to go there. Besides, who am I that I should question Philadelphia's right to make itself ridiculous?' Judgment was reserved, eventually to be granted in favour of the players.

In Chicago there were further protests, but by now the

protestors were losing all hope of stopping the plays. The solid American public held firm in their appreciation of the plays and players. On 12 February Lady Gregory concluded her diary entry: 'I can hardly believe we shall sail next week! It will be a great rest surely . . . Well, we have had a great victory!'[10]

Gruelling as the tour was for the players as well as for Lady Gregory, it had dispelled for ever a falsely sentimental idea of Ireland and persuaded the intelligent American theatregoers of the importance and vitality of the Irish theatre. For the future it was to make possible subsequent tours, and thereby provide the theatre with a much needed source of revenue. Through the developing interest of critics and public in Irish drama, playwrights like Lennox Robinson, Sean O'Casey, Paul Vincent Carroll, and of recent years Brian Friel, Hugh Leonard and Tom Murphy have found a ready market for their plays both on and 'off' Broadway, while at home increasing numbers of American tourists have flocked to the Abbey Theatre.

But this first American tour gave something also to the American theatre; Eugene O'Neill was to tell an interviewer many years later, 'It was seeing the Irish Players that gave me a glimpse of my opportunity. I went to see everything they did. I thought then and I still think that they demonstrate the possibilities of naturalistic acting better than any other company.'[11]

At home

During the players' absence in America, Nugent Monck, a disciple of William Poel and later founder of the Maddermarket Theatre in Norwich, was summoned by Yeats to train a second company to take over the theatre while the main body of the players was on tour; this would make it possible to maintain a permanent touring policy upon which the economics of the theatre depended. This second, or number two company, was also intended to tour in Ireland when the number one company returned.

As a disciple of William Poel, Monck was a principal pioneer of the revival of medieval drama in England. It was Yeats's hope that a new company trained by him would create an audience for a poetic and visually more artistic form of theatre.

Monck opened the season with a production of the six-teenth-century morality, *The Interlude of Youth* (16 November 1911). This was followed by other morality and liturgical dramas, as well as productions of Yeats's plays — *The Land of Heart's Desire* and *The Countess Cathleen*. There were, too, productions of plays by Rutherford Mayne and Lady Gregory and a revival of Douglas Hyde's play in Irish, *An Tincéar agus an tSídheóg;* but, despite Monck's gifts as a director of the more poetic type of drama, habitual Dublin playgoers were not to be weaned of their popular diet.

Among the new players who worked with Monck were Una O'Connor, later to make her name in New York and Hollywood, Cathleen Nesbitt who became a leading actress in London, Harry Hutchinson and A. P. Wilson, both of whom were to join the main company, the latter as manager and play director. When the number one company returned from the States, Monck returned to Norwich; he came back briefly at the end of the year to join the players for their second American tour.

Stage design — Craig and Ricketts

One of the short-lived benefits Monck brought to the Abbey was an awareness of more modern forms of staging and design. For his productions of the medieval plays he employed processions through the auditorium, steps leading up to the stage from the auditorium, removing the footlights in order to provide a shallow forestage. In his spectacular production of *The Countess Cathleen* (14 December 1911), as in other productions, Monck was one of the few play directors who was able to make effective use of Gordon Craig's screens.

Yeats's interest in Craig's staging of Purcell's operas in 1901 has already been mentioned. Since that time he had cultivated Craig's acquaintance and helped to organise an exhibition of his designs in Dublin in 1904. In 1910 Craig offered to design a set of his patented screens for the Abbey. These were used for the first time in any theatre for a revival of *The Hour Glass* and a new play by Lady Gregory, *The Deliverer;* both plays opened on 12 January 1911. Craig was above all a powerful influence on stage design, rather than a practical man of the theatre. In designing his screens his intention was that they should be moved during the course of the action to form a variety of different shapes and angles. Had this been attempted at the Abbey the result would have been certain disaster, as Stanislavsky was to discover when Craig's screens, designed for the 1912 production of *Hamlet* at the Moscow Art Theatre, collapsed like a house of cards minutes before the curtain was due to rise on the first performance. Furthermore Craig's refusal to allow his screens to be used on tour unless he was personally present to supervise their operation made them of little practical use to the Abbey.

Craig also designed costumes and masks for *The Hour Glass,* as well as for a production of *On Baile's Strand.* However, there appears to be no record of their being used. Once again Craig insisted on being present to show the actors how his masks were to be worn.

A more practical collaboration was that between Yeats and Charles Ricketts, the distinguished British painter and stage designer. In April 1908 Ricketts designed costumes and settings for a revival of Synge's *The Well of the Saints* and in June 1914 he designed costumes for the London production of *The King's Threshold* by the Abbey company for which Yeats designed a flexible setting not unlike Craig's screens. Greatly excited by Ricketts' heroic costumes, Yeats wrote to him,

> I think the costumes the best I have ever seen. They are full of dramatic invention, and yet nothing stands out, or seems eccentric. The company never did the play better, and such is the effect of the costumes that the whole scene got a new intensity, and the passages of action that seemed commonplace became powerful and moving.[12]

From 1914 the employment of guest designers — indeed of any designers — for many years to come was virtually abandoned. Stock scenery, literally knocked together by Seaghan Barlow, became the rule, partly conditioned by economic reasons, but largely due to a singular lack of visual appreciation by those responsible for staging the plays. The repetition of the same wallpapered setting for bedroom or parlour and ill-joined whitewashed flats for cottage kitchen, earned for the Abbey a reputation for dreariness in its staging that persisted until the nineteen-thirties.

The fall in artistic standards

When the main body of the players returned from their American tour in February 1912 their stay in Dublin was brief. Two new plays were introduced, William Boyle's *Family Failing* (28 March) and Lennox Robinson's *Patriots* (11 April). The latter which concerns the disillusionment of an Irish patriot at the indifference shown by his countrymen to his call for action, opened on the same day as the third Home Rule Bill was introduced into the House of Commons; Irish patriots were once again to be disillusioned when parliament failed to implement it. In another four years the frustration of a small group of patriots was to burst forth into an action that was to bring about the eventual independence of the country.

In May the company set forth for what was now becoming an annual tour of British cities, including Oxford and London. At the Royal Court Theatre in London two new plays were produced, T. C. Murray's moving play, *Maurice Harte* (20 June) and Lady Gregory's *The Bogie Man* (4 July). The company then accepted a somewhat surprising offer from Oswald Stoll of a five-week engagement at the London Coliseum followed by a tour of Stoll's music-hall circuit, presenting Lady Gregory's one-act comedies, *Hyacinth Halvey* and *Spreading the News*. The engagement provided a welcome addition to the players' salaries, but did nothing to improve their artistic standards. Playing twice nightly in the vast spaces of theatres such as the London Coliseum and the Glasgow Alhambra required a considerable broadening of their acting style. This, coupled with their arduous American tour with its problems of adapting performances to different theatres and audiences, clearly took its toll of the freshness, simplicity and truth that had once characterised the Abbey style. E. A. Baughan seemed to be aware of this when he wrote in the *Daily News* on 19 July, 'the acting has deteriorated in simplicity without becoming more effective . . . their plays are becoming more mechanical'. William Boyle had some harsh things to say about the production of his play, *Family Failing,* when it was presented in London. He wrote to Holloway on 1 July,

> The play went remarkably well considering the atrocious way it was produced. Few of the players were at home in their words, and the whole thing was done in the slowest manner possible, speeches left out here and repeated there in a way to make many of the retorts pointless. . . . Clearly it had not been rehearsed enough, and no one seemed to care whether the words spoken were mine or the actor's own 'make-up' on the spur of the moment.[13]

The players returned to Dublin for a brief visit in the autumn presenting two new plays, St John Ervine's play, *The Magnanimous Lover* (17 October) and Lady Gregory's *Damer's Gold* (21 November). Ervine's play drew the now familiar complaints of 'bad language': the critic of the *Independent* wrote, 'The thing is too foul for dramatic criticism, and I am not a sanitary inspector.'

In December the company set forth again on a four months' tour of the States, this time Canada was included; Lady Gregory once more undertook the arduous task of managing the company. Their departure was not without criticism at home; on 27 December Ernest A. Boyd wrote in the *Irish Times,* 'It is evident that nationalism and patriotism, which were once the watchwords of the Irish dramatic movement have been relegated to a position of secondary importance.'

During their second American tour Irish-American opposition largely disappeared, being mainly confined to the newspapers rather than noisy demonstrations. In Philadelphia, previously the scene of the greatest hostility, the Playgoers Club presented Lady Gregory with a silver loving-cup inscribed 'In appreciation of Her Great Work for Dramatic Art.'

In Dublin the number two company under Lennox Robinson's direction held the stage with a repertoire that included plays by Strindberg, Gerhardt Hauptmann and the Indian dramatist, Rabindranath Tagore. It was in harness with Tagore's play that Padraig Pearse was invited to present his pupils of St Enda's College in a play in Irish, *An Rí* (The King), written by Pearse himself, in which the prophetic line occurs, 'Welcome is death if it is appointed to me.' ('Mochion an bás ma's é ordaitear dhom.') Prophetic, too, in the light of future events, was the title of Tagore's play – *The Post Office*.

When the number one company returned in May 1913 their sojourn in Dublin was again short before setting forth on their spring tour of the British cities which included a six-weeks engagement at the Court Theatre. Sara Allgood now left the company to join a tour of Arnold Bennett's play, *The Great Adventure,* directed by Granville Barker. Later she was to waste her talents in a seemingly endless tour in England, Australia and New Zealand of Hartley Manners's sentimental comedy, *Peg O' My Heart.* Her absence and that of her sister, Molly O'Neill, was a severe loss to the company.

The Abbey is exhausted

The American and British tours had made a handsome profit, but few plays of importance had been seen on the Abbey stage. 'The Abbey is exhausted, 'wrote the future novelist and playwright, Brinsley Macnamara, in the *Independent* on 9 May 1913, 'The halo has fallen from the head of Mr Yeats. His gesture has lost its eloquence. He has put on the garment of the commonplace and dwells among the businessmen of his time.'

In fairness it should be remembered that without Miss Horniman's subsidy the theatre depended for its existence on the income it derived from its tours overseas, but the initial impetus had come to a halt. There was a dearth of good new plays; Synge was dead; Lady Gregory's talent was drying up; Robinson was heavily engaged in the administration of the theatre, as well as directing all the plays; Yeats, disillusioned by the indifference of the public to poetic drama, was turning from the theatre to the drawing-room where he could bring together a select audience to appreciate his new interest

CARL A. RUDISILL LIBRARY
LENOIR RHYNE COLLEGE

in discovering through the Noh drama of Japan a way of combining the spoken word with music and dance.

Returning to Dublin in the autumn of 1913, the number one company presented R. J. Ray's *The Gombeen Man,* first produced at the Court Theatre on 30 June and T. C. Murray's *Sovereign Love* which opened at the Abbey on 11 September; otherwise the season contained little of interest except for a savage, but amusing, attack on the Dublin critics by St John Ervine in a one-act sketch, *The Critics* (20 November).

On 30 January 1914 the dramatic critic of the *Irish Independent* had reason to complain that 'a season that has been thoroughly uneventful will close at the Abbey this week'. A week later the company left for their third tour of the States, while in the Abbey itself A. P. Wilson carried on a somewhat desultory season with such actors as he could gather together. Among these were two players who were to bring new life to the theatre in the course of time, Arthur Shields, at that time a part-time player from the Civil Service, later to become a leading actor and play director, and the incomparable comedienne, Maureen Delany. Another new recruit, Sean Connolly, was to play a more tragic part on a different stage two years later. Shields and Maureen Delany made their first appearance in Edward McNulty's comedy, *The Lord Mayor* (13 March) which was to prove a mainstay of the theatre's repertoire for some years to come.

The 1914 American tour was to be the last for many years. To Lady Gregory's intense disappointment, this tour under Lennox Robinson's management lost money. She had fixed her hopes on a sufficient profit to rescue the theatre from its financial difficulties, and for this failure she blamed Robinson. Lennox resigned, and, after an unsuccessful attempt to enlist in the Munster Fusileers, he became an Organising Librarian to the Carnegie Trust. He was to be recalled to the Abbey eight years later.

Apart from the financial loss suffered, there was a more potent reason for the end of the American tours: over Europe the storm clouds of war were gathering; soon the Atlantic no longer offered a safe passage between the old world and the new. The sources from which the Abbey derived the greater part of its revenue had dried up.

5
The Troubled Years
1914–1923

Drama on another stage

To add to the financial difficulties the Abbey was now facing, the Lockout and Strike dragged on through the winter of 1913 until the early months of the new year. It was to protect the strikers from clashes with the police that the tiny Irish Citizen Army was formed, its flag the Plough and the Stars and its secretary Sean O Cathasaigh. Some ten years later under the name of Sean O'Casey he was to bring new life to the ailing Abbey Theatre and win for himself international renown.

But now the year was 1914. Throughout Europe the nations were manoeuvring in a ruthless struggle for power; Germany was arming; in Russia there was social and political unrest; the Austrian empire was crumbling in the face of nationalist aspirations in the Balkans. On 28 June the Archduke Francis Ferdinand of Austria was assassinated at Sarajevo by a Bosnian nationalist; on 4 August Britain entered a war that was to act as a catalyst for Irish nationalism, a war that was to divide the nation in two.

After bitter struggles between the Lords and Commons the Home Rule Bill eventually received Royal Assent in September 1914, only to be indefinitely postponed until the end of hostilities. In the North opposition to Home Rule, led by Edward Carson, had been steadily mounting. One hundred and fifty thousand Ulstermen pledged themselves to resist it by force; arms were smuggled in and in January 1913 the Ulster Volunteers were formed.

In retaliation, the Irish Volunteers were formed, soon to be taken over by John Redmond, leader of the Irish Parliamentary Party. When war broke out many of the Volunteers followed Redmond to serve with distinction on the battlefields of Flanders, but a small determined body refused to fight under an alien flag; for them England's difficulty was Ireland's opportunity. Following Ulster's example, arms were smuggled in and in May 1915 a military committee was secretly set up, largely staffed by the Irish Republican Brotherhood with Pearse as Director of Military Organisation. Among his colleagues were Joseph Plunkett and Thomas MacDonagh, the former a minor poet and MacDonagh, like Pearse, an incipient playwright as well as poet; both had helped Martyn to form the Theatre of Ireland and MacDonagh's play, *When the Dawn is Come,* prophetically portraying a future war against England, had been produced at the Abbey in 1908. Of these men and others like them, consumed with the fire of revolutionary romanticism, Yeats was to write those lines, already quoted, that haunted his sleepless nights,

> Did that play of mine send out
> Certain men the English shot?

On Easter Monday, 24 April 1916 Dublin woke to the sound of gunfire, and in front of the General Post Office Pearse read a proclamation declaring an Irish Republic. On the same day the bills outside the Abbey announced a new play for the following evening — *The Spancel of Death.*

In fact this play, written by T. H. Nally, was never produced. The Abbey lay in the centre of the battle zone, midway between the G.P.O. and Liberty Hall, the headquarters of the Citizen Army. The young Abbey actor, Sean Connolly, died in an abortive attack on Dublin Castle, whilst in the G.P.O. Arthur Shields was to surrender and be interned with the last remnants of the Volunteers.

When Pearse and Connolly together with their colleagues fell before the guns of their executioners in Kilmainham Gaol the country was profoundly shaken. But it is to be doubted if their blood sacrifice alone would have led to the war of attrition that followed had it not been for the frequent arrests, the drawn out executions and, not least, the Military

Service Bill of 1918 giving the government power to introduce conscription into Ireland. By the end of the Great War
the Irish Republican Brotherhood had penetrated the nationalist societies, and in January 1919 an Irish parliament (Dáil
Éireann) ratified the establishment of the Irish Republic.
British troops were rushed to Ireland, including the dreaded
'Black-and-Tans'; guerrilla war ensued, escalating into the
terror and counter-terror of the Anglo-Irish War. The Treaty
of 1922, establishing the Irish Free State (Saorstát Éireann),
brought no end to terror. Irishmen now fought against Irishmen, Free Staters against Republicans. Ireland knew no peace
till 1923. From these years of strife, stretching from the
General Strike of 1913 to the end of the Civil War, came
O'Casey's five plays – *The Shadow of a Gunman* (the Anglo-
Irish War), *Juno and the Paycock* (The Civil War), *The
Plough and the Stars* (the Easter Rebellion), *The Silver Tassie*
(the Great War of 1914–18), and *Red Roses for Me* (the
Lockout and Great Strike of 1913).

The purging of the Abbey

During these years of anxiety and strife the theatre's financial position was precarious; from 1919 to 1923 it was little
short of desperate. In March 1921 Dublin was under curfew
from eight o'clock in the evening; in common with other
theatres the Abbey was forced to close and lay off its players
and employees. Lady Gregory hastened to London to raise an
Abbey Theatre Fund, appealing to her influential friends and
to the theatre's many admirers. The playwright and play
director, J. B. Fagan, organised a series of subscription lectures by Shaw, Yeats, St John Ervine and Lady Gregory;
special matinees were given of *The Whiteheaded Boy,* then
running at the Ambassadors Theatre; and on 12 June Lady
Gregory was able to record in her diary, 'Yesterday by
second post a letter from Lady Ardilaun with a cheque for
£500! So the Abbey is safe for a long time, I hope for ever!'
But the respite was short. During the long drawn-out Treaty
negotiations and the ensuing Civil War, Dubliners were in no
mood for serious plays; comedy and farce were the only sure
ways of attracting an audience. New plays tended to be stereo-

typed or crudely melodramatic. As a result acting standards were slack; what remained of the group spirit nurtured by the Fays gave way to opportunism; many of the players left to seek higher rewards elsewhere, and leadership was spasmodic as managers came and went with alarming frequency. Yeats was out of Ireland for the greater part of the time; disillusioned by the political situation, he even considered accepting a professorship in Japan. On 9 December 1921 he wrote to Lady Gregory suggesting that the theatre be handed over to the Provisional government.

Lady Gregory, now in her sixties, had other problems on her hands. In 1915 her favourite nephew, Hugh Lane, was drowned in the sinking of the Lusitania, and much of her time was spent in endeavouring to secure his unique collection of pictures for the nation. In 1918 she suffered a shattering blow when her only son, Robert Gregory, was killed on active service in Europe. The years of the Black-and-Tans and of the Civil War brought her constant anxiety and distress, for her home lay in the centre of one of the most terror-ridden districts in the country. Yet, despite her sorrows and anxieties, she did her best to keep the theatre alive, sometimes directing the plays herself, and on one occasion playing the part of 'The Old Woman' in *Cathleen Ni Houlihan.*

'The Abbey is mortally sick,' wrote the dramatic critic of *New Ireland* on 4 March 1916, 'its greatest work is past. . . . Its mortal shell still remains with a sort of mechanical life struggling in it, drawing its vitality not from within itself but from echoes of its past.' The sickness was not, however, a sign of mortality but a painful process of purgation. Like the nation, the Abbey had to bleed before new life could arise. Slowly and painfully it was shedding its past. 'Romantic Ireland's dead and gone,' wrote Yeats. Cuchulain, Diarmuid and Grania appeared as ghosts, masked and strangely stylised, in the fashionable London drawing-rooms of Lady Cunard and Lady Islington. Divorced from European influences Irish drama had become increasingly parochial, a stale imitation of its past vitality. Yet despite the mediocrity of many of the plays, we can see in hindsight how the subject matter was gradually changing to express the consciousness of the emerging nation.

The plays

O'Casey was not the first to portray the lives of those who lived in the teeming slums of Dublin. In 1914 A. P. Wilson, who was at that time manager of the theatre, presented a grim picture of the conditions in which the workers and their families lived in his play *The Slough* (30 November) in which one of the characters, 'Jake Allen', was based on the leader of the 1913 General Strike, James Larkin. *Blight* (11 December 1917) by Oliver St John Gogarty, writing under the pseudonym of A and O (Alpha and Omega), also depicted the filthy condition of the Dublin slums in a more objective light.[1] Daniel Corkery's play, *The Labour Leader* (30 September 1919), contained a critical portrait of Larkin as the exploiter of the poverty and degradation of the working class. Nor was O'Casey the first to make use of the 1916 Rising as a subject of drama. Maurice Dalton in *Sable and Gold* (16 September 1918) showed the effects of the Rising upon a middle-class Dublin family. O'Casey, however, scored over his predecessors because, like all great playwrights who depict the particular conditions and events of their time, he depicted them in terms of the universal human condition. It is his creation of characters and their reaction to these events and conditions that make his plays reach out to audiences beyond the frontiers of time and place.

Political and social problems were reflected in a variety of ways as playwrights sought to come to grips with the complexity of the changes that were taking place. Often their attempts to do so resulted in crude melodrama and contrived situations. Melodrama was present in the plays of J. Bernard MacCarthy, a rural postman who contributed five plays, the best of which, *The Crusaders* (19 January 1917) concerns a young priest, the son of a publican, who arrives to conduct a temperance mission in his native village, only to find that if his campaign succeeds his family's business will be ruined and his father unable to repay the money which the young priest's brother has embezzled.

Of a higher quality are the plays of Seumas O'Kelly whose first play, *The Shuiler's Child,* dealing with the problems of adoption, had been presented by The Theatre of Ireland in

1909. In *The Bribe* (18 December 1913) he dealt with nepotism in local authority appointments, a problem only too prevalent at the time.

A new playwright of considerable potential emerged in Brinsley Macnamara, a successful novelist and later a member of the Board of Directors. In *The Rebellion in Ballycullen* (11 March 1919) he satirised the pseudo-patriotism of the inhabitants of an Irish village in their reactions to militant nationalism. In *The Land for the People* (30 November 1920) he portrayed the betrayal of the movement for the redistribution of the land by a leader of that movement who himself becomes the largest landowner in the district. Macnamara, however, is best known as a writer of comedy, the first of which, *The Glorious Uncertainty,* was presented on 27 November 1923.

T. C. Murray returned to play-writing after a gap of five years with a harsh satire of the peasant-farmer's rapacity for money. *Spring* (8 January 1918), a one-act play, portrays a poverty-hardened peasant woman who condemns her father to the workhouse only to relent when the Old Age Pension Act is passed. Ironically his death prevents her from laying her hands on his pension.

Lennox Robinson contributed two political plays, *The Dreamers* (2 February 1915) and *The Lost Leader* (19 February 1918). In the former he adopted the device of turning back to history to illustrate recent political attitudes. The play deals with Robert Emmet's ill-fated rebellion in 1803, showing the young patriot on the one hand as the true dreamer of Irish independence, and on the other as the victim of the shiftless futility of his followers and of the people's lack of spirit and co-operation. *The Lost Leader* is based on the popular myth that Parnell did not die in 1891 but lived on in obscure retirement. An old man, Lucius Lenihan, part-owner of a hotel in a remote corner of Ireland, reveals under hypnosis that he is, or believes himself to be, Parnell. Confronted with a gathering of sceptics representing the various factions of Irish political life, he condemns them for destroying the unity that he (Parnell) had achieved 'until Home Rule became merely the exchange of government by English shop-keepers for government by Irish gombeen-men'. In the ensuing riot Lenihan is killed by a chance blow from a blind man, the only one who implicitly believes him to be Parnell, leaving open the question of his true identity.

Protestant attitudes in the North of Ireland were represented in St John Ervine's plays: *Mixed Marriage* (30 March 1911), a play that retains its topicality today, *The Orangeman* (13 March 1914), a one-act play satirising religious fanaticism in Belfast during the annual celebrations of the Battle of the Boyne, and his finest play, *John Ferguson* (30 November 1915), a powerful portrait of the religious zeal and dourness of a North of Ireland peasant standing 'Learlike' against the buffets of fate.

From the North, too, came the first plays of George Shiels, one of the most prolific contributors to the Abbey's repertoire. His early plays, *Bedmates* (16 January 1921) and *Insurance Money* (13 December 1921) are one-act farces of no great dramatic value, but in *Paul Twyning* (3 October 1922) Shiels reveals himself as a master of the well-made comedy. For many years his comedies with those of Robinson and Macnamara were to provide the popular bulwark of the theatre's repertoire. If Shiels's plays are not great drama they provided two generations of Abbey players with splendid vehicles for popular character studies.

Lady Gregory found a new outlet for her love of folk drama in the fantasy world of her 'Wonder Plays': *The Dragon* (21 April 1919), *The Golden Apple* (6 January 1920), and *Aristotle's Bellows* (17 March 1921). In these, for the first time children's drama was catered for.

Fantasy of a different kind was supplied by Lord Dunsany. *A Night at an Inn* (2 September 1919), *The Tents of the Arabs* (24 March 1920), and an earlier play, *King Argimenes and the Unknown Warrior* (26 January 1911) stand apart from the main stream of Irish drama. His plays based on a fictitious world of vaguely oriental mysticism proved more popular in American little theatres than in Ireland. His first play, however, *The Glittering Gate* (29 April 1909) might well have provided a subject for Samuel Beckett. Two Cockney burglars wait expectantly at the gates of Heaven; one of them endlessly opening empty beer bottles that descend mysteriously from above. When eventually the gates open

they disclose a void — 'empty night and stars' — whilst from
above comes mocking laughter.

> *Bill:* Stars! Blooming great stars! There ain't no heaven,
> Jim.
> *Jim:* That's very like them. Yes, they'd do that.
>   *Curtain*

It was above all comedy that kept the doors of the theatre
open during these trouble-ridden years. Yeats recognised this,
though he despised the mediocrity of many of the plays. In
1919 he contributed his only full-length comedy, except for
The Herne's Egg (1939), but *The Player Queen,* which was
first produced in London by the Stage Society, was above the
heads of a popular Dublin audience.

It was Lennox Robinson who set the tone for the new
popular, undemanding comedy of middle-class family life
with *The Whiteheaded Boy,* first produced at the Abbey on
13 December 1916, and later to run in wartime London for
nine months. In turning from his early ironic and pessimistic
view of Irish character to good-humoured satire, liberally
sprinkled with sentiment, he discovered his real strength as a
dramatist. His next play *The Round Table* (31 January 1922)
has much of the whimsy nature of J. M. Barrie's plays. In the
same year, 1922, he wrote his delightful comedy of manners,
Crabbed Youth and Age (14 November). In dedicating his
Essays to Lennox, Yeats wrote,

> I dedicate this book to you because I have seen your ad-
> mirable little play, *Crabbed Youth and Age,* and would
> greet the future. My friends and I loved symbols, popular
> beliefs and old scraps of verse that made Ireland romantic
> to herself, but the new Ireland, overwhelmed by responsi-
> bility, begins to long for psychological truth.[2]

Management and players

In July 1915 Patrick Wilson, the then manager, was dismissed for 'turning to his own purposes, offers that were
intended for us'.[3] It appears that Wilson was carrying on a
theatrical business of his own, even going so far as to con-

tracting Abbey players to perform in his ventures. He was succeeded by St John Ervine, who was already becoming known as an important playwright in Ireland as well as in Britain. In the sensitive climate of the time the appointment of a Protestant from the North of Ireland, known to be antagonistic to Home Rule, was hardly opportune. Ervine had no scruples in expressing his views on the future of the Abbey which he regarded as merely one of a chain of repertory theatres spread throughout the British Isles. His public relations were equally provocative. In a lecture to the Dublin Literary Society on 11 January 1916 he declared that Ireland was not only 'a sick nation' but 'very nearly a lunatic nation'. He had already ridiculed the Dublin critics in his one-act sketch, *The Critics,* in which four Dublin critics discuss a play that none of them have seen throughout, and one has not seen at all, condemning it as 'dirty', 'immoral' and 'a slight upon our pure Irish womanhood'. The play turns out to be *Hamlet.* During the Easter Rising Ervine's sympathies were far removed from those of the players, his only regret being that the British gun-boat, Helga, had not blasted the Abbey to pieces. Small wonder that his relations with the players were far from happy. When he demanded that, contrary to their custom, they rehearse twice a day while on tour, they refused to co-operate. Ervine replied by giving Sinclair and his fellow players a week's notice of dismissal. The players telegraphed to Lady Gregory, asking whether the manager had the power to dismiss them without an opportunity to state their case to the Board. Unfortunately they acted hastily without waiting for her reply. Patrons arriving at the Abbey on 29 May 1916 were handed a slip of paper reading: 'To the Patrons of the Abbey Theatre. The Players regret having to disappoint their Public this week as they will not appear at the theatre under the present Manager, Mr St John Ervine.' In the circumstances Yeats and Lady Gregory felt they had no option other than to confirm their manager's notice of dismissal.

Once again the Abbey lost its best players. Arthur Sinclair, Sydney Morgan, Harry Hutchinson, J. A. O'Rourke, Kathleen Drago, Eithne Magee and others left to form their own touring company, The Irish Players, which for many years proved a formidable rival to the Abbey in the British touring circuits, as well as in London. In July 1916, to the relief of the two Directors, Ervine handed in his resignation.

In fairness it should be stated that Ervine inherited a serious financial situation when he took over the management and a thoroughly disgruntled company. The losses that the theatre had sustained during the 1914 American tour and the ensuing London season under Wilson's management had made it necessary during subsequent tours to abolish the profit-sharing arrangement by which the players were able to augment their meagre Dublin salaries. Moreover, by October 1915 the financial situation was such that the players' salaries had to be reduced. Inevitably, there was severe discontent; in fact Sinclair had already announced his intention of resigning at the end of the season. If Ervine's manner of dealing with the players was 'abrupt' and 'imperious', they themselves were by no means easy to manage and there were frequent complaints of players playing for a laugh, or for a round of applause, and not infrequently 'gagging' their lines. If Ervine had not been the catalyst that brought about the dissolution of what had been one of the best acting companies, a drastic change would have been inevitable.

Ervine was succeeded by J. Augustus Keogh whose reputation was based on his productions of Shaw's plays. The Abbey now proceeded to embark on a repertoire of Shavian drama, opening the autumn season with a much belated production of *John Bull's Other Island* (25 September 1916). During this season Maire O'Neill returned to the Abbey to play, among other parts, that of 'Aunt Ellen' in *The Whiteheaded Boy*. Thereafter she left to join Arthur Sinclair whom she later married. Fred O'Donovan and J. M. Kerrigan who were filming in England at the time of the Sinclair split, returned to a company that included Arthur Shields, now liberated from internment, Maureen Delany, May Craig, Christine Hayden, and a part-time actor, Barry Fitzgerald.

Keogh's reign was, like Wilson's and Ervine's, a short one. Yeats complained that he was becoming increasingly commercial in outlook, and when he sought a more advantageous contract the Directors seized the opportunity of accepting his resignation. Fred O'Donovan now took over the management. In August 1917 the company was back in the Coliseum under Oswald Stoll's management, staging among other plays Edward McNulty's one-act comedy, *The Lord Mayor*. By the end of 1918 O'Donovan, like Sinclair, was looking for more lucrative employment. In December he informed Holloway that he was thinking of going to America[4] and in the following February he left the Abbey, complaining of Yeats's 'interference' in rehearsals, and of his 'not getting more pay'.[5] It would seem he, too, had fallen a victim to the broad acting of the music halls; in March 1919 Dr Larchet remarked to Holloway, 'O'Donovan's artistry has fled from him of late, and he plays the buffoon in all comedy parts he attempts.'[6]

With O'Donovan went the last remnants of the old company.

Yeats and Lady Gregory have been accused of resenting any authority other than their own in the management of the theatre. Certainly the Abbey has had an unhappy record of ridding itself of managers and play directors, and this not only under the directorship of Yeats and Lady Gregory. Yeats, in particular, has been criticised for the devious way in which he 'nudged out' those whose usefulness appeared to be declining or who appeared to be a threat to the authority of the Board. Such criticisms are partly true: Yeats was both devious and ruthless in his methods. Even before the departure of the Fays, Martyn, Moore and Russell found themselves manouevered into positions where they could no longer continue to serve. Nor can it be denied that both he and Lady Gregory were autocrats. Lady Gregory had her favourites and was ever reluctant to give major responsibility to others, more especially to the players and managers, believing that to do so would be to open the doors to mediocrity and commercialism. Others would argue that the Abbey would never have survived had it not been for the talent and popularity of its players, and that those upon whose livelihood the theatre depended should at least have had some share in its management. In recent years the Abbey, in common with other theatres, has admitted players and theatre technicians to its Board; but no theatre, whether controlled by playwrights, artistic directors, business managers, players or independent shareholders, can hope to survive without a strong hand at the helm. Once the Abbey had become a professional theatre involved in full-time performances and touring activities, neither Yeats nor Lady Gregory could give sufficient time to provide the day-to-day attention that was essential to the running of the theatre; the result was artistic and managerial frustration and the loss of many valuable artists.

Yeats was eventually to admit that the time had come to engage a younger person to manage the theatre, whose artistic judgment and loyalty he could trust. He accordingly summoned his protégé, Lennox Robinson, back to the Abbey. 'Lennox Robinson represents the Ireland that must sooner or later take the work from us; the sooner that some young man who feels that his own future is bound up with the Abbey is put in charge the better,'[7] he wrote to Lady Gregory. Lennox had never been one of her favourites; in her diary for 24 February 1919 she wrote, 'I have rather reluctantly consented. He grew very slack before and very careless about keeping up the acting and lost us much money on our American tour.'[8]

Lennox proved more resilient than his predecessors in his relations with his two autocratic Directors partly because, as a playwright, he was a major contributor to the theatre's repertoire, and partly because Yeats, recognising his talents, arranged for him to become a shareholding member of the Board, though both he and Lady Gregory stipulated that his membership should be reviewed annually. But above all Lennox possessed, as his biographer has pointed out, 'a wiry strength concealed beneath his vague unworldly air and weary voice, that enabled him to give way on lesser problems — that some mistook for weakness — and hold tenaciously to his basic artistic principles.'[9] Above all he had no greater ambition than to serve what he called 'that strange Irish thing', a cause that he followed, not only in his work for the Abbey, but as the founder of the Dublin Drama League through which he sought to enlarge the perspective of players, playwrights and audiences.

The Dublin Drama League

Lennox founded the Drama League in 1918 under Yeats's

W. B. Yeats

2. Lady Gregory

Edward Martyn

4. George Moore

5. W. G. Fay

6. Frank Fay

7. J. M. Synge

8. Miss Horniman

9. Cathleen Ni Houlihan, 1902

The Hour Glass, 1903: Dudley Digges (the Wiseman), Frank Fay (the Fool)

11. The old Abbey

12. The green-room in the thirties

13. Design by Charles Ricketts for
    Cuchulain in *On Baile's Strand*,
    1908

14. Mask by Hildo Krop for *The
    Only Jealousy of Emer*, 1929

15. Barry Fitzgerald as Fluther
Good in *The Plough and the
Stars*

16. F. J. McCormick as 'Joxer'
Daly in *Juno and the Paycock*

17. Maureen Delany as Widow Quin
in *The Playboy of the Western
World*

18. Sara Allgood as Juno in *Juno
and the Paycock*

19. Ria Mooney as Rosie Redmond in *The Plough and the Stars*, with the author, Sean O'Casey

0. Lennox Robinson

21. Frank Dermody

22. A philosophical discussion — Seaghan Barlow and Mick Judge

23. Hugh Hunt

24. Tanya Moseiwitsch

presidency with himself as secretary. Yeats had always intended that the Abbey should include plays by continental dramatists in its repertoire; in this he was not supported by Lady Gregory or Synge, both of whom wished to confine the theatre's work to Irish plays upon which its reputation was based. After fourteen years of an almost exclusive diet of Irish drama, most of which was conceived in the well-made play tradition, and set in the only too familiar stock scenery, the Abbey had bred an audience resistent to any of the new forms of theatre that were emerging on the continent. By 1918 both players and playwrights had reached a point where repetition and insularity were seriously stifling creative work.

At a public discussion held in the Abbey to promote the aims of the League Lennox declared,

> Here in Ireland we are isolated, cut off from the thought of the world, except the English world, and from England we get little in drama, except fourth-rate. I ask you, for the young writer's sake, to open up the door and let us out of our prison. Seeing foreign plays will not divorce our minds from Ireland . . . but being brought into touch with other minds who have different values of life, suddenly we shall discover the rich material that lies to our hand in Ireland.[10]

The League continued giving occasional productions on Sunday and Monday nights until 1929. Among authors whose works were presented — many of them for the first time — were D'Annunzio, Sierra, the Quintero brothers, O'Neill, Lenormand, Andreyev, Cocteau, Schnitzler, Evreinov, Verhaeran, Bjornson, Pirandello and Strindberg. By making use of the Abbey stage and company the Drama League did much to extend the work of the players and to build up an audience that was eventually to make possible the creation of the Gate Theatre as a full-time professional theatre for continental drama. Among the dramatists who were influenced by the new drama, apart from Lennox himself, were O'Casey and Denis Johnston.

The new company

Despite the loss of many established players, the company

Lennox gathered around him showed again that Ireland possessed a seemingly inexhaustible supply of acting talent.

Barry Fitzgerald (Will Shields) made his first big success as 'The King' in Lady Gregory's *The Dragon*. 'A masterpiece of unforced, richly comic humour', wrote the *Irish Times* critic on 21 April 1919; while the critic of the *Daily Telegraph* declared, 'his picture of "The King" was one of the finest comedy studies I have seen for years — broadly sketched yet always in artistic moderation, unctuous yet never degenerating into clowning. It was one of the cleverest studies amongst those given last night by fifteen clever players.' Amongst those fifteen were his brother, Arthur Shields, P. J. Carolan, Eric Gorman, Maureen Delany, May Craig and one who was to become the greatest actor on the Irish stage for over thirty years, F. J. McCormick.

McCormick's entry into his career as an actor was typical of that of many of the Abbey actors, few of whom had any professional training. Like Barry Fitzgerald, Gabriel Fallon, Arthur Shields, and Eric Gorman, he held a minor position in the Civil Service, acting in his spare time in the Workman's Club at 41 York Street where he played in melodramas — *The Shaughraun, Arrah na Pogue* and the 1798 plays — the popular one-act farces and short thrillers, like *The Monkey's Paw*. From York Street he graduated as a part-time professional to play at the Queen's, concealing his identity under the stage name of McCormick lest he be charged with breaking the terms of government service. In November 1917 he was engaged by Frank Fay to play the leading part in an Irish comedy, *Flurry to the Rescue* at the Theatre Royal. 'During those three weeks' rehearsal I learnt more from Frank Fay than I had learnt before,' he was to declare many years later.[11] There followed further engagements. It was while playing in another comedy, *The Courting of Mary Malone*, that he was spotted by Fred O'Donovan and asked to play a small part at the Abbey in a revival of *The Bribe* by Seamus O'Kelly in April 1918. Rehearsing during his lunch hours McCormick was frequently late back to work and was finally told to choose between the office and the Abbey. He chose well. The following year he played his first major part in Constance Powell Anderson's play, *The Curate of St Chad's*

(20 May 1919).[12] The press was unanimous in its praise of the young actor: 'There are few roles he could not undertake with distinction . . .' 'I am going to back every cent I have on this sincere artist to be at the top of his profession . . .' The critics were right; F. J. was to become a great actor. Over the years he was to compass every kind of part from Oedipus and King Lear to his definitive characterisation of Joxer Daly in *Juno and the Paycock*. McCormick was an instinctive actor; he knew nothing of Stanislavsky's system, nor did he claim to have any conscious method of building a character, yet in many ways he was the embodiment of Stanislavsky's ideal. 'More than any other actor in the history of the Abbey', wrote Gabriel Fallon, 'it might be said that the character possessed him rather than he the character.'[13] Had he wished he could have become a leading actor in London or New York, but McCormick appeared to be totally lacking in ambition. Outside Ireland he remained almost unknown except to those American audiences who saw the Abbey players during their occasional tours. Shunning publicity and intensely religious, he was content to devote his talents to the Abbey, demanding no more than a meagre wage in return.

As an actor Arthur Shields possessed a very different quality from that of his brother, Barry Fitzgerald. The latter's strength lay in his slightly roguish, easy-going personality which he was never completely able to suppress any more than he could overcome a slight stutter, excelling in such parts as 'Captain Boyle' in *Juno and the Paycock* and 'Fluther Good' in *The Plough and the Stars*. Arthur ('Boss') Shields was intense, earnest, and slightly withdrawn. His best work was as a play director in which capacity he shared much of the burden with Lennox Robinson. As an actor he could suggest the weakness of 'Donal Davoren' in *The Shadow of a Gunman* and 'Johnny Boyle' in *Juno and the Paycock* on the one hand, and the austerity of Canon Skerritt in Paul Vincent Carroll's play, *Shadow and Substance* on the other.

Another actor who was to share part of the burden of management and play direction was M. J. Dolan who joined the company after demobilisation from service in the British Army. Michael Dolan retained much of a soldier's sense of discipline; like McCormick he was meticulous in everything he undertook whether in theatre management, play directing, as a teacher of acting or in his careful study of a part. He, too, was to devote the rest of his life to the Abbey.

If comedy was to be the mainstay of the repertoire for many years to come, then the new company was doubly blessed, for not only did it possess in Barry Fitzgerald a great comedian and considerable box-office 'draw', but also Maureen Delany — large, warm-hearted, with a permanent twinkle in her eye. Maureen was not a great actress, but she was a superb performer. For over twenty years she was to play herself on the stage without varying her characterisation by a twitch of her eyebrow, to the utter delight of her public. The parts she played seemed to be tailored to her personality — Maisie Madigan in *Juno and the Paycock,* the Widow Quin in *The Playboy of the Western World,* Aunt Helen in *The Whiteheaded Boy* — these and many others were Maureen Delany to more than one generation of playgoers.

The new company might have been hand-picked to serve O'Casey's plays; for, besides F. J. McCormick, Arthur Shields, Barry Fitzgerald and Maureen Delany, there were May Craig for Mrs Gogan, P. J. Carolan for Adolphus Grigson, Michael J. Dolan for the quarrelsome Young Covey, Eric Gorman for Peter Flynn, Gabriel Fallon for Mr Gallogher, Eileen Crowe, later to become a leading Abbey actress, for Mary Boyle, Christine Hayden for Mrs Henderson and Sara Allgood who returned for a brief season to create her definitive characterisation of Juno Boyle; while waiting 'in the wings' were two talented young recruits, Shelah Richards and Ria Mooney, who were to join the company in 1924 and play the parts of Nora Clitheroe and Rosie Redmond. Both were to become leading actresses and distinguished play directors: Shelah Richards directing her own company at the Olympia Theatre, Dublin, where, among othe plays, she directed the first performance of O'Casey's play *Red Roses for Me* in March 1954 — later she became one of the first play directors for Irish Television (R.T.E.); Ria Mooney as director of productions at the Gaiety Theatre, Dublin, and for many years at the Abbey Theatre and the Queen's.

The stage was now set for the Abbey to be reborn through the marriage of players with the plays of a great playwright.

6
The Free State Theatre
1923–1932

'A nation once again'

Ireland in 1923 was not just a nation once again, it was a very different nation from the one about which the founders of the Abbey had written their plays. No longer a romantic anachronism perched on the fringes of western civilisation, the new Ireland was preparing to take its place in a not very 'brave new world'. It was this reality that the younger dramatists endeavoured, however inadequately, to express: no longer the twilight legends of a heroic past, nor the shebeens of a picturesque peasantry, for Cuchulain had died in the G.P.O. and 'the springtime of the local life [had] been forgotten, and the harvest [was] a memory only, and the straw [had] been turned to bricks'.

The Civil War ended in the spring of 1923 but the bitterness remained — the bitterness and the disillusion. Reality now lay in a nation divided against itself: antagonism between Orangemen and Catholics in the North, Free Staters and Republicans in the South, between Capital and Labour, conservative priests and progressive schoolmasters; among petty bureaucrats, political nepotists and grasping gombeen men; it lay in hydro-electro works, in the charred ruins of the 'big houses', in the diminishing remnants of the Protestant population with their proud traditions of Swift and Burke, Grattan, Emmet and Parnell; it lay in the tragi-comedy of the Dublin slums.

For those who had dreamed of a nation united, free and at

peace with itself the new Free State with its puritan outlook, its literary and film censorship, was a bitter awakening. Nor had self-government brought a solution to social problems; in the country agricultural difficulties led to political unrest, emigration was still a serious menace; in the cities there was little sign of a brighter outlook for the labouring classes. For many who had lost husbands, sons and lovers it was not easy to accept that 'bloodshed is a glorious and a sanctifying thing'.

Sean O'Casey

Sean O'Casey was forty-three when *On The Run,* later re-named *The Shadow of a Gunman,* was accepted by the Directors of the Abbey. Born and bred in Dublin, he was the youngest of thirteen children, eight of whom died in infancy. His father, a commercial clerk, who worked during his latter years for the Irish Church Mission, a Protestant organisation, was a man with some pretensions to learning. His small library of books included the works of classical authors as well as theological treatises. When Michael Casey died the family under its indomitable mother had to face a severe, and no doubt humiliating, fall in living standards, but at no time was this respectable lower-middle-class family reduced to living in the appallingly overcrowded conditions of Dublin's slum tenements, as eagerly reported by the press, and luridly described by some of his biographers who, as Sean McCann has pointed out, have been misled by an inadequate knowledge of Dublin 'combined with the wild inaccuracies of O'Casey himself'.[1] However, let it be said that nowhere in his auto-biographies — often inaccurate and certainly highly drama-tised — does O'Casey state that his family lived in the teem-ing tenements described in the *Medical Press* of the time and in government inquiries as worse than those of Moscow and Calcutta.

Sean's early years were plagued with a chronic eye com-plaint that hampered his education; this, together with the family's religious difference from their almost exclusively Catholic neighbours, kept him somewhat alienated from his young contemporaries, earning him the title of 'Sean the

Proud'. It was indeed his pride that steeled him and his mother to overcome the humiliation of their poverty. It was his pride and his sensitivity to the criticisms of more privileged writers that produced the rebellious, the belligerent Sean O'Casey. 'Oh, dear Sean, don't be too belligerent,' wrote Charlotte Shaw,[2] but Sean could not easily keep 'the two-edged sword of thought tight in its scabbard'.

There was in his nature an ambivalence, as Gabriel Fallon has pointed out. Sean, the often venomous critic of society — more especially of the Church — the revolutionary Communist, blind to the worst excesses of Stalin, was also a man of great compassion: a hater of all forms of bloodshed and of the bigotry that denies the gaiety and fullness of life.

Largely self-educated, he developed in early life a passion for the theatre. Through his brother, Archie, who organised amateur theatricals in a disused stable, Sean played in excerpts from the plays of Boucicault and Shakespeare, his favourite playwrights; and, on one occasion, he was called upon to play the part of Father Dolan in a professional production of *The Shaughraun* in the old theatre in the Mechanics' Institute, soon to be transformed into the Abbey Theatre. From his mother he inherited a love for the language of the Bible. At the age of seven he won a Sunday school prize for proficiency in Holy Scripture. As a young man he worked in a variety of tough manual jobs and, like many of his fellow labourers, he fell under the spell of the fiery labour leader, Jim Larkin. For a time he became secretary of the Irish Citizen Army, eventually resigning in protest against its association with the largely middle-class nationalists of the Irish Volunteers.

Sean was never a routine nationalist, though he joined the Gaelic League, attending classes in the Irish language with Ernest Blythe — and was for a time a member of the Irish Republican Brotherhood. But the national cause was for him secondary to the cause of a workers' republic, and Sean was too much of a humanitarian to condone bloodshed.

The Shadow of a Gunman

It was in the middle of 1921 that he submitted his first plays to the Abbey. Written in long-hand on poor paper and with worse ink, they made difficult reading. 'After reading ten pages,' Lennox Robinson declared, 'one felt inclined to throw the manuscript aside and reach for a rejection slip, but then suddenly one would come across a character or a scene startling in its truth and originality, a flash of undoubted genius.'[3] 'I believe there is something in you and your strong point is characterisation,' Lady Gregory told him.[4] Strangely enough it was Lady Gregory the aristocrat, alone among Dublin's literary hierarchy, with whom O'Casey felt most at home. After her death he wrote to her biographer:

> I loved her and I think she was fond of me – why God only knows. Our friendship affinity was an odd one; she an aristocrat, I a proletarian Communist. Yet we understood each other well . . . It was (and still is) a bitter memory within me that the difference between the Directorate and me over *The Silver Tassie* separated us for ever.[5]

When *The Shadow of a Gunman* opened on Thursday, 12 April 1923 for a meagre three evening performances and a matinée, neither the size of the audience, nor the critics, suggested that anything unusual had occured to change the fortunes of the rapidly declining Abbey. Only the critic of the *Evening Herald* saw in it the marks of genius.

> It was indeed a welcome and wholesome sign to sit in the Abbey last night and listen to an audience squirming with laughter and revelling boisterously in the satire which Mr Sean O'Casey has put into his two-act play. Not for a very long time has such a good play come our way. It was brilliant truthful, decisive . . . His characters were as perfect and his photography, for one really felt his men and women were but photographs, was nothing less than the work of genius.

Word of mouth travels quickly in Dublin and on the following night the house was filled to three-quarter capacity. Saturday matinée was sold out and on Saturday night Lady Gregory recorded to her grief that many had to be turned from the door. When the play was revived in the opening week of the new season not a seat was empty.

In October, O'Casey contributed a satire of contemporary political attitudes, *Cathleen Listens-In,* a one-act play that added little to his reputation; but on 3 January 1924 he handed in the script of his first full-length play that was to win him the Hawthornden Prize and world-wide renown.

'Juno and the Paycock'

The play opened on 3 March 1924, breaking all records by being continued for a second week to satisfy the crowds turned away from the door. Lady Gregory, inspired no less by the queues outside the theatre than by this 'wonderful and terrible play of futility, of irony, humour, tragedy,' wrote in her diary for 8 March, 'This is one of the evenings at the Abbey that makes me glad to have been born.'[6]

When *Juno* was revived in August, playing again to full houses, Holloway wrote, 'Certainly he [O'Casey] has written the two most popular plays ever seen at the Abbey.' But for Holloway it was above all the acting that drew his greatest praise. 'The acting . . . reaches the high water mark of Abbey acting. It looks as if the Abbey is coming into its own at last, and it's about time. In December next it will reach its twentieth year of existence.'[7] Critical approval, however, was by no means universal. For many, O'Casey's mixture of tragedy and comedy was not only strange and unorthodox, there were those who questioned the play's 'morality'. When *Juno* was presented in Cork in June 1924 under Sally Allgood's management for a week's run of twice-nightly performances, the management insisted that references to Mary Boyle's seduction by the schoolmaster, Charlie Bentham, be omitted and her pregnancy changed to tuberculosis.[8] As this demand was made between the first and second 'houses' Sara Allgood who was playing her part of 'Juno' was understandably distraught. Gabriel Fallon who was playing the part of Bentham records that 'somebody told her not to bother until she reached the third act and then to meet the lines as they came'. Predictably this ended in disaster.

Fitzgerald as Boyle was standing still and apprehensive, holding up his moleskin trousers as he asked her what the doctor had to say about Mary. Allgood sat down and tapped the table with nervous fingers saying 'Oh, Jack, Jack . . .' which was rather far off script. Something in Fitzgerald's manner made the house titter. Suddenly to my utter amazement I heard Allgood quickly say: 'Oh, Jack, Jack; d'ye know what Bentham's after doin' to Mary?' This was capped by the loudest laugh I have ever heard in a theatre.[9]

In November 1925 the play opened at the Royalty Theatre, London, directed by J. B. Fagan with a cast that included Arthur Sinclair as Captain Boyle, Sydney Morgan as Joxer Daly and Sara Allgood as Juno Boyle.

The Plough and the Stars

In August 1925 O'Casey's next full-length play reached the Directors and was unanimously accepted. But trouble lay ahead when rehearsals began under M. J. Dolan's direction. Dolan disliked both the play and the playwright. 'At any time I would think twice about having anything to do with it,' he wrote to Lady Gregory, 'the language is — to use the Abbey phrase — "beyond the beyonds". The song at the end of the second act, sung by the "girl-of-the-streets" is impossible.'[10] For Lennox Robinson who now took over the direction troubles multiplied. Eileen Crowe who was to play Mrs Gogan refused to say the line 'any kid Jinny Gogan has had since was got between the borders of the Ten Commandments!' She was replaced by May Craig. F. J. McCormick, now married to Eileen Crowe, refused to use the word 'snotty', and Ria Mooney who was cast as the prostitute, Rosie Redmond, recalled that some of the players tried to frighten her out of playing the part 'because they felt they would be besmirched by the fact of one of them playing such a role'.[11]

In the little world of Dublin playgoers word quickly spread that the Abbey was about to produce another 'immoral' play. Small wonder that there was, as Holloway wrote, 'electricity in the air before the curtain' on Monday, 8 February 1926 when the play was first presented.[12] However, to the relief of the players nothing untoward occurred. On Tuesday there was some hissing; on Wednesday 'a sort of moaning sound' was heard when the flags of the Volunteers and Citizen Army were carried into the pub. On Thursday night let those present speak for themselves.

Ria Mooney (Rosie Redmond): On the Thursday night, however, there was a changed response. After the curtain went up on Act 2, I heard voices raised above a whisper in the House. The voices grew louder.

Irish Times: There began a pandemonium which continued until after the curtain fell. It was carried on mostly by women, who shouted, booed and sang, occasionally varying their demonstration by a set speech.

Holloway: Mrs. Pearse, Mrs. Tom Clarke, Mrs. Sheehy-Skeffington, and others were in the theatre to vindicate the manhood of 1916 . . .

Ria Mooney: Then lumps of coal were thrown at me, and pennies fell noisily beside me on the stage. There were shouts from members of the audience, urging me to "get off", which only made me more determined to stay on.

O'Casey: The high, hysterical, distorted voices of women kept squealing that Irish girls were noted over the whole world for their modesty, and that Ireland's name was holy; that the Republican flag had never seen the inside of a public house; that this slander on the Irish race would mean the end of the Abbey Theatre; and that Ireland was Ireland through joy and through tears . . .

Irish Times: At the start of the third Act, notable for Mrs. Clitheroe's description of what she saw of the fighting in the streets, when, half demented she sought her husband, about a dozen women made their way from the pit on either side of the theatre . . .

Shelah Richards (Nora Clitheroe): I then noticed there were several female figures climbing up from the auditorium onto the stage. I watched transfixed as they huddled around the front-of-house curtain. Somebody shouted "Fire!" I screamed and dashed to the curtain followed by the other actors on stage and a hand-to-hand battle took place. We somehow managed to get the ladies off the stage up some steps and out to a little landing that led to the stage door and to the front-of-house. It was a pitched battle — fisticuffs, bums' rush, the lot.

Holloway: Some of the players behaved with uncommon roughness to some ladies who got on the stage, and threw two of them into the stalls.

O'Casey: Barry Fitzgerald became a genuine Fluther Good and fought as Fluther himself would fight, sending an enemy, who had climbed onto the stage, flying into the stalls with a Flutherian punch on the jaw.

Holloway: One young man thrown from the stage got his side hurt by the piano.

Ria Mooney: The entire cast wandered on to see the excitement: to see Barry Fitzgerald having a boxing match with one of the men from the audience who tried to rush the stage; to hear F. J. McCormick disassociating himself and his wife from the play . . .

Shelah Richards: Some of us felt this was a betrayal: we were involved, the play was a masterpiece, O'Casey our hero and we were prepared to fight, literally, for him and his play. The pro-O'Caseyites summarily manned the curtain and brought it swinging down on that actor. Meanwhile the Directors were being phoned all over Dublin.

Gabriel Fallon (Captain Brennan): Yeats, I was told, was already on his way to the theatre. I made up my mind to note everything he said and did.

Shelah Richards: I slipped away from the stage to see how

the ladies [dedicated members of Cumann na mBann who had been deeply involved in 1916 Easter Week and the Civil War] were and what they were up to. When I reached the top of the stairs and opened the door to the little landing where we had incarcerated them, I found them happy, smiling-faced, listening to somebody, hidden from me, who was talking to them smoothly and wittily; I had to look and see who had turned these furious females of ten minutes ago into sweetly smiling girls – it was Sean O'Casey!

Sean O'Casey: There wasn't a comely damsel amongst them.

Ria Mooney: Then Yeats came striding on stage . . .

Gabriel Fallon: One would imagine that the senior director of a theatre at which rioting was taking place would have looked somewhat perturbed on arriving there in the middle of a riot. Not so Yeats. He was smiling broadly as he came through the stage door and down the seven wooden steps leading to the stage itself . . . I said to him: 'This looks like a rather serious state of affairs, Mr. Yeats; what do you propose should be done about it?'

W. B. Yeats: Fallon, I am sending for the police, and *this time* it will be *their own* police!

Gabriel Fallon: Knowing that he (Sean) would be violently opposed to the idea of sending for the police, I managed to get word to him that Yeats had already taken that step. Leaving the women in the midst of their clamour, he made his way back-stage and told Yeats . . .

Sean O'Casey: The police! Sean to agree to send for the police – never! His Irish soul revolted from the idea . . . No, no, never! But a wild roar heard in the theatre seemed to shake the room where they all stood, told him to make up his mind quick; and swearing he could ne'er consent, consented.

Gabriel Fallon: As coolly as if he were pacing his eighteenth-century drawing-room in Merrion Square, Yeats walked up and down the stage still smiling to himself, apparently oblivious to the pandemonium that raged beyond the curtain . . . The old war-horse was hearing again the trumpets sounding the vindication of Synge . . .

W. B. Yeats: Tell O'Malley (the stage electrician) to raise the curtain the very moment I give the signal.

Gabriel Fallon: Yeats then placed himself close to the curtain opening and after a moment's pause gave the signal.

Shelah Richards: . . . advancing slowly to the footlights with raised hand, looking like an ancient Roman Senator.

Gabriel Fallon: . . . even the finest of actors would have stood transfixed in admiration of Yeats' performance. Every gesture, every pause, every inflection, was geared to a tolerance calculated to meet an angry mob. From his well-considered opening, with flashing eyes and upraised arm . . .

W. B. Yeats: I thought you had got tired of this, which commenced fifteen years ago. But you have disgraced yourselves again. Is this going to be a recurring celebration of Irish genius? Synge first and then O'Casey. The news of the happening of the last few minutes here will flash from country to country. Dublin has again rocked the cradle of a reputation. From such a scene as this theatre went forth the fame of Synge. Equally the fame of O'Casey is born here tonight. This is his apotheosis. [Not one word of this was heard by those in the auditorium but Yeats had taken the precaution of handing the speech he intended to make to the press before he came to the theatre.]

Sean O'Casey: . . . His anger making him like unto an aged Cuchullain in his hero-rage; his long hair waving, he stormed in utter disregard of all around him, confronting all those who cursed and cried out shame and vengeance on the theatre, as he conjured up a vision for them of O'Casey on a cloud, with Fluther on his right hand and Rosie Redmond on his left, rising upwards to Olympus to get from the waiting gods and goddesses a triumphant apotheosis for a work well done in the name of Ireland and of art.

The Irish Times: Suddenly and unexpectedly the shrieks and turmoil from the pit and from the invaded stalls died down, almost before Dr. Yeats had finished. The explanation was found with the arrival of half-a-dozen men of the detective branch . . .

Sean O'Casey: Then the constables flooded into the theatre, just in time. Rough and ready, lusty guardians of the peace . . . mystified, maybe, at anyone kicking up a row at a mere play. They pulled the disturbers out, they pushed them out, and, in one or two instances, carried them out, shedding them like peas from the pod of the theatre, leaving them in the cold street outside to tell their troubles to their neighbours or to the stars.

Irish Times: The next unexpected incident was the raising of the curtain and the continuance of the interrupted Act 3. This was hailed with a wild enthusiasm from the general body of the audience, in which the counter-demonstration was entirely drowned.

Sean O'Casey: Sean went home feeling no way exalted by his famous apotheosis. He was bewildered and felt sick rather than hilarious. Slandered the people! He had slandered his class no more than Chekhov had slandered his. Did these bawling fools think that their shouting would make him docile? He would leave them to their green hills of holy Ireland. His play (*Juno and the Paycock*) was doing well in London, and the producer, J. B. Fagan, had written several times asking him to come over. Why didn't he go, and leave the lot of them? The land of Nelson and Clive was beckoning to him more clearly than ever before; and he was ready to leave the land of Patrick and Tone.[13]

For the rest of the week the play, under police guard, drew full houses. No further demonstrations took place, though an abortive attempt was made to kidnap Barry Fitzgerald, presumably in the belief that this would effectively cause the play to be withdrawn. During the following weeks, controversy raged in the press. The *Independent* called for theatre censorship to protect the morals of the young; to which the *Irish Times* replied that 'the morals of the young were more likely to be perverted on the Dublin Streets than in the Abbey Theatre.' Mrs Sheehy-Skeffington, whose husband was perhaps the most tragic victim of the 1916 Rising, conducted a lively correspondence in the press with Sean O'Casey over the nationalist issue. At a public meeting on 1 March they both aired their views in open debate, accompanied by much irrelevant argument from their supporters on issues that had little to do with the rights or wrongs of O'Casey's treatment of the 1916 Rising.

But it was the criticisms of the literary fraternity, rather than the onslaught of the ardent nationalists, that wounded the sensitive pride of O'Casey. The novelist Liam O'Flaherty, the playwright Brinsley MacNamara, the poets F. R. Higgins and Austin Clarke, and the leading critic and theatre historian Andrew E. Malone, each for different reasons dismissed his plays with ill-concealed contempt. 'So Sean, at first bewildered by the riot, was now puzzled by the Irish critics, for innocent gawm that he was, he didn't realise then that these fellows didn't know what they were talking about.'[14] He was hurt, too, by the coolness of the Abbey players, for his lack of tact in criticising their work had left him with few friends. Lennox Robinson was aloof, Yeats remote. On 5 March he packed his bag and went to London.

The Silver Tassie

It was two years later, on 1 March 1928 that Lady Gregory received a letter from Sean, informing her that he had just finished typing his new play. 'I hope it may be suitable and that you will like it. Personally I think it is the best work I have done.'[15] But neither Lady Gregory nor her fellow Directors shared his opinion. Yeats, who had accused the Abbey audience of disgracing itself by failing to appreciate *The Plough and the Stars,* now disgraced himself and his theatre by rejecting *The Silver Tassie.*

Let it be said, however, that *The Silver Tassie* with its mixture of expressionist techniques and naturalism is greatly dependent upon imaginative direction and design. In neither was the Abbey of the twenties capable of doing it justice, let alone appreciating its experimental style. The mistake the Directors made was not so much in rejecting the play, but in the manner of its rejection. Ironically, it was Lady Gregory, who might claim to know Sean's prickly temperament better than Yeats or Robinson, who made the mistake of underestimating his reaction to their criticisms. In her belief that these might give him the chance to amend the play before its publication, she sent him Yeats's and Robinson's criticisms as well as her own. 'But I had a bad night or early morning thinking of the disappointment and shock he will feel.'[16] Sean was not merely shocked, he was furious. 'Curse o' God on them! . . . His anger grew with every line he read . . . He would send a salvo of words that would shake the doors of the Abbey and rattle the windows.'[17] Point by point he voiced his indignation at Yeats's criticisms. Worst of all was the suggestion that he might avoid the embarrassment of an outright rejection by informing the press he had withdrawn the play for revision.

In reply Sean sent copies of Yeats's letters, together with others by Robinson and Lady Gregory to the *Irish Statesman* whose editor, George Russell (AE), declined to publish them without the writers' consent. Anticipating Russell's scruples, O'Casey sent copies to St John Ervine who was only too delighted to press the case for their publication in *The Observer*. They appeared for the first time in that newspaper on Sunday 3 June 1928. Ervine wrote to O'Casey:

You are perfectly justified in publishing the correspondence. The production of a play by you at the Abbey is a matter of public interest. The Abbey is the nearest thing we have to a national theatre in these islands: it is subsidised by the Government of the Free State; and therefore the rejection of a play by an author who, as Yeats himself asserts, saved the theatre from extinction is a matter of considerable public interest . . . I do not object to Yeats regarding himself as the Holy Ghost, but I complain that he is sometimes inclined to regard himself as the entire Trinity.

On Monday following the letters appeared in the *Irish Times*.[18]

Now it was Yeats's turn to be furious: the letters were private; they were not written for publication; he would sue for breach of copyright; he would appeal to the Society of Authors. Sean replied that 'Yeats could take the dispute to the League of Nations for all he cared.' Yeats now authorised the *Irish Statesman* to publish the letters with additions. 'So far as Dublin is concerned I think we will gain out of the controversy, and elsewhere when the play is published,' he wrote to Lady Gregory.

Far and wide the dispute raged in the English and Irish press; Echoes of it resounded in the press of America and Europe. Those who had never heard of Yeats or O'Casey learnt about them for the first time.

But in the quiet groves of Coole Park an ageing Lady Gregory mourned her action. Her *Journals* record: 'I am sad about it all,' (4 May); 'Very, very, sad,' (10 June); 'We were wrong and I fully confess it.' (Letter to Walter Starkie who, alone among the Directors of the National Theatre Society had written, 'Sean O'Casey has given so many fine works that we ought to leave the final decision with the audience that has laughed and wept with him.') Shaw now waded in, adding salt to her wounds: 'Starkie was right, you should have done the play anyhow . . . It is certainly a hell of a play . . . He [W. B. Yeats] has fallen in up to the neck over O'C.' On 30 June Lady Gregory received the published copy of the play in which Sean had written, 'with pride and warm affection from Sean O'Casey.' She wrote, 'I am glad to have it, though I cannot look at it without pain for that loud quarrel, but I am glad he can think kindly of my part in it, all meant in kindness if he but knew.' In October 1929 she saw the play at the Apollo Theatre, presented by C. B. Cochran with Charles Laughton in the leading part and Augustus John's superb setting for the war scene. 'I am convinced we ought to have taken it and done our best to put it on,' she wrote in her diary.[19]

But the last had not been heard of *The Silver Tassie* as future years were to tell; nor did the tragedy of its rejection end in 1929. To Sean it brought a life-time of self-imposed exile from his native city; but Ireland and her people, whether remembered in love or rancour, remained the fountain of his inspiration until the day he died on 18 September 1964. In a broadcast tribute Micheál Ó hAodha said,

> A tale told to life itself! That is what O'Casey has left us in over twenty books and plays. Time may muffle *The Drums of Father Ned, The Bishop's Bonfire* may become a ring of grey ashes, a few feathers may even be ruffled in the gorgeous *Paycock's* tail. But the blue and silver of *The Plough and the Stars* will still float bravely in the breeze.[20]

For the Abbey, however, the rejection of *The Tassie* was to rob it of a playwright who might have weaned its audience of the deadly diet of popular comedy and spurious realism.

Coming of age

On Sunday, 27 December 1925 the Abbey celebrated its twenty-first birthday. During those twenty-one years two hundred and sixteen plays, the work of eighty-six authors, had been presented; some had enriched the stages of Europe and America; not a few had been acclaimed as classics of the modern theatre. Two hundred guests filled the stalls; the pit and gallery were crowded with the theatre's devotees. Three plays from the theatre's earliest years were presented, *In the Shadow of the Glen, Hyacinth Halvey* and *The Hour Glass*. In the latter play Frank Fay returned to play his old part of the Wise Man. Perhaps some who were present were reminded how far away were the ideals of the founder playwrights from the popular realism that now dominated the theatre's repertoire. For better or worse, the theatre, like the nation, had shed its early idealism to face the harsh facts of its economic existence.

The need for subsidy

'Yet we did not set out to create this sort of a theatre, and its success has been to me a discouragement and a defeat'[21] wrote Yeats in an open letter to Lady Gregory. Success, as we have seen, was scarcely an accurate description of the Abbey's financial situation when O'Casey's *The Shadow of a Gunman* was first presented. In fact the theatre was on the verge of bankruptcy. Since 25 March 1923, it had been under armed guard against threatened reprisals by the Republicans for failing to close its doors as a token of disapproval of the Provisional government's acceptance of the Treaty — a situation that was hardly conducive to theatre-going. Its account was so heavily overdrawn that the bank refused to cash its cheques, and O'Casey was offered the alternative of receiving his royalties — amounting to the lordly sum of four pounds — in cash from the box-office, or waiting until such time as the theatre's bank balance was again in credit. Obviously the theatre could not continue to appeal to the charity of Lady Gregory's wealthy friends, most of whom were English or Anglo-Irish, not could it survive artistically by a policy of continuous touring. In 1922 the state of the theatre's finances was such that the Directors could only afford to engage three of the players on full-time salaries, the remainder being 'part-timers', receiving little more than their bus fares.

The first official approach to the government was made in a statement by the Directors in 1922, setting out the precarious state in which the theatre found itself and the reasons why it should receive help from the Provisional government. At the same time they held out the bait of their wish 'to engage a Gaelic-speaking producer of plays and to form a company of Gaelic players . . . If the Government intend to make a great National Theatre the Abbey Theatre might eventually be turned into the Gaelic Theatre.' On 18 February 1923 Lady Gregory recorded in her diary:

At 5 o'clock I went to the Government buildings to see the Minister of Education, Eoin MacNeill. As to the Abbey, he is anxious we should have the subsidy, it is to come on in the next Budget debate. He is asking for it as an aid to an educational work: our teaching of acting and dramatic writing. He is by no means sure we shall get it but thinks even a discussion on the Abbey will do it good, get more interest aroused in it. I told him of our desire to give it over. He was rather startled and said he didn't want to manage a theatre and was sure the Government didn't, anyhow for some time to come.[22]

The offer to hand the theatre over to the government was repeated in a letter to President Cosgrave, dated 27 June 1924, signed by Yeats and Lady Gregory. Ernest Blythe, then Minister of Finance, to whom the letter was forwarded, considered this offer was more tactical than serious, and that in fact it was only an emphatic way of asking for a subvention. Indeed it seems hard to believe that Yeats was so naïve as to believe that the Free State government, faced with the manifold problems of creating the machinery of the new state, not to mention its economic regeneration and the establishment of law and order, would welcome the prospect of running a highly controversial theatre. Lennox Robinson, however, assures us that this was a 'perfectly serious offer'. In which case it adds weight to the view that after twenty-one years the Directors were increasingly weary of running a theatre whose economic existence depended on a diet of popular comedies. Yeats as we have said, was anxious to shed some of the burden of decision-making and it was in April 1924 that Lennox Robinson was appointed a Director of the National Theatre Society.[23]

If government help was to be forthcoming, the Directors realised they would first have to put the theatre's financial affairs in order. The Society's investments were sold to offset the bank overdraft and a mortgage was raised on the premises. On 20 December Blythe was able to tell Lady Gregory that the Executive Council was 'inclined' to help the Abbey. 'I told him our need, our actors underpaid, our actor-manager (M. J. Dolan) getting only £6.7.0. a week, our building so shabby and wanting repair. He asked me how much we wanted to keep going, and I asked for £1,000 a year and £1,000 down for repairs.'[24]

The theatre was fortunate in that three powerful members of the Executive Council, Ernest Blythe, Eoin MacNeill and Desmond Fitzgerald, Minister for External Affairs, as well as the leader of the Labour Party, Thomas Johnson, were all keen patrons. Moreover, Yeats had been appointed to the Senate in 1922, and in the following year was awarded the Nobel Prize; two events that redounded to the theatre's national and international prestige.

A subsidy of eight hundred and fifty pounds was voted for the financial year 1925–26. From the following year onwards this was raised to one thousand pounds, and Blythe expressed the hope that the actors' salaries would be increased. Thus the Abbey became the first theatre to receive a government subsidy in the English-speaking world.

Government representation

Money from the public purse entailed some form of government representation in the theatre's affairs. There were those who feared that the appointment by the government of Dr George O'Brien, Professor of Economics at University College, Dublin, would entail a loss of that artistic freedom for which Yeats and Lady Gregory had fought since the earliest days of the dramatic movement. Indeed the danger was increased by the fact that the responsibilities of Dr O'Brien were never clearly stated; a situation that led to trouble when O'Brien, who made no claim to be 'an author or a dramatic critic' became highly alarmed by Dolan's refusal to direct *The Plough and the Stars*, and by his fears that the play 'might provoke an attack on the theatre of a kind that would endanger the continuancy of the subsidy'.[25] To which Lady Gregory replied, 'If we have to choose between the subsidy and our freedom, it is our freedom we choose.' O'Brien asked for the second act to be largely re-written and for a general toning down of the vituperative language. At a hastily summoned Directors meeting, Lady Gregory bluntly informed him that 'Blythe had made no conditions in giving the subsidy, and certainly no hint of appointing a censor.' Faced with the formidable opposition of Yeats and Lady Gregory, O'Brien gave way, admitting that he had 'mistaken' his position. For a time at any rate the danger of government interference in the artistic life of the theatre was averted.

The increase in the subsidy in 1926 enabled the Board of Directors to comply with Blythe's wish that the players' salaries should be increased and placed on a regular scale. Up to now the salaries of the players largely depended on the financial state of the theatre, or on how much the manager and Board thought individual players were worth. The salaries of existing full-time members of the company were now fixed at seven pounds ten shillings when playing; half salaries were paid for non-playing weeks. New full-time members were paid three pounds ten shillings for the first year of their engagement, and increased by one pound annually until their salaries reached the top level. Part-time players were paid according to the size of the part, the minimum being one pound ten shillings a week. M. J. Dolan, as manager, received an extra four pounds a week, and Lennox Robinson as play director received four hundred pounds a year.

Salaries remained more or less static until 1946; ludicrous as they seem today, they were at the time comparable to those of lower grades in the Civil Service.

The Peacock Theatre

The subsidy was to bring further benefits to the Abbey. In November 1926 the Board was able to plan the transformation of the portion of their premises that was currently let to the College of Modern Irish into a small theatre.

Yeats commissioned Michael Scott, a young architect who occasionally played with the company as a part-time player, to undertake the conversion. The accommodation consisted of a café on the ground floor that also served as a rehearsal room; a small theatre on the first floor with a stage stepped down to the auditorium, and a scene dock. The auditorium held a hundred seats whose blue upholstery matched by the colour of the walls gave the theatre its name of the Peacock Theatre. The third floor housed dressing rooms and an additional rehearsal room. Many years later Michael Scott was to design the new Abbey Theatre.

Yeats hoped this well-equipped little theatre would serve as an experimental theatre for poetic drama. This hope was never fully realised since financial reasons required it to be let as often as possible to outside organisations. The opening performance took place on Sunday, 13 November 1927, when

Georg Kaiser's expressionist play, *From Morn to Midnight,* was presented by the New Players, an amateur organisation stemming from the Dublin Drama League. The play was directed by the future playwright, Denis Johnston, under the pseudonym of 'E. W. Tocher'.

From 1928 to 1930 the Peacock provided the first home of the Dublin Gate Theatre, founded by Hilton Edwards and Micheál MacLiammóir. It also provided a permanent home for the Abbey School of Acting, and from 1927 to 1933 the Abbey School of Ballet.

The latter was formed by Ninette de Valois, later to found The Sadlers Wells Ballet, now the Royal Ballet. Yeats had admired her work as a choreographer and dancer at the Cambridge Festival Theatre where he had witnessed Terence Gray's choreographed production of *On Baile's Strand.* He now sought to obtain her collaboration in the performance of his 'Plays for Dancers'. Ninette de Valois, herself an Irish-woman from County Wicklow, had trained under Diaghilev; her work for the Abbey provided a series of ballet perform-ances in the Peacock and the main theatre, including the first staging of Yeats's dance drama, *Fighting the Waves* (13 August 1929).

Popular drama

The government subsidy and O'Casey's plays were not the only sources from which the Abbey gained for a time greater financial stability. The decade 1924 to 1934 yielded a valu-able harvest of popular drama that could be relied on to pro-duce, if not full houses, at least respectable returns at the box office. George Shiels had already endeared himself to play-goers with *Paul Twyning* in 1922; he now followed this up with five of the most popular comedies in the theatre's reper-toire: *Professor Tim* (12 September 1925), *Cartney and Kevney* (29 November 1927), *Mountain Dew* (5 March 1929), *The New Gossoon* (19 April 1930) and *Grogan and the Ferret* (13 November 1933).

Lennox Robinson, no less prolific than Shiels, contributed two often revived comedies, *The Far-Off Hills* (22 October 1922) and *Drama at Inish* (6 February 1933), presented out-

side Ireland as *Is Life Worth Living?*. Less popular were his
more serious plays, *Portrait* (31 March 1925) and *The White
Blackbird* (12 October 1925). *The Big House* (6 September
1926), in which he treated the decline of an Ascendancy
family under the impact of the Anglo-Irish and Civil Wars,
proved, together with *The Lost Leader,* among his most
popular serious plays.

Lennox's growing interest in Continental drama was reflected in *Ever the Twain* (8 October 1929) in which he made
use of expressionist techniques, *All's Over Then* (23 July
1932), a drama owing much to Strindberg in its theme of a
battle between the sexes for domination and power, and
Church Street (21 May 1934) with its debt to Pirandello's
Six Characters in Search of an Author.

Brinsley Macnamara, whose first comedy *The Glorious Uncertainty* had drawn full houses in 1923, contributed a no
less popular comedy *Look at the Heffernans* (13 April 1926).
The Master (6 March 1928) dealt with the consequences for
his father (a schoolmaster) that ensued from the publication
of his much discussed novel *The Valley of the Squinting
Windows.* 'Not since the production of Mr. O'Casey's *The
Plough and the Stars* has a new play in Dublin created so
much interest,' wrote the critic of the *Irish Times;* while the
New York Times devoted three columns to an appreciation
of the play. *Margaret Gillan* (17 July 1933), a powerful
drama of the fury of a woman against the man who spurned
her love for the love of her daughter, provided May Craig
with an opportunity to show her considerable strength as a
tragic actress.

Tragedy was also powerfully represented by T. C. Murray's
finest play, *Autumn Fire* (8 September 1924), which treated
the same theme as Eugene O'Neill's *Desire under the Elms.*
The play was later acquired for production in London and
New York. *The Blind Wolf* (29 April 1928) in which Murray
departed from Abbey tradition by laying the scene in Hungary, and *Michaelmas Eve* (27 June 1932) of which the *Irish
Press* somewhat extravagantly claimed 'Mr. Murray has written
a masterpiece for the Irish National Theatre and for the
drama of the world', were for a time amongst the popular
plays that could be counted on to draw an audience.

Unpopular theatre

'I want to create for myself an unpopular theatre and an audience like a secret society where admission is by favour and never to many' Yeats wrote in his essay, *A People's Theatre, a Letter to Lady Gregory.*

In the same month as Dubliners flocked to see *Juno and the Paycock,* an entertainment of a very different kind was provided for a select audience in Yeats's house in Merrion Square. On 3 March 1924 members of the Drama League were invited to witness the first performance in Dublin of *At the Hawk's Well,* the earliest of Yeats's 'Plays for Dancers' based on the techniques of the Noh drama of Japan.

The play was performed by members of the Abbey company with music composed by Edmund Dulac, who also designed the costumes and masks. Dulac's music and designs were originally created for a performance of the play in Lady Cunard's drawing-room on 2 April 1916. For this first performance in London, Henry Ainley appeared as 'The Young Man' and the Japanese dancer, Michio Ito as 'The Guardian of the Well'.

Yeats's interest in Noh drama was stimulated by his contact with Ezra Pound who had published *Certain Noble Plays of Japan: From the Manuscripts of Ernest Fenollosa* in 1916 for which Yeats had written an introduction. The conventions of the Noh with its masks and stylised stage-craft, its combination of music, dance, chanted speech, and its appeal to a refined and aristocratic audience, provided Yeats with a dramatic form that seemed to be immediately sympathetic to his own ideas of poetic theatre. Sean O'Casey, who witnessed the Dublin performance, was at first bewildered and then frankly amused by 'the sight of Mr Robinson doing a musician, and Mick Dolan, the Abbey actor, acting Cuchullain, so serious, so solemn . . . No, the People's theatre can never be turned into a poetical conventicle,' he wrote many years later. 'A play poetical to be worthy of the theatre must be able to withstand the terror of Ta-Ra-Ra-Boom-Dee-Ay.'[26]

The contrast between the exclusive audience who gathered in Yeats's drawing-room and the laughter-seeking crowds who flocked to the Abbey to see *Juno and the Paycock* revealed,

as Liam Miller has pointed out, 'the extent of the gap between the concept of theatre at which Yeats had arrived and
the style which the Abbey had developed'.[27]

The nearest Yeats came to attracting a wider audience to
his 'Plays for Dancers' was achieved with the collaboration of
Ninette de Valois and Hedley Briggs, together with the
Abbey on 13 August 1929. The masks for this performance
were borrowed from the Dutch sculptor, Hildo Krop, who
had designed them for a production in Amsterdam of *The
Only Jealousy of Emer* (*Vroue Emer's Groote Stryd*) on 2
April 1922. For the Dublin performance the music was com-
posed by the avant-garde American composer George Antheil.
'The steam whistle of a merry-go-round discourses heavenly
music by comparison,' wrote the ultra-conservative Joseph
Holloway.[28]

In 1931 Yeats made a further attempt to interest a popular
audience in this sophisticated and esoteric form of theatre.
The Cat and The Moon (21 September) was presented for a
week's run in harness with the popular comedy *The Lord
Mayor*. The result was not encouraging. 'There was', wrote
Holloway, 'a very thin audience for the first night.'[29] The
Irish Times, whilst praising the play, added, 'it is quite impossible to believe that it can ever become a part of the
regular repertory of the Abbey or any other theatre.' Yeats
now accepted the fact that the time was still 'out of joint'
for poetic drama, and in December when his Noh drama, *The
Dreaming of the Bones,* was produced it was restricted to a
single performance on a Sunday night (6 December 1931).

In another convention, however, Yeats was more successful in drawing an audience. His translations of Sophocles'
King Oedipus (7 December 1926) and *Oedipus at Colonus*
(12 December 1927) commanded general respect, and the
former drew full houses. For F. J. McCormick in the name
part it was a triumph. 'His masterly treatment in this play has
put him in the forefront of all the great ones,' wrote the
critic of the *Evening Herald.*

In his only realistic play, *The Words upon the Window
Pane* (17 November 1930) the action of which is centred on a
séance held by a female medium through whom Swift, Stella
and Vanessa speak, Yeats showed that he could rival any of

the realists of the time in commanding the attention of a popular audience.

In *W. B. Yeats and the Idea of a Theatre* Dr James Flannery maintains that developments in theatre today, as exemplified by the plays of Beckett, Ionesco and Pinter, and by the laboratory work of Grotowski and Brook, indicate that a new interest in Yeats's poetic plays is about to occur.[30] Such an interest is, however, unlikely to spread much beyond the limited circle of students of drama; for the major difference between Yeats's plays and contemporary theatrical developments lies in their literary primacy and aristocratic appeal. To the general public Yeats's theatre remains 'a mysterious art', 'a theatre for ourselves and our friends and a few simple people who understand from sheer simplicity what we understand from scholarship and thought.'[31] The greatness of Yeats's contribution to a people's theatre lies not in his plays but in his championship of a theatre that bowed the knee neither to popular favour, nor to political and religious pressures; a theatre that expressed the consciousness of the nation without fear or favour; above all a theatre that proved an inspiration and a focus for many generations of young writers who, but for its existence, would never have contemplated writing for the stage.

New playwrights

Amongst these new playwrights of the post-Treaty generation were Denis Johnston, Paul Vincent Carroll and Teresa Deevy.

The title of Johnston's first play (originally called *Shadow Dance* and later *Symphony in Green*) was changed to *The Old Lady Says No!* after its rejection by the Abbey, its new title implying that it was Lady Gregory who turned it down. Whether this was so or not, Johnston's multi-scene, expressionist satire of Irish idealism was far better served by Hilton Edwards in an historic production by the Gate Theatre than it would have been by the unimaginative production methods of the Abbey in the twenties.

Yeats was fully aware of the Abbey's weakness in staging anything other than the eternal repetition of farm kitchen and front parlour scenes; and it was partly to stimulate a

more creative approach to play directing that he invited
Denis Johnston to direct *King Lear,* the Abbey's first attempt
at a Shakespeare play.

The production, with futurist designs by D. Travers-Smith,
opened on 26 November 1928, providing McCormick with
the opportunity to prove himself once again in a major tragic
role. '*Lear* last night wonderful, McCormick magnificent —
there is no other word — all through,' Lady Gregory wrote.[32]
Yeats was shrewd enough to recognise Johnston's potential as
a playwright and it was no doubt to keep him from becoming
too closely attached to the rival theatre that he persuaded his
fellow Directors to soften the blow caused by the rejection of
his first play by offering a fifty pound guarantee against loss
for its production by the Gate. The Abbey reaped its reward
when Johnston offered it his second play *The Moon in the
Yellow River.* The play is undoubtedly one of the master-
pieces of Irish drama, but strangely enough has never received
the critical acclaim nor the popularity that are its due. This is
partly due to the complexity of its themes, and partly to
Johnston's refusal to commit himself to any easy optimistic
philosophy in his distinctly cynical view of the contradictions
in Irish character and behaviour. In *The Moon* he mirrors the
confused state of Ireland in the birth pangs of its nationhood
with its bombs, political murders and relentless self-devour-
ing. 'Last night's audience was frankly bewildered and so
divided in its opinions that prolonged hissing was mingled
with dominant applause,' wrote the critic of the *Irish Times*
on the occasion of its first production (27 April 1931).

In June 1931 the Directors decided to offer a prize of fifty
pounds for the best full-length play. the award was shared
between Paul Vincent Carroll', a schoolmaster from Dundalk,
and Teresa Deevy, a deaf spinster from County Waterford.
Carroll's play, *Things that are Caesar's* (originally called *The
New Procrustes*), was presented on 15 August 1932, gaining
a universally appreciative press reception. 'Vincent Carroll
will without doubt rank in the future with the greatest of Irish
writers,' wrote the *Daily Express* critic. Miss Deevy had al-
already had two plays presented by the Abbey, *The Reapers*
(18 March 1930) and a one-act play *A Disciple* (24 August
1931). *Temporal Powers,* her prize-winning play which

opened on 12 September 1932, received a less flattering press, though the *Irish Times* wrote, 'The author has produced one of the most thoughtful works seen for some time at the Abbey Theatre.'

The charwoman of the Abbey

In 1924 and 1927 Lady Gregory contributed her last plays to the Abbey, *The Story Brought by Brigid* (14 April 1924), *Sancho's Master* (14 March 1927), and *Dave* (9 May 1927). Shaw called her 'the charwoman of the Abbey', she was in fact not only its servant ·but its mistress. In 1932 she died; her last years saddened by the knowledge that her home to which she had devoted so much loving care was to pass out of the hands of her family. Coole Park was taken over by the Forestry Commission; its lawns and gardens neglected, the great house that had played so vital a part in the history of Irish theatre was wantonly destroyed. Yeats had written in 1929,

> Here, traveller, scholar, poet, take your stand
> When all those rooms and passages are gone,
> When nettles wave upon the shapeless mound
> And saplings root among the broken stone,
> And dedicate — eyes bent upon the ground,
> Back turned upon the brightness of the sun
> And all the sensuality of the shade —
> A moment's memory to that laurelled head.[33]

With her death there ended what might be called the domestic Abbey; the family theatre whose members were held together by her matriarchal rule, whose green-room with its homely furniture and photographs was the centre of family life; a quarrelsome family sometimes, liable to sudden flare-ups, abrupt departures and petty jealousies, with the patriarchal Yeats held in fearsome awe in his presence but good for 'great gas' behind his back, and 'Lady G.' prone to have her favourites, dispensing tea and barmbrack, a strict but kindly matriarch; now all that was changing; parental rule was to be replaced by an oligarchy.

7
The New Directorate
1932–1951

A clash with government

Lady Gregory's death was not the only loss the theatre suffered in 1932. In March of that year the Cosgrave government fell and with it the theatre lost the powerful support of Ernest Blythe in the corridors of power.

The new government, led by Eamon de Valera, embarked on a militant policy of economic nationalism aimed at achieving national self-sufficiency, thus precipitating an economic war with the United Kingdom that lasted until 1938. Stringent economies were made, especially in those areas not considered directly productive. In 1933 the Abbey's annual subsidy was cut to £750 a year; once more the theatre was in economic difficulties.

Meanwhile a clash with the government over representation on the Board of Directors seemed likely. Dr Walter Starkie, who had succeeded Dr George O'Brien as the government appointee although a Catholic, was, as a Fellow of Trinity College, unacceptable to the Fianna Fáil party with its strong republican sympathies. Yeats, ever resentful of political intrusion in the theatre's affairs, retaliated by appointing Starkie as an ordinary shareholding member of the Board. Dr Richard Hayes, the government nominee whose appointment would have been acceptable to the Board, felt himself to be insufficiently versed in theatrical affairs to accept appointment. Without consulting the Directors, the government announced its intention of appointing a politician known to be hostile to the Abbey, whereupon Yeats threatened to close the theatre. A head-on clash was averted by Hayes who, anxious to avoid a quarrel between Yeats and the government, withdrew his objections to joining the Board. Further difficulties lay ahead.

The cut in the subsidy and the economic depression of the thirties made it necessary for the Abbey to seek additional finance by resuming its American tours. In October 1931 the players resumed their visits to America with a mammoth coast-to-coast tour of seventy-nine centres, opening on their old battlefield, Philadelphia, this time to a rapturous reception at the Academy Theatre with George Shiels's comedy, *Professor Tim*. The tour included the Canadian cities of Ottawa, Montreal, Toronto, Vancouver and Winnipeg ending in April 1932. Three more tours were to follow (October 1932–May 1933, September 1934–April 1935, August 1937–April 1938) before another world war was to bar their passage across the Atlantic. In all, the four tours covered some 36,000 miles and over one hundred centres with stays varying between one night and two to seven weeks. During the 1932–33 tour the players once again met their old critics in New York when the United Irish-American Societies passed a resolution requesting the Irish government to withdraw its subsidy from the theatre on the grounds that 'the Abbey players at present touring America are giving wrong impressions of Irish life and character by presenting such plays as *The Playboy of the Western World* and *The Plough and the Stars*'.

The Fianna Fáil government, more sensitive to Irish-American relations than its predecessor, requested the Directors to withdraw the two plays from the repertoire of its next tour; whereupon Yeats, declaring he would prefer to forgo the subsidy rather than submit to government censorship, sought an interview with de Valera. The meeting between the poet and the mathematician proved that personalities are more powerful than politics: 'I was impressed by his simplicity and honesty though we differed throughout. It was a curious experience, each recognising the oth point of view so completely. I had gone there full of suspicion, but my suspicion vanished at once.'[1]

A compromise was found: a note in the programme of subsequent tours explained that, while the government subsidised the theatre, it did not accept responsibility for the selection of its plays.

The new Abbey policy

Lady Gregory's death also brought a major change in the management and policy of the Abbey. Up to 1930 she had come regularly to Dublin and kept a close watch on the theatre's affairs. Since then control had largely been left to Lennox Robinson who was rapidly falling a victim to alcoholism. Among the contract players discipline was slack; on first nights the voice of the prompter was too often heard; in the revival of well-worn comedies 'gagging' and 'milking' the lines for laughs were again apparent. When called upon to direct plays, Arthur Shields and M. J. Dolan, as players themselves, felt inhibited from taking disciplinary action. Punctuality at rehearsals was spasmodic and rehearsals little more than a run-through for lines and moves; while evening rehearsals — the only time the part-time players who worked elsewhere could attend — were resented by those in full-time employment.

This state of affairs offered the worst possible example to the younger players, whose worth was being tested during the absence of the contract players in America. Among the talented newcomers were Ann Clery, Nora O'Mahony, Denis O'Dea, Fred Johnson, Paul Farrell, W. O'Gorman, Joe Linnane and Cyril Cusack, of whose first appearance on the Abbey stage in A. P. Fanning's one-act play *Vigil* (24 October 1932) Holloway wrote: 'This young actor is the stepson of Breffni O'Rourke and shows great promise as an actor, and has a very soft musical voice.' Later he was to add, 'Someday he'll do something by which he'll be remembered for ever on the Irish stage.'[2] Holloway was a shrewd judge of actors.

Up to 1930 the Abbey enjoyed a virtual monopoly of Irish plays and players, as well as the support of the more serious-minded playgoers. Now there was a threat of the latter being

enticed away by the Gate. The Abbey's audience, except on
first nights of new plays, was increasingly composed of those
who went to the theatre for a good laugh; too often the players gave them what they wanted. Something had to be done
if the National Theatre was not to sink into second-class
citizenship.

Yeats, who had now taken up permanent residence in
Rathfarnham on the outskirts of Dublin, found himself in an
embarrassing situation. It was clear that under Robinson the
theatre was in a decline, but he was embarrassed by Lennox's
loyalty to the theatre and the genuine friendship that existed
between them. However, if the Abbey's prestige was to survive something had to be done. Yeats temporised, believing
that this could be achieved by engaging a play director from
abroad responsible for the production of foreign plays, which
he declared to be necessary in view of the 'slackening of
activity among Irish dramatists'. The temporary engagement
of a play director, limited to a period when the contract players were on tour, would not seem a threat to Lennox's more
permanent relationship with the theatre.

After much searching Bladon Peake, who had been trained
under Nugent Monck at the Maddermarket Theatre, Norwich,
was engaged for a brief season, bringing with him James
Bould, a designer of imagination and considerable technical
skill.

Peake must have wanted to tempt Providence by deciding
to open this experimental season with that most unlucky
play, *Macbeth* (25 October 1934). Despite all his innova-
tions — the abandonment of the front curtain, the removal of
the footlights, the building of a forestage, the revolutionary
lighting — the evil powers were not to be appeased; *Macbeth*
was a failure.

Peake's reputation was redeemed by his subsequent productions of Molière's *School for Wives* in black and white
settings and costumes, accompanied by a somewhat bizarre
production of Schnitzler's *Gallant Cassian* (12 November).
Of his production of Pirandello's *Six Characters in Search
of an Author* (3 December), the critic of the *Irish Times*
wrote: 'It can be said without exaggeration that it is one of
the best productions staged at the Abbey within recent

years.' But despite critical approval, receipts fell disastrously. The contracts of Peake and Bould were terminated in January 1935 and the theatre was closed down.

New Directors

'We have got to make a fresh start' Yeats announced in an interview published in the *Daily Express* on 31 December 1934. 'How we shall do it will be discussed when I return to Dublin.' How he did it is an example of his devious diplomacy. At a Board meeting held on 31 January 1935, from which Lennox was significantly absent, Yeats produced an anonymous memorandum, addressed to him personally entitled 'Proposals to the Board of the National Theatre Co. Ltd.' After deploring that 'The Abbey Theatre, once the headquarters of Irish literary affairs, has largely ceased to exist and drama enticing to the intellect and to the eye is now found on another stage,' the memorandum went on to propose the creation of an Advisory Committee 'to advise and confer with the Board of Directors on all matters relating to the management of the theatre'. Since the recommendations of this so-called 'Advisory' body could only be turned down by the unanimous vote of the full Board, its object was clearly to take over the management of the theatre and remove control from Lennox Robinson. Yeats's proposal that two of Lennox's bitterest critics, the poet F. R. Higgins and the playwright Brinsley Macnamara, should be appointed as the first members of this committee leaves little doubt that they were the authors of the document. It also suggests that their proposals were known to Yeats and submitted with his approval.

Apart from its doubtful legality this cumbersome arrangement would have had the effect of handing the theatre over to amateurs who, as yet, were totally unversed in the problems of theatre management. Fortunately its worst effects were averted by Richard Hayes' proposal that a more effective way of introducing new blood into the theatre would be to seek powers to enlarge the membership of the Board. This process involved a six weeks' delay during which the press was liberally sprinkled with letters on what should, or should not, be done to revive the ailing Irish theatre.

In the forefront of the theatre's critics were two of Ireland's most promising young writers, Frank O'Connor (Michael O'Donovan) and Sean O'Faolain, who maintained that there was no 'slackening of activity amongst Irish dramatists', but that dramatists were discouraged from writing for the Abbey by the discourteous treatment they received. At the same time they, and others, strongly deplored Yeats's announcement that 'from now on the theatre's policy would be orientated to include regular productions of contemporary Continental plays'.

On 9 March the Board was able to put an end to the controversy by announcing the appointment of three new Directors: Higgins, Macnamara and Ernest Blythe — the latter now a member of the Senate.

In Fred Higgins there entered upon the scene a genial, witty and lovable personality; a master of intrigue and a man of considerable ambition. Higgins set out to wean Yeats from his loyalty to Robinson, for if a successor had to be found to the ageing poet, who more suitable than the man whom Yeats had described as 'undoubtedly the finest of our young poets: he may bring back to the Irish theatre something of its first poetic impulse'?

It could not be said of Ernest Blythe that he was in the running for the restoration of 'poetic impulses'. Eminently practical and almost totally indifferent to criticism, Blythe's nearest approach to a poetic impulse was his life-long attachment to the Gaelic language. Time would tell which of these three was to be the future master of the Abbey. Certainly not Brinsley Macnamara; for it was no time before that impulsive and emotional man had entangled himself so completely with the players and the Board that his resignation became imperative.

In the early summer of 1935 Yeats and O'Casey made up their quarrel over the rejection of *The Silver Tassie*. With the unanimous consent of the Board the play was accepted for production. *The Silver Tassie* opened at the Abbey on 12 August, directed by Arthur Shields and designed by Maurice McGonigal, provoking, as might be expected, a storm of protest in the press and fierce resolutions at meetings of Catholic and Nationalist societies. On 27 August a meeting of the Galway Catholic Young Men's Society passed a resolution, 'condemning violently the dramatic work of the Abbey Theatre in so far as it infringes canons of Christian reverence or human decency, and in so far as it injures the nation's prestige at home and abroad'.[3] Father Gaffney, O.P., who, of course, had not visited the Abbey, was moved to declare that the inclusion of O'Casey's plays in the current tour of America might well bring shame and dishonour to 'our Irish-American brothers'.[4]

The *Irish Catholic* (7 September) called for a law banning O'Casey's plays. The *Standard* (30 August) demanded that the Abbey get rid of Yeats — 'Mr Yeats is no literary leader for a Catholic country' — while the President of the Gaelic League, P. T. McGinley, in the *Irish Independent* of 29 August declared that the Abbey itself should be abolished. Needless to say he had not seen the play. But it was the charges of blasphemy levelled against the play that roused the Catholic sensitivity of the Abbey Director, Brinsley Macnamara. He issued a statement to the press in which he declared he was not at any time in favour of the play's production but, as the only Catholic Director present when the play was accepted, he felt powerless to prevent it. However, he had given instructions 'to have certain excisions from, and amendments to, the printed version of the play made, particularly with regard to the travesty of the Sacred Office in the second act . . . Not only had nothing been done to reduce the offensive quality of the play, but it was more brazenly offensive than when I had seen it in its London production in 1929.' He went on to accuse the audience of showing 'a wholly uncritical . . . almost insane admiration for the vulgar and worthless plays of Mr. O'Casey' and the players for showing 'a reverence for his work that has not been given to any other author who has ever written for the theatre'.[5] The players demanded a public apology; the Board called upon him to resign. Macnamara refused, claiming that his statement was necessary to save the theatre. Stalemate was resolved by the Board's resolution to set up a sub-committee to run the theatre, consisting of all its members except

Macnamara. At this point this impulsive but well-meaning man — more effective as a playwright than as a theatre Director — had no option but to resign. In his place the Board elected Frank O'Connor in October 1935. It was in the midst of these revolutionary movements that I made my first appearance at the Abbey.

Personal encounter

Among the provisions of what came to be known as the 'New Policy' was the re-casting and re-designing of the standard repertory plays. Higgins and Macnamara in their memorandum had also called for stricter control of rehearsals. This they felt could only be achieved by a play director from outside the company; for this purpose Yeats sought the advice of the Poet Laureate, John Masefield. On 8 July, Yeats asked the Board 'to consider the engagement of Mr. Hugh Hunt who was a past President of the Oxford University Dramatic Society, subsequently he had produced plays for six months at Nugent Monck's theatre at Norwich, since when he had been Producer (Director) at the Croydon Repertory Theatre, and had directed *King Lear, Children in Uniform* and *Othello* at the London Westminster Theatre'.

My contract commenced on 19 August 1935 and at my request the Board engaged the young and highly promising designer, Tanya Moiseiwitsch. I should add that my only connection with Ireland was through my mother's side of the family — 'black Protestants' from the North of Ireland; I had only visited Ireland once before, and that for a few weeks at the age of three. I was totally ignorant of Irish politics; and even more so of the traditions of the Abbey. I was twenty four and spoke with an Oxford accent. A more unlikely candidate for the task of directing a distinguished company of Irish players it would be hard to find. During the following three years, I was to direct twenty-two new Irish plays, eight one-act plays, three plays by non-Irish writers and some half dozen revivals. My engagement ended in November 1938. Tanya Moiseiwitsch remained until January 1939 to be succeeded by Anne Yeats, the daughter of the poet.

From then on the engagement of a resident designer became part of the accepted policy. Yeats's attempts to improve the woefully unimaginative visual aspects of the productions by calling on the services of such scenic artists as T. Sturge Moore, Gordon Craig, Robert Gregory and Charles Ricketts had, as previously stated, fallen victim to economic pressures and were, in any case, almost solely confined to his own plays and those of Lady Gregory. From 1914 onwards the dreary repetition of white-washed cottage kitchen and wall-papered parlour had been only occasionally relieved by an imaginative design by an artist such as Nora McGuinness or Dorothy Travers-Smith. The standards set by James Bould, Tanya Moiseiwitsch, Anne Yeats and their successors Michael Walsh, Alicia Sweetman, Carl Bonn and Vere Dudgeon were at least a partial answer to those who had long pointed to the superior staging of Hilton Edwards and Micheál Mac Liammóir at the Gate Theatre.

The story of those troublesome years is amusingly, if not entirely accurately, recounted in Frank O'Connor's auto-biography, *My Father's Son.*[6]

The policy rejected

The policy of presenting non-Irish plays as a means of reviving the Abbey's fortunes proved no more successful under Hugh Hunt's direction than it had been under Bladon Peake's. A cautious start was made with Shaw's *Candida* and *Village Wooing* (30 September). André Obey's *Noah* (11 November) proved successful despite its unusual technique; but *Coriolanus* (13 January 1936) and James Elroy Flecker's *Hassan* (1 June) neither recaptured the so-called 'lively minds' who had deserted to the Gate, nor pleased the groundlings of the Abbey. Clearly the Irish theatre could not be rescued by challenging the Gate's policy. Its immediate regeneration lay in a vigorous and creative approach to the work upon which its national and international reputation had been founded.

For this purpose greater help and encouragement had to be given to new playwrights, and established writers treated with greater courtesy than had been the case in recent years. The Abbey had to face the fact that it no longer held a market monopoly of Irish plays, nor of Irish players. The School of Acting was reorganised under Ria Mooney's direction, and from its pupils past and present arose a lively Experimental Theatre in the Peacock in which new plays were tried out. In the production of new plays, as well as in revivals, the standards of visual presentation had to be improved if the theatre was to keep abreast of the new movements in scenography, and the same care given to the design of farm kitchen and Dublin tenement as was given in the past to the plays of Yeats and Lady Gregory. Players must no longer be required to rummage in the wardrobe to find suitable costumes for themselves, nor must the peasant girls in *The Playboy* adorn themselves with eye shadow and permanently waved hair. In the revivals of repertory plays younger players must take the place of those who had outgrown their parts. Hunt's radical changes might have produced open hostility among players and staff; that they did not do so was due to the support of the senior players and the talent and tact of his designer. It was in the Board room that antagonism arose, for it was here in the power struggle that ensued that the real threat to the regeneration of the theatre lay.

The struggle for power

In the summer of 1936 five of the senior players were contracted by R.K.O. to appear in the film of *The Plough and The Stars,* an engagement that led to the loss of Barry Fitzgerald to the greater rewards of the film industry. Opportunity was taken in their absence to re-cast with younger players some of the repertory plays, including *The Playboy* and Yeats's *Deirdre.* These two plays appeared on 27 July and 10 August with new designs by Tanya Moiseiwitsch. In Yeats's play the leading parts of Deirdre and Naisi were played by Micheál MacLiammóir and Jean Forbes Robertson. It was, wrote Holloway, 'one of the great first nights of the Abbey'.[7] But, as A. E. Malone pointed out in his *Irish Times* review, 'This revival will not hearten the traditionalists of the Abbey', adding, 'but it is surely time another mode has its day.' This was not the view of the traditionalists.

Both productions were the subject of acrimonious debates

in the Board room — while there were full houses in the
theatre. Hunt's interpretation of *The Playboy* and Cyril
Cusack's fine performance as Christy Mahon were assailed as
travesties of the Abbey style, while other members claimed
the performances to be examples of what was now called
'Peasant Quality'. *Deirdre* was considered a deliberate challenge to Yeats's theories of verse speaking in what O'Connor
called his 'Senecan style'. 'Yeats was furious, and Higgins
stormed against Hunt, without, however, having the faintest
idea of how to produce the poetic ideas he talked of.'⁸

So far as the young and headstrong director was concerned,
the Abbey style of speaking Synge was a mindless sing-song,
and Seneca as dead as the Dodo.

It was, however, decreed that Hunt should be debarred
from directing the plays of Yeats and Synge in the future, a
decree that Yeats was to ignore by asking him later to direct
his new play, *Purgatory*. At the time, however, Hunt's self-
esteem was considerably deflated. He was further shocked
by the Board's decision to make cuts in the salaries of those
players who, in the opinion of some members, failed to live
up to their demands for 'Peasant Quality'; among these were
such loyal and long-serving players as Maureen Delany and
May Craig. In September 1936 Hunt resigned his position as
manager, a duty that he had mistakenly undertaken in December 1935, and concentrated on the direction of the new plays
that were now flooding into the theatre.

Management was now assumed by the Board; this led to
prolonged weekly meetings and increasingly acrimonious debates; it also led to a struggle for power. Signs of antagonism
between Robinson, Higgins and O'Connor had shown themselves in the winter and spring of 1935—6 when Yeats was
absent in Majorca, where Higgins had predicted his imminent
death.

Higgins and O'Connor set out to neutralise Robinson, and
at the same time to neutralise each other; while Hayes attempted to keep the peace by siding alternately with O'Connor and Higgins; and Starkie felt it his duty to rescue Robinson from himself. Although intent on playing a martyr's part,
Robinson was quite capable of emerging from his despondency
to strike an effective — and surprisingly venomous — blow at

his warring colleagues. Meanwhile, Blythe, the inscrutable, watched and waited.

The unexpected return of Yeats from the grave avoided an open conflict, but from now on a 'Dance of Death' took place between the Abbey and Rathfarnham with each of the candidates for the succession vying to catch the ear of the supposedly dying 'king'. Yeats, who had no intention of dying, was thoroughly enjoying playing one Director against the other.

While the Board was engaged in these manoeuvres, more vital matters arose, matters that were closer to the function of a Board of Directors than quarrelling over who should play what part, or whether Synge's plays should, or should not, be treated as fossils of an outworn tradition.

A new theatre

Early in 1936 the opportunity arose to purchase White's premises occupying the corner site between the front entrance to the Abbey and Lower Abbey Street. Subsequent discussions with the young architect, Michael Scott, led to proposals for the reconstruction and enlargement of the theatre. In August 1937 these premises were purchased with government consent; at the same time the then Minister of Finance, Sean MacEntee, suggested that Government finance might be available for a theatre complex housing the Abbey, the Gate and the semi-professional Gaelic Players (An Comhar Dramaíochta). Ernest Blythe was asked to prepare a scheme, with Michael Scott's assistance, to meet the needs of all three parties. The result was Scott's imaginative plan to extend the area of the proposed complex to incorporate some six or seven houses on the river front.

Whether such a scheme would have been acceptable to the Gate, or would have proved to be in the best interests of either theatre, was not put to the test. The General Election in July 1937 left the government with a reduced majority and more urgent preoccupations. In August 1938 hopes were raised by the suggestion that the government might provide £100,000 towards the costs of the new building, subject to the agreement of all parties; but now war clouds were once more gathering over Europe; in September came the Munich crisis and the dismemberment of Czechoslovakia; a year later the Second World War broke out; the government of the twenty-six counties comprising the Irish Free State, bent on a course of precarious neutrality and dependent upon dwindling resources, was in no position to indulge in a grandiose scheme for building a national theatre.

New plays, 1936–9

If the years immediately preceding the war failed to see the birth of a new building to house the Irish theatre, they did at least see something of a re-birth of Irish drama.

Among the best new plays of 1936 were Brinsley Macnamara's *The Grand House in the City* (3 February), a Chekhovian comedy which A. E. Malone claimed as his best play; St John Ervine's much revived *Boyd's Shop* (24 February); Teresa Deevy's *Katie Roche* (16 March) of which David Sears in the *Independent* wrote: 'Masterpiece is a word to be used sparingly, but I have no hesitation in applying it to Miss Deevy's *Katie Roche,*' while Holloway wondered 'how future audiences will take the piece'.[9] In fact this search for self-discovery by a young, romantic and strangely ingenuous girl of 'irregular parentage', married to a man far older than herself, belongs too closely to the twilight world of Teresa Deevy to appeal to the extrovert young audiences of today.

Later in the same year Teresa Deevy was to contribute her only historical play, *The Wild Goose* (9 November). George Shiels, vying with Lennox Robinson as the Abbey's most prolific writer of popular comedy, unexpectedly provided a bitter and merciless drama of almost Strindbergian proportions in *The Passing Day* (13 April). This was followed by one of his most warm-hearted comedies, *The Jailbird* (12 October). The year ended with a popular court-room drama, *Blind Man's Buff* (26 December) billed under the joint authorship of Denis Johnston and Ernst Toller, though in fact it owes little to Toller's *Blind Goddess* (Die Blinde Göttin) from which it was freely adapted.

The year 1937 opened with what David Sears in the *Independent* called 'the most remarkable play produced at the

Abbey for many years', Paul Vincent Carroll's *Shadow and Substance* (25 January). In this, Arthur Shields gave a masterly performance in the part of the austere Canon Skerritt, and Phyllis Ryan, a sixteen-year-old pupil of the School of Acting, won all hearts as the visionary servant girl Brigid. In New York, Carroll's play with Cedric Hardwicke and Julie Haydon in the leading parts, won the Critics Award for the Best Foreign Play of the Year 1936—7. In 1940 Hunt directed the play at the New Theatre in London with Cecil Parker and Joyce Redman.

The rejection of Carroll's second major play, *The White Steed,* in 1938, on grounds somewhat reminiscent of those advanced by the Abbey's Directors against *The Silver Tassie,* led to a temporary breach between the playwright and the Abbey. Fortunately the success of *The White Steed* in New York, with Barry Fitzgerald, summoned from Hollywood to play the leading part, helped to heal Carroll's wounded pride. In 1939 he made what he described as 'an honourable peace' when his play *Kindred* was produced at the Abbey on 25 September. However, Carroll never again achieved the success of his earlier plays.

Between 1937 and 1939 the flow of new plays continued. George Shiels added two more popular comedies to the repertory of his money-spinning revivals, *Quin's Secret* (29 March 1937) and *Neal Maquade* (17 January 1938). A third play, *Give Him a House* (30 October 1939) was one of the very few failures by this almost consistently successful playwright. The decline of the Anglo-Irish gentry was the theme of Lennox Robinson's *Killycreggs in Twilight* (19 April 1937) as it was of Maura Mulloy's *Who will Remember . . .?* (17 May 1937) and Andrew Ganly's one-act play *The Dear Queen* (4 April 1938).

In 1938 Lennox also contributed *Bird's Nest* (12 September) but neither this, the second of his plays to be laid in the imaginary seaside resort of Inish, nor *Killycreggs in Twilight* were 'vintage' Robinson. However a considerable success was scored with a revival of his Parnell play *The Lost Leader* (31 August 1937) in which the young William Devlin, whose Lear at the Westminster Theatre in London in 1934 had won the unqualified praise of James Agate, appeared as a guest artist in the part of Lucius Lenihan. 'The audience was entranced — at times a pin could have been heard to drop — and the *Abbey* audiences are seldom so sensitive', wrote Malone in the *Irish Times*.

Meanwhile the power struggle in the boardroom was threatening to develop into an open breach. Hunt's adaptation of O'Connor's short story, *In the Train* (31 May 1937) had led to their collaboration in a full-length play, *The Invincibles* (18 October 1937) based on the assassination of Lord Frederick Cavendish, the Chief Secretary for Ireland and his Under-Secretary, T. H. Burke, in Phoenix Park in 1882. The first night was not without a degree of tension as rumours of a hostile demonstration circulated, reinforced by the presence of the venerable Maud Gonne, arrayed in the deepest mourning and accompanied by a group of known extremists. Frank O'Connor in *My Father's Son* recalls:

> There was no riot that night because Maud apparently decided that it might not be understood, and the only protest came from a Nazi visitor who thought the play was directed against Hitler and wrote to the papers to say how shocked he was at this defence of· tyrannicide.

On the same evening Lennox Robinson, who had agreed to the production, attended a debate at the Gate Theatre where he denounced the authors for having dramatised a subject that, so he claimed, was bound to cause pain to the relatives of the men who had been executed some fifty years before. In fact the sister of Joe Brady, the leader of the Invincibles, called at the theatre on the night of the dress rehearsal to offer the players the suit in which her brother was hanged and the ivory crucifix sent to him on the eve on his execution by Lady Frederick Cavendish.

At the following board meeting Richard Hayes tabled a motion that Robinson should be dismissed. Yeats, however, managed to persuade the members to reject the motion, declaring that Robinson would provide a written apology — an apology that Yeats had eventually to write himself for Robinson to sign. Further trouble followed.

The players at that time consisted of a talented company formed during the absence of the contract players in America.

Among these were Ann Clery, Moya Devlin, Josephine Fitzgerald, Christine Hayden, Nora O'Mahony, Ria Mooney,
Shelah Richards, Shelah Ward, Brian Carey, Frank Carney,
Cyril Cusack, Eric Gorman, Fred Johnson, W. O'Gorman and
Liam Redmond. In December, Sean O'Faolain's play, *She
Had to do Something,* was scheduled for rehearsal. The cast
list was already posted when the Board acceded to the
author's insistence that the leading part be changed and an
actress from Britain be imported to take the part of a French-
woman who invites a company of Russian ballet dancers to
visit an Irish provincial town. Evelyn Bowen was the attractive and talented wife of the actor and author, Robert
Speaight, but her stage experience was confined to the amateur theatre. The players considered her engagement a reflection on their own abilities to play anything other than Irish
parts. A strike was threatened. Frank O'Connor, who had
undertaken the job of managing director, dissuaded them
from taking this action, arguing that it would be regarded by
the public as an act of discourtesy to a guest. His subsequent
elopement with the lady in question, however, not only
severely shocked the pieties of the time, but considerably
undermined his influence as a member of the Board and with
the company, causing him to withdraw more and more from
the theatre's affairs and eventually from Ireland. In 1938
O'Connor contributed two plays, *Moses' Rock* (28 February)
written in collaboration with Hunt, and *Time's Pocket* (26
December).

Before the year 1938 drew to a close the Board was again
in turmoil. During the absences of Yeats and O'Connor, Paul
Carroll's play *The White Steed* was rejected on the grounds
that it would prove offensive to the priesthood. Carroll, like
O'Casey over the rejection of *The Silver Tassie,* was incensed
by the way in which the rejection was conveyed to him, and
threatened to withdraw his plays from the repertoire, declaring he would never again submit a play to the Abbey. O'Connor demanded that the play be reconsidered. Meanwhile it
had been accepted for production in New York, and O'Connor's attempt to heal the breach was not helped when he
himself turned it down on aesthetic grounds.

Less creditable still was the Board's rejection of Yeats's

play, *The Herne's Egg,* on grounds of obscenity. For Richard
Hayes, as government representative and the most devoutly
Catholic member of the Board who had been totally misled
by Higgins as to the meaning of the symbolism, there was
some excuse, but for Higgins who rejoiced in a smutty tale
and a bawdy song there was none. More typical was Blythe's
reaction claiming that the play was so obscure that no one
would notice that it was obscene.

Somewhat disillusioned by the bickerings and intransigence
of the Board now that Yeats — a sick man — had left for the
South of France and O'Connor had largely withdrawn, Hunt
resigned in November 1938 to direct *The White Steed* in New
York with Barry Fitzgerald, Liam Redmond and Jessica
Tandy. O'Connor's suggestion that Denis Johnston should
be invited to become the play director when Hunt left was
turned down on the grounds that 'he would want to have his
own way'. In the event Louis D'Alton, the son of a well-
known Irish melodramatic actor-manager, was appointed in
January 1939. D'Alton, happier as a playwright than as the
employee of a Board of Directors — his first play, *The Man in
the Cloak,* had been produced at the Abbey in September
1938 — only remained for a brief five months, resigning in
May 1939 to be succeeded by Frank Dermody who had
served his apprenticeship at the Gaelic theatre (An Taibhdhearc
in Galway. Founded in 1928, the Galway Gaelic Theatre is
to-day the only theatre in Ireland presenting an exclusive
repertoire of plays in Irish. Like the Abbey, it receives an
annual subsidy from the government.

Plays in Irish

Blythe's vision of making the production of plays in the Irish
language a regular feature of the National Theatre's policy, a
policy that had always been among the early objects of the
Irish Literary Theatre, was accepted in principle by the Board
early in 1938. In May of that year Hunt directed a revival of
Casadh an tSúgáin. It was the first play in the Irish language
to be presented by professional actors on the Abbey stage.
The presence of its venerable and revered author, Douglas
Hyde, who had now become President of Eire, at the first

performance (9 May) assured reasonable audiences. There was, however, a dearth of Irish plays to implement Blythe's dream. The Board offered a prize for the best one-act play in Irish, and the two plays that divided the prize, *Baintighearne an Ghorta* by Séamus Wilmot, and *Donnchada Ruadh* by Séamus Ó hAodha, were presented on 12 December 1938 and 15 May 1939, directed by Dermody. But not only was there a dearth of plays, there was also a dearth of Irish-speaking players and, more seriously, of Irish-speaking play-goers, at least amongst those who frequented the Abbey. Dermody's decision to add a class in Irish to the School of Acting did something to encourage young players to learn Irish, but there was no easy solution to the problem of the audience. It was not until the 1940s that a policy of presenting plays in Irish on a more regular basis was begun.

One-act plays

While Blythe was endeavouring to encourage the writing of one-act plays in Irish, the tradition of writing one-act plays in English, one of Ireland's greatest contributions to world drama, and one in which the genius of her writers shone with particular brilliance, was fast disappearing. Indeed the years before the Second World War were to see the last major flowering of this miniature art. The years 1934 to 1938 saw the production of *Church Street* (Lennox Robinson, 21 May 1934), *The Resurrection* and *The King of the Great Clock Tower* (W. B. Yeats, 30 July 1934), *A Deuce o' Jacks* (F. R. Higgins, 11 September 1935), *The End of the Beginning* (O'Casey, 8 February 1937), *In the Train* (O'Connor/Hunt, 31 May 1937), *Coggerers* (Paul Vincent Carroll, 22 November 1937), *A Spot in the Sun* (T. C. Murray, 14 February 1938),[10] *The Dear Queen* (Andrew Ganly, 4 April 1938), *The Great Adventure* (Charles I. Foley, 19 September 1938), and – most distinguished of all – Yeats's *Purgatory,* presented for a single performance in August 1938 at the Abbey Theatre Festival.

A festival and a farewell

On twelve successive nights (8–20 August 1938) seventeen

plays, many of them the one-act classics of the Abbey's repertoire, were presented to an audience, a large percentage of which was gathered from America, Britain and the Continent. By day there were lectures on the Abbey and its dramatists, exhibitions of pictures and manuscripts connected with the theatre, and visits to places of cultural interest. The extent of this festival of plays with the limited resources of a small theatre would by today's standards seem impossible. It must, however, be remembered that the players at that time were accustomed to carry a repertoire of twelve or more plays on their American tours, and nightly changes of bill were not infrequent. The American and overseas tours had also resulted in the creation of what was now a talented team of home players who had already taken over the revival of some of the repertory plays and some of the new plays as well.

On 10 August Yeats's *Purgatory* was presented, a masterpiece in miniature, comparable only to Synge's *Riders to the Sea* and Lady Gregory's *The Rising of the Moon* as one of the great one-act plays of the world. When, at the end, the familiar white-haired figure walked onto the stage, no longer as upright as in former days, a wave of emotion seemed to sweep through the audience, for the Festival was a salute to the theatre he had inspired, and *Purgatory* was his farewell to Ireland. 'I have put into this play, not many thoughts that are picturesque, but my own beliefs about this world and the next.'

On Saturday, 28 January 1939, Yeats died at Cap Martin, close to Menton in the South of France. 'Ireland has lost one of her greatest sons and the world has lost one of its greatest poets,' declared Lennox Robinson in a statement to the *Irish Times*.

At a special meeting of the Board of Directors Lennox was asked to go to Menton to see if it was possible to bring the poet's body back to Ireland. He arrived too late: Yeats was buried in the little cemetery at Roquebrune between Menton and Monaco. It was not till after the war in 1948 that his body could be brought home to rest, as he had wished, under the shadow of Ben Bulben in the county of Sligo.

Under bare Ben Bulben's head
In Drumcliff churchyard Yeats is laid.
An ancestor was rector there
Long years ago; a church stands near,
By the road an ancient cross.
No marble, no conventional phrase;
On limestone quarried near the spot
By his command these words are cut:
        Cast a cold eye
        On life, on death.
        Horseman, pass by![11]

The Abbey after Yeats

When Yeats left Ireland for the last time in October 1938, Higgins — by now acknowledged as his heir — was appointed managing director.[12] During the company's 1937/38 tour of the States under Higgins's management, O'Connor had taken over the management of the theatre, the Board having by then discovered that corporate control of day-to-day business was both wearisome and inefficient. Higgins's appointment inflamed the growing antagonism between O'Connor and the rest of the Board, and on 2 May 1940 O'Connor resigned. 'With Yeats permanently gone,' he wrote in later years, 'I began now to realise that mediocrity was in control, and against mediocrity there is no appeal.'[13]

O'Connor was unfair in attributing the mediocrity of the ensuing years solely to those who controlled the theatre's destiny. Other events, beyond the control of the Abbey, were to rob it of much of its artistic purpose. On 3 September 1939 war broke out and the government declared its neutrality. Inevitably war had an effect on the Irish theatre, though the effect on its economy was less severe than in the belligerent countries. While shortages of electricity, coal, petrol and clothing created problems for the management, and the prohibition of salary increases under the Emergency Powers Act (1940) produced hardships for the players, the Abbey's box-office recorded an unprecedented number of 'full houses'. But neutrality had more serious consequences: it was, as Professor Lyons has pointed out, the psychological rather than the material effects of the war that were eventually to prove more significant.[14]

At the very moment when nationalism had achieved its aim and parochial attitudes could be set aside, Irish writers found themselves cut off from their European roots, roots that might now be expected to spread out into a universal growth. When, after seven years, the country emerged from the 'Plato's cave' in which not only the writers but an entire people had been cut off from the events that shaped the future of mankind, it was to face a very different world, in the making of which they had played no part. Some, like Denis Johnston and Frank O'Connor, found it necessary to leave the country; nor should it be forgotten that 50,000 persons from the twenty-six counties served in the British forces. For many writers isolation resulted in the gradual drying up of creativity, or the stale repetition of past formulae.

In fairness to the playwrights it must be said that the leadership of the Abbey offered little to inspire them, and there was little to encourage experiment with new forms and ideas.

The new management

In January 1941 Fred Higgins died at the early age of forty-four. 'I dare say,' wrote Lynn Doyle in the *Irish Times* (9 January), 'that he had within him to become a greater poet than W. B. Yeats had he lived long enough to discipline a little the strong exuberant rush of his inspiration.' Yet without Higgins's Rabelaisian exuberance his undisciplined and betimes malicious – spirit contained within that burly Johnsonian frame, there would not have been so likeable a man, nor – I dare say – so good a poet.

In Higgins's place the Board appointed Ernest Blythe as managing director. In Eárnan de Blaghd, as he sometimes preferred to be known, the Abbey had not only acquired an ex-Minister of Finance who knew his way round the corridors of power, but a man whose character had been tempered in the heady years leading up to the 1916 Rising and the Anglo-Irish conflict and hardened by the tragic consequences of the Anglo-Irish Treaty.

Blythe's background was widely different from the world

of politics and theatre in which he was to become involved. Son of a North of Ireland farming family — staunch Protestants and Loyalists — he was brought up to work on the land. In 1905, however, he sat for and passed the examination for the British Civil Service and in March of that year was posted to Dublin. Here his first evening was spent at the Queen's, a theatre that was to play a leading role in his future life. Visits to the Abbey followed, and, at the same time, he was caught up in enthusiasm for the revival of the Irish language, joining the Keating branch of the Gaelic League where Sean O'Casey went to Irish classes. Later he was to perfect his mastery of the language by working as a farm labourer in Kerry. Enthusiasm for things Gaelic led to his commitment to the national cause and to his internment in Reading gaol in 1916.

In many ways Blythe remained a true son of his native province: a man of shrewd judgment but narrow artistic views, of impeccable rectitude, impervious to criticism, steadfast in his decisions and often ruthless in their enactment. In October 1918 he wrote in an article entitled *Ruthless Warfare:*

If England decided on this atrocity (the imposition of conscription), then we, on our part, must decide that in our resistance we shall acknowledge no limit and no scruple. We must recognise that anyone, civilian or soldier, who assists directly or by connivance in this crime against us, merits no more consideration than a wild beast, and should be killed without mercy or hesitation as opportunity offers . . . Thus the man who serves on an exemption tribunal, the doctor who treats soldiers or examines conscripts, the man who voluntarily surrenders when called for, the man who in any shape or form applies for an exemption, the man who drives a police car or assists in the transport of army supplies, all these having assisted the enemy must be shot or otherwise destroyed with the least possible delay.[15]

For thirty years, as the most abused man in Ireland, Blythe was to control the theatre with firmness, much wisdom and little inspiration. Caution was his watchword and art declined — for caution untouched by the inspiration of the artist breeds mediocrity. In fairness to Blythe and his fellow Directors, it

should be said that the theatre had to be kept in business at
all costs until such time as the government was in a position
to carry out its grandiose plans of building a trefoil national
theatre, though this became more and more remote as the
effects of war and its aftermath brought more pressing problems to the fore. In one respect, however, Blythe fulfilled
what he believed to be the artistic destiny of the Abbey.

Amharclann na Mainistreach

The vacancy on the Board brought about by O'Connor's resignation was filled in October 1940 by the appointment of a
poet and Gaelic speaker, Roibeárd Ó Faracháin, at that time
Director of Talks at Radio Eireann. Backed by his two Gaelic-
speaking colleagues, Hayes and Ó Faracháin, Blythe now put
his dream of a Gaelic-speaking theatre into practice. On theatre
programmes the Abbey's name appeared in its Gaelic form,
'Amharclann na Mainistreach', and the players' names began
to appear in their Gaelic form in the programmes. From 1942
onwards it became theatre policy to accept new junior players only if they could perform in Irish as well as English.

On 22 February 1942, *Cách,* Blythe's translation of the
fifteenth-century morality play *Everyman,* was presented
alongside a one-act play by Traolach Ó Raithbheartaigh, *Gloine
an Impire* (The Emperor's Glass). While these productions
demonstrated the Abbey's superiority to the amateur Gaelic-
speaking companies in matters of staging, they also exposed
the difficulties of attracting an audience large enough to
make professional productions in Irish economically viable.
Blythe was not to be defeated by this problem. In March
1942 he persuaded the Gaelic theatre organisation, An Comhar
Dramaíochta, to sub-let its production of plays to the Abbey.
Thus he was able to lay hands on this organisation's annual
grant which, at the time, amounted to £600; of this £500 was
now allocated to the production of five plays a year to be
performed on Sunday and Monday nights in the Abbey, and
£100 to provide scholarships for Gaelic speakers to study in
the Abbey School of Acting. A joint committee was formed
to select the plays, consisting of members of the two Boards
of Directors with a chairman nominated by the Ministry of

Education. There still remained, however, three major problems — shortage of good plays in Irish, shortage of good Irish-speaking players, and shortage of Irish-speaking audiences.

The first problem was temporarily solved by translations of foreign plays and by play competitions with substantial prize money. For the other problems no quick solution was possible. Frank Dermody's Irish class for actors and the granting of scholarships to Gaelic speakers prepared the way for a future reservoir of dual-speaking players, but Blythe's decision to restrict the contracts offered to new players to those who were competent Gaelic speakers was to lose the theatre valuable acting talent, while the problem of drawing an audience remained intractable until 1945 when the Abbey presented its first pantomime in Irish using Mícheál Ó hAodha's adaptation of Lady Gregory's play *The Golden Apple* as a basis. *Muireann agus an Prionnsa* opened for a scheduled six nights' run on 26 December; it ran for forty-three performances. From 1945 until recent years pantomimes in Irish became an annual event. Whether their success can be attributed to the fact that they were written in Irish is open to question; but if the Gaelic pantomimes could hardly be said to justify Blythe's belief that they were a powerful weapon for popularising the native language, at least they gave pleasure to the young of all ages.

The Abbey's Gaelic policy, however, based on what appeared to be linguistic rather than artistic grounds, seemed to some a betrayal, or at least a distortion, of the Abbey's primary purpose, and disruptive of its regular work. The ageing Holloway wrote in his diary for 30 May 1943:

> It is a pity to see the childish efforts of the Gaelic three Directors of the Abbey to graft on the Gaelic Theatre to the far-famed Abbey, and to behave like children in interfering with the regular work of the theatre by encroaching on their rehearsals and interfering in many ways with the Abbey players' progress. They also have been calling the theatre by a Gaelic name on the cover of the programme and printing Gaelic poems in the ordinary Abbey programme. All three Directors have the Gaelic bee in their bonnets and behave like children in foistering Gaelic plays on the Gaels who have no love for sitting out Gaelic plays.[16]

Holloway, however, did not live long enough to justify his criticisms. After keeping a written record of the Dublin theatres for forty-eight years, this great old gossip and diarist died on 13 March 1944. Whether the policy of linguistic revivalism had any bearing on the decline in the number of new plays in English, as some of the theatre's critics maintained, is extremely unlikely.

Plays, players and audiences, 1940–1950

Throughout the forties and fifties there was a marked decrease in the number of new plays. During the decade 1930/40 one hundred and four new plays were produced; from 1940 to 1950 the number fell to sixty-two; in the following decade there was a further decrease. Yet despite this decline in the output of original plays, there was a considerable increase in audiences. This phenomenon was not confined to the Abbey, for although the war prevented the commercial theatres from importing popular plays and musicals from Britain, the Gaiety and Olympia theatres, largely relying on Irish talent, did a flourishing trade.

While no single factor can account for the increase in the Abbey's audience, it was perhaps partly due to the claustrophobic atmosphere of a city cut off from the rest of the world to which the theatre offered some form of escape. It must be remembered, too, that the whole attitude of the general public to the Abbey had radically changed since the earlier years of the century. It was no longer regarded as an art theatre reserved for the exclusive patronage of a small clique of intellectuals. The Abbey had become a theatre for the people, offering an evening's entertainment at which the average citizen could feel at home. For this change in the public's attitude, the plays of O'Casey and the popular comedies of George Shiels, Lennox Robinson and Brinsley Macnamara, as well as the undemanding dramas of Louis D'Alton, and Frank Carney, were largely responsible.

Larger audiences brought about a change in the repertory policy. Instead of the old system of limiting the initial run of a new play to a week or a fortnight, no matter how popular it proved, and thereby keeping it alive for revival in the theatre's repertoire, new plays were run until their audience was exhausted. This policy was also applied to such popular revivals as *Professor Tim,* retained for two months in 1944, *The Plough and the Stars,* for three months in 1945, and even *Katie Roche,* never a popular play, was dragged out for eleven weeks to diminishing audiences in 1949. This change in policy which was brought about partly by the shortage of new plays, was to have serious consequences in future years when the Abbey found its stock of popular revivals exhausted. To its critics it appeared that the theatre under Blythe's management had adopted a shamelessly commercial policy.

Nevertheless, the Abbey's record of new plays still remained unique by comparison with repertory theatres elsewhere. From the established playwrights came two plays by Lennox Robinson, *Forget Me Not* (26 December 1941) and *The Lucky Finger* (23 August 1948), neither of which would he have wished to have classified amongst his best work. They were to be the last contribution by this loyal and consistent champion of the Irish theatre. Lennox died in 1958. His last years were devoted to promoting the cause of the amateur theatre movement, as well as encouraging by his perceptive criticism the work of new playwrights, and writing the history of the theatre to which he had devoted the greater part of his life.

Another prolific playwright reached the end of his contributions to the Abbey. George Shiels contributed seven plays between 1940 and 1948, of which *The Rugged Path* (5 August 1940) — a tragedy based on the fatal accusation in Ireland of being an 'informer' — was rightly praised by David Sears in the *Independent* — 'George Shiels showed us at the Abbey last night that he is a great dramatist.' Shiels died in 1949.

Paul Vincent Carroll's *The Wise have not Spoken* (7 February 1944), though not a great play, was not helped by Blythe and Hayes who felt it incumbent upon themselves to alter the plot. The fact that the play succeeded would seem to have been largely due to Frank Dermody's production.

Brinsley Macnamara's *Marks and Mabel* (6 August 1945) proved a feeble sequel to his successful *Look at the Heffernans.* St John Ervine's two plays, *William George Mawhinney*

(23 March 1940) and *Friends and Relations* (30 June 1941) possessed little of the skilful characterisation of his earlier work. Other North of Ireland playwrights were Joseph Tomelty — *The End House* (28 August 1944) and Nora Mac-Adam — *The Birth of a Giant* (13 May 1940).

Amongst plays from other new writers came a prize-winning play from Elizabeth Connor, *Mount Prospect* (22 April 1940), *Strange Guest* (9 November 1940) by Francis Stuart, *The Bugle in the Blood* (14 March 1949) by the short story writer Bryan MacMahon, and Walter Macken's *Mungo's Mansions* (11 February 1946), laid in the slums of Galway which some claimed to be a West of Ireland equivalent to O'Casey's Dublin trilogy. Macken was at that time director of plays at the Gaelic theatre in Galway. He was to join the Abbey in 1948 as an actor and many years later as play director. From this theatre, too, came one of Ireland's greatest actresses, Siobhan MacKenna. Siobhan came to Dublin on a Comhar scholarship in 1944, playing her first major part in a revival of *Village Wooing* in 1945. Among other new players who made their first appearance on the Abbey stage during these years were Máire Ni Dhomhnaill (1944), Angela Newman (1948), Micheál O Bríain (1943), Geoffrey Golden (1945), Micheál Ó hAonghusa (1947), Bill Foley (1947), Edward Golden (1948), Philip O'Flynn (1948) and the inimitable Harry Brogan (1944), one of those rich personalities who, like Maureen Delany and Barry Fitzgerald, seemed to be carved out of blackthorn to fit into every comedy of Irish life.

Louis D'Alton, more successful as a playwright than as a play director, contributed four plays, two of which were considerable public successes, *The Money doesn't Matter* (10 March 1941) which ran for nine weeks, and *They Got what they Wanted* (18 February 1947) with a record run of twelve weeks. Amongst the most popular plays from new writers were M. J. Molloy's *The King of Friday's Men* (18 October 1948), and Frank Carney's *The Righteous are Bold* (9 July 1946). In the former, Walter Macken made his greatest success as an actor in the part of the battered shillelagh fighter, a part he played later in the short-lived Broadway production. In Carney's play, a frankly melodramatic 'pot-boiler' about exorcism, Máire Ni Dhomhnaill scored a singular success — many times to be repeated — as a girl possessed by the devil.

Frank Dermody, to whose production the success of the play was largely due, was now to accept an offer to join Gabriel Pascal's Irish film company. He left in February 1947. For the past seven years Dermody had directed the Abbey plays both in Irish and English, trained the newcomers to the company, directed the School of Acting and taught a class in Irish. Like others who worked for the managing director, Dermody was mentally and physically exhausted. Blythe had many qualities as a business manager, but he lacked the warmth, or perhaps the desire, to gain the players' affection; too often his attitude appeared to be that of an employer who regards his workmen as useful, but expendable, items to be worked to the limit of their capacity, and only humoured if illness or departure was likely to interrupt the work in hand. As a result the Abbey lost much of the corporate spirit that the no less dictatorial rule of Yeats, Lady Gregory and F. R. Higgins had drawn forth from its players.

During the war, the players had little chance of finding a market elsewhere, but with the end of hostilities films, radio and television opened up new possibilities of employment. From 1946 onwards film and television offers became a serious problem in planning future programmes. In that year alone Eileen Crowe, Siobhan McKenna, F. J. McCormick, Cyril Cusack, M. J. Dolan, Denis O'Dea and Seamus Locke were all contracted to appear in films in Ireland and England. Obviously the Abbey could never offer salaries to equal those of the film industry, but Blythe believed that a substantial increase in the existing salaries, made possible by the lifting of regulations controlling increases in actors' salaries, coupled with the offer of long term contracts for some of the part-time players, would make the theatre less vulnerable to precipitate departures and more attractive as a career for young players. In 1946 the Board agreed to raise the top salaries from seven to ten guineas a week and other salaries commensurately, pending an application for an increase in the annual subsidy. In 1947 this was raised to £3,000 a year. An Comhár Dramaíochta, too, received an increased subsidy, as a result of which its annual grant to the Abbey for the production of

Gaelic plays was increased from £500 to £2,500.

But more money failed to prevent the drain of players to more lucrative jobs overseas. Shelah Richards and Arthur Shields went to New York in 1938, and in the following year Shields joined his brother, Barry Fitzgerald, in Hollywood. Ria Mooney left in 1944 to join a new company at the Gaiety Theatre. Siobhan McKenna, Denis O'Dea (then married to Siobhan) and Cyril Cusack left in 1947. Death too took its toll. P. J. Carolan died in 1938, Maureen Delany in 1961, Michael J. Dolan in 1954, but the greatest loss the theatre sustained was the death of F. J. McCormick on 24 April 1947. With his death it seemed as if a whole gallery of much loved characters had disappeared from the stage.

More money, too, could do little to improve the quality of Gaelic plays, and nothing to dampen the criticisms that were levelled against the so-called commercialisation of the National Theatre; nor could more money assuage the anger aroused by the refusal of its managing director to listen to those who, rightly or wrongly, claimed to be friends of the theatre and whose criticisms were directed against the falling standards of production and Blythe's policy of Gaelic revivalism.

On Saturday 7 November a young man, Valentin Iremonger, rose in the stalls just before the curtain went up on the last act of a revival of *The Plough and the Stars*.

Ladies and gentlemen, just before the show proceeds, I would like to say a few words. When the poet Yeats died, he left behind him to the Irish nation as a legacy his beloved Abbey Theatre, then the first theatre in the world in acting, in production and in the poetic impulse of its tradition. Today, eight years after, under the utter incompetence of the present directorate's artistic policy, there is nothing left of that fine glory. Having seen what they did to O'Casey's masterpiece tonight, in acting and production, I, for one, am leaving this theatre as a gesture of protest against the management's policy.[17]

His protest was endorsed by the *Irish Times,* and argued by many others. Blythe refused to comment; and it was left to his fellow Director, Roibeárd Ó Faracháin, to try to refute the charges, and, at the same time, to insist that a play director of real artistic merit be appointed in the place of the always efficient, but seldom inspired, M. J. Dolan. His choice was Ria Mooney who, since leaving the Abbey in 1943, had been in charge of the productions at the Gaiety Theatre, Dublin.

Ria took up her appointment in January 1948. Little did she realise at the time that she, too, would be ground down by the lack of artistic understanding and the acceptance of mediocrity that was spreading throughout the theatre like a fatal disease.

I had to direct from twelve to seventeen productions every ten months with a company of young people who had to be trained and disciplined as well. All this had to be done in a rehearsal time of two hours every day for three weeks, plus two dress rehearsals which I had insisted upon, the old company having had but one.

I wanted the public to have colour and excitement in their theatre — the kind of theatre I had known outside the Abbey, except that now I wanted the colour to flow from the work of Irish playwrights. . . . I did not have to wait long before I realised that however much I might strive to implement my theories, which were viewed as being 'grandiose', my engagement in the theatre was looked upon as being a 'holding' position until such time as Irish-speaking Directors could take over. I was told that the nation was at war with the English language.[18]

However, lest it be thought that Blythe was incapable of recognising and using artistic talent when he found it, his report to the Board on the work of a young Gaelic-speaking director, Tomás Mac Anna, indicates that he was a shrewd judge of artistic ability, even if he sometimes abused it. Of Mac Anna's first production for the Abbey, a Gaelic translation of Chekhov's *The Proposal* (16 September 1947), Blythe wrote, 'We have struck a man who will be a tower of strength in the theatre.'

Ordeal by fire

However, the illness the 'Old Lady of Abbey Street' was

suffering from could not be cured by human talents. The cure had to come from the patient herself. The fact that this indomitable old body had not completely lost her spirit was demonstrated on 14 April 1950, six days after the opening of a new play, *Design for a Headstone,* by Seamus Byrne. The play, concerning a group of political prisoners, roused the anger of members of the I.R.A. on the grounds that the views expressed by one of the prisoners were Marxist, whilst members of a religious organisation contended that the play was a smear on the Catholic priesthood. From the ensuing demonstration it might seem for a brief moment that the Abbey was back among the heady arguments over *The Playboy* and *The Plough and the Stars.*

But neither demonstrations by the audience nor criticisms of the Board's policy was capable of restoring the Abbey to its former health.

About 1 a.m. on the morning of Wednesday 18 July 1951, after the curtain had fallen on the last scene of *The Plough and the Stars* — a scene in which the fires of Dublin's Easter Week are seen through Bessie Burgess's attic window — two Dubliners, standing at the corner of Abbey Street, noticed a glow in the upper windows of the theatre. Suddenly flames shot up into the night sky. The Abbey was on fire. Soon five sections of Dublin's Fire Brigade were in action, but in less than an hour the backstage was destroyed, the stage badly damaged, the auditorium roof collapsed; while all the scenery, furniture props, a large portion of the wardrobe, as well as many scripts and prompt copies of plays, went up in flames. The 'Old Lady' had set fire to herself.

8
The Years of Exile
1951–1966

In search of a home

> The Abbey really died with that fire it had. It was as if God struck a match and set the whole thing alight.[1]

The Abbey did not die; but the years of its exile radically altered its character and reduced its standing as a leading European theatre. The fire destroyed more than a building, it destroyed an atmosphere, a sense of dedication to an ideal, however tarnished it had become through the passing years.

If Dubliners are quick to 'knock' institutions and individuals who, through good luck or honest endeavour, raise their heads above the commonality, they are no less quick to give a helping hand to those who fall by the wayside. On the morning after the fire, offers of alternative accommodation came from many different sources. Eventually Lord Moyne's offer of the rent-free use of the Rupert Guinness Hall for a period of two months was gratefully accepted. In the meantime the company transferred its production of *The Plough and the Stars* to the tiny Peacock stage where it continued without the loss of a single performance: a feat made possible by gifts of props and clothing from well-wishers and the heroic efforts of Seaghan Barlow the designer, Vere Dudgeon, and some of the actors in improvising the sets and salvaging what they could of the costumes.

Those who have told the story of the Abbey fire have pointed out that the last words to come from the stage on night of 18 July were those of the song sung by the soldiers as the curtain fell on O'Casey's play: 'Keep the home fires burning'. No less symbolic, perhaps, was the overture played by the Abbey orchestra before the curtain rose in the Peacock on the following night: Beethoven's *Prometheus*.

The gods who condemned Prometheus to be bound to a rock for his theft of fire from Olympus were now to condemn the Abbey to an equally uncomfortable abode.

The Queen's

Early in August Blythe sought an interview with Louis Elliman of Odeon (Ireland) Ltd with a view to leasing the Queen's Theatre. A rental of £227 a week was proposed, and on 24 August the contract for a five-year lease was signed.

The Queen's had long lost the last vestiges of such sleazy glory as it enjoyed in the high days of melodrama. Its noisy, pleasure-seeking audience who cheered and booed and sang their patriotic songs had deserted to the cinema where the celuloid heroes and villains were oblivious to their encouraging improvisations. The building itself was in poor repair; it was draughty; its walls were in need of paint; its carpets and upholstery were shabby; the stage lighting was many years out of date; plaster was falling from the ceiling, and patches of damp disfigured the approach to the dress circle. Like many of the old touring theatres, the Queen's had no foyer space – no doubt to encourage its patrons to frequent the bars; it possessed no workshop or wardrobe store; its dressing-room accommodation was inadequate, and the sight-lines from the sides of the circles were bad. Such disadvantages might easily have been overcome, for the Abbey itself was scarcely eligible for top league rating, had the Queen's possessed the one quality that could be ascribed to the old Abbey, namely that sense of intimacy between actor and audience that had largely shaped the character and acting style of the old theatre. But after all, a long occupancy was not anticipated.

The sympathetic Minister of Finance, Sean MacEntee, was encouraging the Directors to press ahead with planning a new building for which government aid would be forthcoming. Two years, or perhaps three, at the Queen's was all that need be expected, and the new building could be completed at a rough estimate of between £25,000 and £30,000. Fifteen years later, the Abbey company left the Queen's for a home of its own which had cost £600,000. During the time the architects had produced sixteen different sketch plans, over five hundred sheets of drawings and five models.

On 24 September, after eight weeks in the Rupert Guinness Hall, the company opened at the Queen's with a revival of *The Silver Tassie*. The result was a failure. 'We have more than done our duty by *The Silver Tassie* and we should never see it again,' declared Blythe at a meeting of the Board on 24 September. Twenty-one years later *The Silver Tassie* was to celebrate Ireland's entry into the European Economic Community.

The difference in size between the Abbey and the Queen's presented the company with problems that altered the pattern as well as the economics of its productions. The Queen's auditorium had a total capacity of 760 seats, approximately fifty per cent more than the Abbey. In the old theatre a new play, if it proved reasonably popular, would be taken off after a week or fortnight's run, and later revived in the repertoire from time to time. Now with a larger capacity house the audience was used up more quickly; this virtually entailed an end to the repertory system. With very few exceptions revivals were no longer economically viable, and the only hope of covering expenses, far greater than at the Abbey, was in long runs of popular plays on the rare occasions when these could be found. In adopting the long run system the Abbey gained a larger popular audience at the expense of much of its character. Except that its plays were predominantly written by Irish writers the National Theatre seemed to be little different from its commercial rivals.

Blythe estimated that playing to just over fifty per cent of capacity might involve a weekly loss of seventy-five pounds; in fact, by the time the company left the Queen's, with seat prices almost double those of 1951, the loss could be, and often was, anything between £500 and £900 a week. During the first six years of occupancy the operational loss averaged £12,500 a year; in the last six years it was almost £23,000 a year, insurance compensation for the fire had been eaten up, and the company's reserves were spent, while the bank overdraft was running at over £50,000 despite supplementary grants and increases in subsidy. Small wonder that, as the years went by, the prospect of remaining at the Queen's for what seemed a lifetime appeared to Blythe and his fellow Directors little less than purgatory itself.

Architects and economics

For the architects, too, the demands and restrictions of the city authorities, the constant call for new estimates and revised plans, the unforeseen problems of the site itself, and, worst of all, the lost opportunity to provide an architectural and functional theatre second to none on a much larger site, must have been no less galling.

What went wrong? Michael Scott with his personal connection with the Abbey, and his substantial architectural practice, was the obvious choice as the architect. Pierre Sonrel, the distinguished French architect and theatre consultant, was fully qualified to advise on and oversee the plans. There remained, however, a series of hurdles that might well have daunted more experienced architects than Scott, while the Board's goading and harrying did little to create harmonious relations between architect and client.

The architect's brief was to provide a building containing a proscenium-arch theatre, seating six hundred and fifty, and a small theatre suitable for more experimental staging, seating one hundred and fifty, the government having now abandoned the grandiose plan – or folly – of incorporating the Abbey and Gate under one roof. But the existing site owned by the Abbey, which included White's premises and a small tobacconist shop, was inadequate for the requirements of a modern theatre complex bearing in mind the stringent demands of the Fire Department. Moreover, the Corporation's refusal to permit the main theatre's stage and auditorium to be built on top of the small experimental theatre not only complicated, but considerably delayed, the planning.

This made the acquisition of the adjoining public house, The Abbey Bar, imperative to even the most modest scheme. Tommy Lennon, the proprietor, had benefited considerably from the patrons as well as the actors of the Abbey; now that this trade was temporarily lost, he was quite willing to sell his premises, but upon his own terms. A reliable valuation of his business suggested a figure of £7,000; Lennon demanded £40,000. After considerable pressure the Department of Finance reluctantly agreed to the Board raising their offer to £25,000; Lennon refused. It was not until 1957 after nearly six years of bargaining that the premises were purchased for £32,000 – a sum that Lennon did not live to enjoy.

But Lennon was not the only one to exploit the situation. Ellis, the tenant of the adjoining tobacconist shop owned by the Abbey, whose net annual profit was estimated at £600, now claimed compensation for termination of tenancy amounting to £5,000. Once again the Department of Finance refused to allow the Directors to meet this demand, thus involving further delays before a compromise was reached and estimates could be drawn up.

In the meantime Scott had conceived a far more imaginative plan. This consisted of bridging the narrow lane between the old Abbey and the buildings on Eden Quay, and providing the new theatre with a riverside frontage on the Liffey. But the endless delays, the criticisms of press and public, the loss of audiences, the importunities of the bank manager, and the humiliations of constant appeals for increased funds (made no easier by changes of Government and of personnel in the Department of Finance, were beginning to affect the temper of even so imperturbable a character as Blythe. He reacted angrily: he would have no more plans; no more bright ideas; let the architects get down to basic planning; cut out all elaborations; at all costs get the theatre open, and rescue the Abbey from its purgatory. Finally in 1959 plans were approved by the Corporation and estimates submitted to the Department of Finance. In the same year an Act was passed by the Irish Parliament authorising a contribution of £25,000 from what was known as the Suitors' Fund.

The way might now seem open for a start to be made on clearing the site and commencing the new building. Scott's revised plans were expected to be finished by mid-June; notices to quit were given to Lennon's bar and Ellis' shop; but by now the rough estimates for building and equipment had risen to £385,000 and in a climate of national economic stringency the Department of Finance declared that not one penny more than the sum voted would be forthcoming.

Once again new plans had to be drawn up, new economies made. It was not until February 1962 that tenders could be invited. On 15 June the lowest tender submitted by A. J. Jennings & Co. Ltd. was accepted. But estimates were still well above the sum voted under the Act, and with water seepage and other problems delaying the constructional work, the prospect of an early return to Abbey Street grew more and more remote. Moreover, Blythe had to admit to the shareholders that the year ending in July 1962 had been the worst that had been experienced since the company had come to the Queen's. Not a single play had proved anything like a success; receipts had been falling steadily since 1955; the debit balance was approaching £33,000 (it was to rise to nearly twice that figure before the company finally left the Queen's), and there seemed little hope of obtaining the additional funds required to complete the building by appealing to well-wishers at home and in the States. Press criticism of the theatre's policy was mounting; demands for Blythe's resignation were being voiced; and a leading article in the *Irish Times* declared the Abbey was no longer entitled to the name of the National Theatre.

Plays and playwrights

We have seen how the size and economics of the Queen's had changed the character and policy of the Abbey company from that of a repertory theatre, with a good supply of revivals to fill out the weeks necessary for rehearsing new plays, to that of a theatre whose economic survival depended almost entirely on long runs of new plays. The theatre itself was not the only cause of this. From 1961 onwards Telefís Éireann was making heavy demands on the output of playwrights; and Radio Éireann had long supplanted the Abbey as the purveyor of verse drama; while the ever-increasing amateur theatre with its competitive festivals was killing the market for the old favourites. In 1958 the Abbey suffered a severe blow in the loss of almost the only revivals that could still be relied upon to draw a reasonable audience.

Early in that year the Council of the Dublin Tóstal (Festival) announced the production of an adaptation of Joyce's *Ulysses,* entitled *Bloomsday,* and a new play by Sean O'Casey, *The Drums of Father Ned,* for its June theatre festival. The Archbishop of Dublin and Primate of Ireland, the Most Reverend John C. McQuaid, who had read neither play, promptly withdrew his permission for the votive Mass to celebrate the opening of the Tóstal. After much hesitation the Council declared its intention of postponing the theatre festival, but going ahead with its plan to present O'Casey's play, to which the author would be required to make certain amendments. It was then that O'Casey struck. In his own name and in that of the dead Joyce, he forbade the professional performance of all his plays in the Irish Republic.[2]

Ironically, it was upon the Abbey, an entirely innocent party in this affair, that the blow fell. Since the twenties, O'Casey's plays had been the mainstay of the repertoire, and only three years previously the company's production of *The Plough and the Stars* had won the unanimous praise of the Paris critics when it was presented at the Théâtre Sarah Bernhardt during the International Theatre Festival. Now for almost six years the company was to be denied the opportunity of displaying what was its most popular and satisfactory work. Except for the hardy old melodrama, *The Righteous are Bold,* there were no other plays from the repertoire of the old theatre that could be relied upon to pay their way.

However, the company did have its popular successes among the new plays, some of which could be relied upon to stand up to revival. Walter Macken's *Home is the Hero* (28 July 1952) ran for seventeen weeks and proved a useful standby; so, too, did Louis D'Alton's play, *This other Eden* (1 June 1953), with a twenty-four weeks run.

Other successes came from the pen of the most prolific of the Queen's dramatists, John McCann, eight of whose plays were presented, three of them — *Twenty Years A-Wooing* (7 April 1954), *I Know where I'm Going* (26 January 1959) and *A Jew Named Sammy* (27 August 1962) — proving highly popular. John O'Donovan provided five plays in all, one of which, *The Less we are Together* (22 July 1957), ran for twenty-four weeks. John B. Keane, whose plays have been more widely presented by amateurs than by professionals, contributed two plays; one of these, *The Man from Clare,* first produced by the Southern Theatre Group in Cork in 1962 and by the Abbey on 5 August 1963, attracted almost capacity houses. From the North of Ireland came two plays that did good business at the box-office: Joseph Tomelty's *Is the Priest at Home?* (15 November 1954) and John Murphy's *The Country Boy* which was first produced by the Group Theatre, Belfast, and opened in the Abbey on 11 May 1959. But most of these, together with many others, have long since been forgotten; indeed there was, as Tomás Mac Anna has said, 'a grim, grey similarity between most of the plays that went on at the Queen's'.[3]

In the eyes of many of its former friends, the Abbey had sold its birthright for a mess of potage. The picture was not, however, quite as grey as has been painted. Denis Johnston's *The Scythe and the Sunset* (9 May 1958), Bryan MacMahon's *The Song of the Anvil* (12 September 1960) and *The Honey Spike* (22 May 1961), and the plays of two promising playwrights later to become internationally recognised, Hugh Leonard (*The Big Birthday,* 23 January 1956) and *A Leap in the Dark,* (21 January 1959) and Brian Friel (*The Enemy Within,* 6 August 1962) — these helped to break the spell of mediocrity, though they could hardly be counted successful at the box-office. Brendan Behan's *The Quare Fella* (8 October 1956), originally produced at Alan Simpson's Pike Theatre, did however prove a commercial success when it was revived in 1960. No doubt the success of Joan Littlewood's London production of this play (1956) and *The Hostage* (1958) helped to swell the audiences. Blythe, who had obtained a copy of *The Hostage,* expressed himself as glad he had not encouraged the author to submit such filthy rubbish to the Abbey.

In the last years of the Queen's there were some welcome additions to the repertoire in the form of foreign plays, including Eugene O'Neill's *Long Day's Journey Into Night* (24 December 1962) with fine performances by Philip O'Flynn, Ria Mooney and T. P. McKenna, Lorca's *Yerma* (28 February 1966, and a singularly successful production of Brecht's *The Life of Galileo* (21 September 1956) directed

by Tomás Mac Anna, regarded by many as a break-through
in lighting, production and acting.

The Gaelic policy

As we have already seen, Blythe had persuaded his fellow
Directors to endorse his policy of presenting one-act plays
in Irish after the conclusion of the main evening's entertainment, before the Abbey company left the old building. This
practice became a regular feature of the Queen's repertoire.
Whether for reasons of economy, or because he feared that
announcing these plays in advance might discourage his box-
office customers, Blythe adopted the unusual course of not
alerting the audience of the addition to their entertainment
until they opened their programmes — a ruse that might result
in a fifty percent attendance, but more often in far less. However the Gaelic pantomimes continued to flourish, more at
home in the Queen's than in the old Abbey.

Clearly Blythe's aims in promoting Gaelic drama were not
wholly artistic. His boast of presenting one hundred and
twenty nights a year of plays in Irish, including pantomime,
was at least partly aimed at impressing the government with
the Abbey's value as a medium of education in the Irish language, thereby channelling the grants from the Department of
Education to Comhar Dramaíochta directly to the Abbey —
an aim in which he was eventually to succeed.

A Golden Jubilee

Whatever faults Blythe may have had, he lost no opportunity
of pressing the case for government recognition of the theatre's
national importance. The Golden Jubilee of the Abbey, celebrated on 27, 28 and 29 December 1954, was seized upon as
an opportunity to focus national attention on the theatre.
Two hundred guests, including the President, the Taoiseach,
ministers, ex-ministers, and members of the diplomatic corps,
were invited to witness three plays by the founders of the
Abbey, *In the Shadow of the Glen, On Baile's Strand* and
Spreading the News. If such rarefied fare impressed official-
dom, it failed to heal the breach between the Abbey and its

old supporters. Well might the ancestral shades of the founders cast a cold eye on the fate of a theatre that, fifty years
previously, they had created with such high ideals. 'Be bold!
Be bold! and evermore be bold!' Yeats had declared as the
motto of the Abbey when he launched it upon the world.
Now it seemed that 'Be cautious!' had become the theatre's
watchword. The dusty old home of melodrama was indeed
wreaking its revenge on the high idealists who had set out to
destroy its popular fare. Not only had the Abbey grown es-
tranged from its oldest and best friends, but more grievously
it had failed to win the respect of a younger generation who
had deserted to other theatres.

New Directors

For this Blythe has been widely blamed; but the problem of
transforming this old-fashioned, uncongenial building into
a centre of artistic life could only have been solved by a
Jerzy Grotowski, a Joan Littlewood or a Peter Brook. Blythe
was not one of these, nor were his fellow Directors. Perhaps
things might have been different if they had been willing, or
bold enough, to place greater responsibility in the hands of
their professional employees, but the Abbey still followed
the tradition of its founders that artistic direction must rest
in the hands of the Board of Directors. This tradition might
be said to have some justification in the early years when
Yeats, Synge and Lady Gregory were the authors of most of
the plays, but was scarcely justifiable when control was in the
hands of an ex-Minister of Finance, supported by government
appointees and well-meaning amateurs, with the single exception of Lennox Robinson, now lost in a mist of alcoholic
euphoria.

In 1963 Ria Mooney, worn out by the heavy demands of a
thankless and unrewarding task, suffered a break-down that
led to her resignation. Her place was taken by Frank Dermody,
now returned from the film world. But still it was the Managing Director and his fellow members of the Board who selected
the plays, while he himself approved the casts, engaged and
discarded the players, attended rehearsals when he chose to
do so, interviewed the playwrights, and made cuts or in-

sisted upon alterations in the scripts for what were claimed
to be artistic reasons. In 1958 Richard Hayes died and the
government appointed Dr Séamus Wilmot, Registrar of the
National University, to succeed him. With Wilmot and
Ó Faracháin on the Board, Blythe encountered at least some
resistance to his autocratic rule.

On 14 October, three months after Hayes's death, Lennox
Robinson died, his last years dimmed by his affliction and
saddened by the deteriorating standards of the theatre he had
served for the greater part of his life, and which he was no
longer able to re-vitalise. In his will he left the copyright of
all his works, after the death of his widow, in trust to the
Directors: 'the income to be applied in aid of playwrights,
players, producers, stage designers, musicians, and other servants of the theatre'.[4] Ironically, he died a poor man.

Resistance to Blythe's autocracy was further strengthened
when Gabriel Fallon was co-opted to replace Lennox Robinson. At one time a part-time actor in the company, and subsequently combining his work as a civil servant with that of a
dramatic critic, Fallon had, through his criticisms of some of
O'Casey's later plays, incurred that proud old man's severe
displeasure. His appointment to the Board caused some
doubts in Blythe's mind as to his discretion, for, as a journalist,
Fallon could rarely resist the temptation to tell a good story
or to air his views in the press. But it needed more than the
combined resistance of Ó Faracháin, Wilmot and Fallon to
shake Blythe's belief in his policy and the rightness of his
methods.

Opportunity lost

In September 1963 the misfortunes that had seemed to have
become permanent features of the exiled company began to
disperse. On 3 September the foundation stone of the new
theatre was finally laid by the President, Eamon de Valera,
in the presence of a distinguished gathering of ministers and
officials. The omission of Miss Horniman's name among the
names of the other founders engraved on the stone caused
some sharp criticism which Blythe countered by announcing

that her name would be incorporated on a plaque in the vestibule: a promise yet to be fulfilled.

Of greater importance was the opportunity to restore the international prestige of the theatre arising from an invitation to present *Juno and the Paycock* and *The Plough and the Stars* at the Aldwych Theatre in London as part of the 1964 World Theatre Season, followed by a second invitation to the international theatre season in Paris, this time with *Juno and the Paycock*. After the six years absence of these plays from the theatre's repertoire and with an almost entirely different company, it was essential to perform the plays in Dublin before launching them as part of two international seasons. With this in mind, O'Casey lifted the ban on the performance of his plays by the Abbey. Here, at last, was an opportunity to confound the 'dismal Willies' of the Dublin press.

Quick to seize the golden opportunity for greater government support, Blythe applied for the annual grant-in-aid to be raised to £20,000. This he failed to obtain, but a nonrecurrent grant of £11,000 towards reducing the overdraft was added to the theatre's subsidy of £14,000.

On 10 February *The Plough* opened at the Queen's. The house was packed, and on the last night there were twenty more people in the auditorium than the number permitted by the Corporation. Not only did the Abbey appear to be on the threshold of an international triumph but best of all for the ex-Minister of Finance were the house-full boards outside the Dublin theatre and the reports of heavy booking at the Aldwych. Then suddenly the evil powers that had haunted the Abbey ever since the fire returned once more.

On Monday 13 April, just seven days before the company was due to open at the Aldwych, the players gave notice of their intention to strike on the following Saturday, unless their long delayed demands for salary increases were met. At the same time the Irish Transport and General Workers Union instructed the members of the theatre staff to withdraw their labour in support of the players' claims. Blythe had consistantly refused to recognise Irish Actors' Equity as a negotiating body in discussing players' salaries. Now, faced with a strike on the eve of the London visit, he was forced to agree to the Labour Court's decision to appoint a mediator. Dr C. S.

Andrews, whose award would be binding. The strike was called off, and *Juno and the Paycock* opened at the Aldwych Theatre on 20 April. Peter Daubeny, the Director of the World Theatre Seasons, wrote:

> ... When I actually went with John Francis Lane to see the plays in Dublin I experienced a degree of dismay. ... After the old Abbey had been burned down in 1951, the company, crossing the Liffey to the Queen's, had suffered a deterioration of spirit. It was hardly surprising. The place was like a drill-hall and, however full it might be, always felt empty. The productions seemed crammed with faults, some poor acting and very poor sets ...
> I argued bitterly with the Abbey directors, insisting that changes be made before the productions came to London. When I described my problems to O'Casey he wrote of one of the directors, 'He is a mass of obstinacy, so full of his own importance that he will listen to no-one; insensitive, too, utterly impervious to anything said to him. He hasn't the faintest idea what Drama is, and less about the art of the actor; he has become a human limpet fastened to the Abbey Theatre.'[5]

The press was less than enthusiastic — Daubeny described it as 'a muted press'; despite the full houses the Abbey's professional reputation suffered a severe blow.

O'Casey: What a blasted waste, what a glorious opportunity lost!

The Directors: Mr. Sean O'Casey was not present at any performance in the Aldwych Theatre, London, and therefore could not form a personal opinion on the merits, or demerits, of the performances or of the players.

O'Casey: Let them think what they like, but the Directors have been dead for years. They know nothing at all about acting or the drama. No more does Ernest Blythe who may be a good manager, but who is an absolute monarch. All the Directors do is what he tells them.

The Directors: The Directors of the Abbey Theatre have read with great interest Mr. Sean O'Casey's announcement that they have been dead for years. They would like to assure Mr. O'Casey that, as in the case of Mark Twain, the rumour is greatly exaggerated.[6]

On 18th September, two months after this controversy, Sean O'Casey died. O'Casey owed not a little to the Abbey,' wrote the *Irish Times* (19 September 1964); but the Abbey owed not a little to O'Casey and now it had let him down.

The shareholders

On their return from Paris, Blythe and the players gave their evidence to the Court of Enquiry into the players' salaries and awards. The findings of Dr Andrews went far beyond what some would consider his brief. In addition to the overdue increases in salaries and the suggested institution of a superannuation fund for the players, Andrews recommended that the theatre should be converted into a nationally owned state institution, controlled by a Board appointed by the government. Fortunately Dr Ryan, the Minister for Finance, had no intention of following this advice, but he did suggest that it would help to allay criticism of the management if the number of shareholders were increased, while still leaving voting power in the hands of the Board. The new share-holding members of the Society should, he suggested, be people of artistic merit or those having a recognised representative capacity. He further suggested that any ordinary Director, namely a Director not appointed by the Minister, who died or resigned from the Board, should in future be replaced by a successor elected at a General Meeting of all the Members of the Society. At the same time it was agreed that in view of the annual grant and the provision of state funds for a new building, the Minister should be entitled to nominate a second Director to represent the government. In consenting to these suggestions, Blythe made the provisos that the person appointed as a second government representative should be someone likely to work harmoniously with the existing Directors, should not be associated with a competing organisation, and should be an Irish speaker.

In July 1964 the Directors put forward a list of forty names, declaring their willingness to allot thirty shares each to a selected group of twenty-five shareholders known to be interested in literature and the arts, and on 23 February 1965 the Articles of Association were amended accordingly.[7] In July Walter Macken was, with the approval of the Board, appointed by the Minister as the second government representative.

Some relief was afforded to the problems of increased salaries and the formidable overdraft by the provision of a non-recurrent grant of £10,000 for the year 1965–66, and by the government's declaration of its intention to raise the subsidy to £30,000 in the following financial year. But all this was no solution to bridging the gap between the sum voted for the new building and its steadily mounting cost. The only way seemed to be the abandonment of the Peacock, leaving it as an empty shell without a stage, equipment and furnishing until such time as funds could be found to complete it.

It was now that the shareholders began to show their mettle. At their first meeting in May 1965 they passed a resolution declaring their belief in the necessity of completing this essential adjunct to the proper functioning of the National Theatre. They further resolved that the government should be urged to give the new theatre a clear start by paying off its crippling overdraft. This pressure from the newly appointed members of the Society was instrumental in persuading the government to provide a supplementary grant for the completion of the Peacock, but credit must also be given to Blythe who pointed out to Dr Ryan that there was now a considerable surplus in the Suitors' Fund arising from the accumulated interest on the sum voted six years ago for the rebuilding of the Abbey. The ex-Minister of Finance was still a skilled hand at manipulating figures.

All this augured well for the future relations of the Board and its new shareholders, but now that the new members of the Society had got a foothold, they were determined to bring an end to the dictatorship of the managing director. They demanded the appointment of an artistic director with full control of plays and players; in this they had the support of the players themselves. A further demand was the inclusion of works by foreign authors, old and new, in the repertoire.

An artistic adviser

Blythe urged the Board to resist these demands. 'They want the Abbey like a British repertory theatre,' he declared. The appointment of an artistic director would, he believed, destroy the function of the Board. Furthermore, 'the national character of the Abbey could not be achieved by appointing someone, possibly a foreigner, or an Irishman without much national feeling' — here he had in mind a suggestion that Tyrone Guthrie might be approached — 'and giving him a free hand in the selection of plays, players and play directors'. When pressed, he was prepared to consider Seamus Wilmot's suggestion of appointing an artistic adviser, working in a consultative capacity. In November 1965 the Board appointed Walter Macken to this post as artistic adviser and assistant manager. Strangely enough the anomaly of appointing the government representative as artistic adviser and assistant manager to a theatre that had always prided itself on its artistic independence did not seem to occur to anyone. However Macken's tenure of office gave rise to no complications, though had he taken up the posts a month earlier it might well have done so, for at that time the committee appointed by the government to plan the fiftieth anniversary of the 1916 Rising had expressed strong views against the Abbey presenting any of O'Casey's plays, as being 'cynical in outlook and disparaging in their commentary on events of Irish history,' to which Blythe replied strongly deprecating the committee's views. In the event, the plays decided upon for this commemoration week were Lady Gregory's *Dervorgilla*, Padraig Pearse's *The Singer*, and Roibeárd Ó Faracháin's *Lost Light*. Pearse's play, written in the autumn of 1915, was not at that time submitted to the Abbey lest its production should reveal the plans that were forming for a country-wide rising. Joseph Plunkett was profoundly impressed when he read it, declaring that, 'if Pearse were dead this would cause a sensation'.

In June 1966 Macken announced his intention of resigning, stating he was 'not the man for the job', agreeing, however, to remain as government representative on the Board until the new theatre opened. In his place the Minister appointed Micheál Ó hAodha, Head of Radio Drama at

R.T.E. The position of artistic adviser was taken over in December 1966 by Tomás Mac Anna; at the same time Ernest Blythe, now in his late seventies, announced his intention of gradually retiring from the post of managing director, and the Board appointed Phil O'Kelly as deputy manager.

Staff and players

The staff was changing too. Eric Gorman after thirty-two years as secretary of the Society, retired and his place was taken by John Slemon, a young and energetic accountant. 'Dossie' Wright, a 'jack of all trades', but master of the switchboard, had died in 1952. In 1954 Leslie Scott replaced his brother, Charlie, as chief electrician and, as such, acted as consultant engineer to the architects of the new building. In 1964 Brian Collins was appointed resident designer. Scenic designers were regarded as a necessary evil by the Managing Director who had no sympathy for their fanciful ideas. For much of the time Mac Anna bore the burden of re-painting and papering the stock flats, a task that he shared with his manifold duties as director of the Gaelic plays, composing lyrics, writing the pantomimes, and on one occasion an opera, *An Fear Phos Balbhan,* for which Gerald Victory composed the music.

Of the old company only Eileen Crowe, May Craig, and Harry Brogan remained. Of the young players who grew up in the Queen's and the latter days of the Abbey, some had left to work elsewhere, including Marie Kean, Siobhan McKenna, Denis O'Dea, Ray MacAnally, Jack MacGowran, Joe Lynch, and T. P. McKenna; but others were to become the mainstay of the new Abbey. Among them were: Kathleen Barrington, Máire Ní Dhomhnaill, Joan O'Hara, Aideen O'Kelly, Brid Lynch, Fidelma Murphy, Maire O'Neill, Angela Newman, Micheál Ó Bríain, Desmond Cave, Vincent Dowling, Philip O'Flynn, Bill Foley, Clive Geraghty, Edward and Geoffrey Golden, Micheál Ó hAonghusa, Patrick Laffan, Peadar Lamb, Patrick Layde and Donal McCann.

In the workshop, Seaghan Barlow assisted by George Howard of the Queen's, still sawed away — though less vigorously than in earlier years. From the wardrobe, backstage, front-of-house and administrative offices of the Queen's came those loyal servants of the Abbey, too numerous to mention, whose proud privilege it is to serve without credit; many of them were to have a life-time of service behind them when the National Theatre moved forward to its new home.

As Blythe's reign drew to its end, it was clear to him, as well as to his colleagues on the Board, that his crusade for the gaelicisation of the theatre was losing support. In May 1966 his fellow members of the Board insisted that when the company opened at the new Abbey the name of the theatre be printed in English on the cover of the programmes, and that no longer should new recruits to the acting company be required to speak Gaelic; while the majority of the players preferred to use the English form of their names. In other ways the players were demanding a greater say in the affairs of the theatre. Regular meetings with the management were demanded by the Players' Council, now officially recognised by the Board; a minimum of four weeks rehearsal for new productions; the engagement from time to time of guest directors; and a general improvement in the staging of plays. The shareholders, backed by the players, were demanding the introduction of a pension scheme for actors, and salaries related to inflationary trends; above all, they demanded that a serious effort be made to revitalise the international reputation of the Abbey: that the dirt, the frustrations, the pinched economies of the Queen's be forgotten, and that the company emerge from its exile to meet the demanding standards of international theatre.

9
The Abbey Comes Home
1966–1969

The theatre opens

On Saturday 9 July 1966, the curtain fell for the last time on
'The Abbey at the Queen's'. Fifteen years of exile were
ended. The old home of melodrama was shortly to fall a victim to the bulldozers of progress.

Across the Liffey chaos reigned. For better or worse it had
been decided to open the new building on Monday 18 July,
fifteen years to a day since the Abbey burnt down. Blythe,
for once showing signs of anxiety, reported to the Board that
the place was a shambles — the stage lifts were not synchron-
ised, all the lights had fused, and the electricians threatened a
strike if the actors held them up by rehearsing on the stage.
Meanwhile, the opening production, *Recall the Years*, a
hotch-potch of highlights from the theatre's history, scripted
by Walter Macken and incorporating film, sound tracks and
elaborate lighting, needed every moment on the new and un-
tried stage to get it into shape. In fact no full rehearsal with
lights and sound was possible before the opening night. The
lighting had to be largely improvised and the sound only
came on half an hour before the audience entered the theatre.
To add to the Directors' anxieties it was not until the end of
June that their attention had been drawn to the fact that the
theatre's patent had expired shortly after the fire. While temporary arrangements could be made to permit performances
to take place, no bar licence could be issued until the patent
was granted, a situation hardly conducive to the success of a

reception to foster better relations with the press. It was only at the last moment that the Revenue authorities relented and a temporary bar licence was granted in anticipation of the patent. The patent itself was finally granted on 30 October.

In view of the number of invitations to politicians, diplomats, Corporation officials, shareholders, relatives of the players and staff, contractors, sub-contractors and old friends of the Abbey, it was decided to spread the opening formalities over a Gala Week during which addresses would be given from the stage on successive nights by political and other personalities, including Senator Michael Yeats, the son of the poet, and the President of the Institute of Architects deputising for Michael Scott. The opening night was the occasion for the President of the Republic to declare the new Abbey open; on the Saturday night it was the turn of the Taoiseach, Sean Lemass, to express the good will of the government and unveil a plaque to those connected with the theatre who had fought or died for the country's freedom in 1916.

> Sean Connolly, killed in action, Maire Nic Shuibhlaigh, Helena Molony, Ellen Bushell, Arthur Shields, Barney Murphy and Peadar Kearney, author of 'The Soldier's Song' (the National Anthem).

At eight o'clock on Monday 18 July four trumpeters sounded the Presidential salute, and Eamon de Valera, on behalf of the people of Ireland, declared the theatre open. Then, amidst heartening applause, the veteran of the theatre, eighty-six year old Seaghan Barlow, stepped on to the stage to strike the three strokes on the gong that traditionally herald the opening of an Abbey play. Thereafter, I turn to Tomás Mac Anna who, with Frank Dermody and Edward Golden, had the unenviable task of staging this first performance.

> The light control board did its very best, not quite managing to light all of the actors all of the time, or even some of the actors some of the time, until suddenly, as May Craig moved regally across the stage to her seat where she was to tell us about the "Playboy" riots of 1907 (she was Honor Blake in that far-off famous production) it gave up the ghost. . . . Two spotmen, who, like the Wise Virgins,

had managed to keep some oil in their lamps, held on to the actress and guided her home. . . . Leslie Scott plunged into the rear end of the machine, the Creator's name was rather emotionally invoked, as well as those of the Holy Family, and back came the lights, slow as be damned, not the sign of a hurry on them. Then the news-strip stopped right in the middle of announcing King Edward's death and Miss Horniman's huff, away back in 1910. . . . Then the sound went . . .[1]

Nevertheless the Abbey had come home.

The new Abbey

Technically the new building conforms to most of the demands of contemporary theatre architecture. Its fan-shaped auditorium — sixty feet from stage to back wall — has a seating capacity of 628 of which ninety-seven are located in a shallow balcony. Every seat commands a full view of the stage, and the foyers and bar arrangements are generous. The open stage, with its forestage mounted on two lifts that descend to form an orchestra pit, can extend forward to a total of fourteen feet from the curtain line, and provides a sense of intimacy between players and audience. The stage itself has a full complement of counterweights for flying scenery, and three large lifts extending across its full width make the stage floor adaptable to various levels. Lighting and sound desks are housed in control rooms located at the rear of the auditorium commanding a view of the stage. The lighting console with its 120-way dimmer-bank controls some 200 outlets of which a generous proportion are located in the front of the house, concealed in wall recesses in the auditorium and in the movable ceiling flaps.

The new theatre, however, presented its problems to a company whose repertoire largely consisted of plays with naturalistic interiors. The wide stage with its seventy-two foot opening has a depth of only twenty-eight feet from the curtain line. Moreover, the position of the front curtain causes a large area of the forestage to become isolated when a traditional box-set with its ceiling and walls has to be set behind it. As a result the play's action tends to be remote from the audience. The new Abbey seemed to have turned its back on the old naturalistic stage craft, and now demanded the poetry of light and the sculptural forms of Appia and Craig. To some extent this has had its influence on the type of play presented, being one of the reasons why many of the plays from the old repertoire seem out of place in the new theatre.

These and other problems, including those concerned with the policy, administration and manning of the two theatres, required careful planning by a team of experienced artistic and administrative personnel possessing a reasonable security of tenure and enjoying the confidence of the Board. The delegation of responsibility to its executive officers was, as we have seen, something the Board had consistently resisted. Indeed, much of the trouble the new theatre encountered in its early years arose from the failure to train administrative and artistic personnel, and provide them with the experience necessary for planning and organising the vastly different operation of running a fully-fledged national theatre. Although Mac Anna had been appointed to succeed Walter Macken, his appointment, like that of the deputy manager, did not become effective until 1 December 1966, and his responsibilities were strictly limited, as the adoption of the title 'artistic adviser' indicated; indeed, Blythe had originally suggested that this appointment should be on a part-time basis. Mac Anna's contract was limited to one year with a possible further year's extension. The deputy manager, too, was on a year's probation, and although O'Kelly had previous experience of theatre management he was, as yet, unfamiliar with the particular managerial problems of the Abbey. In these circumstances the chances of immediate change in the artistic policy, or of a distinctive house-style emerging to complement the opening of the new National Theatre, were remote.

The shareholders and the Board

Blythe's determination to confine all decision-making inside the board room threatened a head-on clash with the new shareholders who felt their advice was being ignored or only half-heartedly adopted. On 12 November 1966 fifteen members requisitioned an Extraordinary General Meeting of the Society to determine the function of the shareholders in the formulation of the theatre's policy. The immediate cause of discontent was the Board's failure to notify them of the terms of appointment of the new artistic adviser and deputy manager, and the nature and scope of their authority. Apart from the particular issue, this clearly raised some awkward questions of a more general nature. Could the theatre operate effectively under a two-tier government of shareholders and Directors? What precisely was to be the interpretation of the shareholders' function as worded in the new Articles of Association, 'to aid and advise the Directors'? A resolution was eventually agreed whereby 'the advice of shareholders shall be sought in specific terms before any important decision is taken which affects the policy of the theatre'. Whilst the Board effectively established its right to govern since it was the Board itself that decided what was or was not important, the shareholders had shown that from now on it must do so under the watchful eye of an influential pressure group.

Ernest Blythe retires

For better or worse, democracy was slowly setting its foot in the doorway of the Abbey. The National Theatre Society Limited of the Fays, Yeats, and Lady Gregory was becoming a nationalised theatre.

On 31 August 1967 Ernest Blythe retired as managing director, having first secured the completion of the Peacock, the outstanding costs of which were met in November of 1967 by a government grant of £75,000. Phil O'Kelly was now promoted from deputy manager to manager but without a seat on the Board, while Blythe remained an influential member of the Board until 1972.

The new Peacock Theatre

On Sunday 23 July 1967, a little over a year from the opening of the Abbey, the Peacock was formally opened by the

Minister for Finance, Charles Haughey. On this occasion no performance took place. Guests were shown some of the features of this comfortable and intimate theatre with its 157 seats and its flexible arrangement by which it can be changed by a mechanical device from an end stage with an acting area of twenty-eight feet wide by nineteen feet deep, to an arena stage with a playing area of twenty feet square.

As an example of new trends in theatre architecture the Peacock can be counted as one of the most successful intimate theatres to be built in recent years, but how to integrate its operation into the artistic and administrative structure of the Abbey proved to be, and still is, a major problem. The very variety of tasks it is expected to undertake would seem to deny the Peacock any consistent or unified policy.

> We will, we hope, make the most fruitful use of what, in all our prolonged negotiations with an enlightened, but prudent State, we harped on incessantly: the Peacock Theatre — the experimental arm of the Abbey, in which the fledgling Irish playwrights, players and others may find the warm nest for their future soaring — and in which all may find model and tutelage from foreign classics and experimental daring. In this Peacock Theatre, the verse-drama which William Butler Yeats, our master-founder, so ardently sought and wrought, will again be mustered. Drama in the Irish language, an objective since the first thoughts of our theatre, we hope to cherish, foster and promote.[2]

Rhetoric apart, this indicates a somewhat confused policy for a theatre to embark on. Its purpose has been further complicated by adding to its functions those of a workshop for the actors, a home for a theatre in education team, a showcase for the finalists of Gaelic drama competitions, a lunchtime theatre, and a venue for 'pop' concerts. Too often the designation of 'experimental theatre' is a cover for the not quite good enough, and so long as the Peacock is dependent on the Abbey for its finance and its players, as well as in its servicing requirements, it inevitably takes second place to the needs of the larger theatre. In recent years under the direction of Tomás Mac Anna, Vincent Dowling, Joe Dowling and

Pat Laffan, productions have been mounted in the Peacock that rival any seen in the Abbey itself. But no matter how successful its productions, the Peacock remains dependent for its very existence upon the fortunes of its senior partner. When economies are called for, the Peacock is the first to suffer, while its policies have changed with each successive incumbent. Yet the Abbey needs the Peacock as a re-vitalising force that can extend the frontiers of drama beyond the more formal limitations imposed by majority audiences. A grant ear-marked exclusively for the smaller theatre would seem to be called for, together with coordinated planning of the repertoires of the two theatres so as to complement each other.

Plays and players, 1966—1969

The last play seen on the stage of the old Abbey was, as we have recorded, *The Plough and the Stars*. It was therefore thought fitting that O'Casey's master work should be the first play presented in the new theatre. On 15 August a new production by Frank Dermody of *The Plough* with designs by Liam Miller succeeded the rather laboured historical revue that celebrated the opening of the theatre. After a seven-weeks run *The Plough* was followed by two new plays, *One for the Grave* (3 October) by the poet and playwright Louis MacNeice, and *Death is for Heroes* (31 October) by Michael Judge. Neither play succeeded in overcoming these somewhat doom-laden titles. The first really successful production of the opening year was an adaptation by P. J. O'Connor of Patrick Kavanagh's novel, *Tarry Flynn* (22 November), in which the young actor Donal McCann scored a notable triumph in the leading part. In this picture of rural life, with its multiple scenes, the particular characteristics of the new stage were used to their best effect by the play director, Tomás Mac Anna, in a production that frankly recognised the stage as a place for acting rather than scenic adornment. The year closed with the last of the Abbey's Gaelic pantomimes, *Férnando agus an Ríonn Óg,* directed once again by Frank Dermody.

1967 saw two of the greatest popular successes of recent

years, Boucicault's great Irish melodrama, *The Shaughraun*
(31 January) and Frank McMahon's adaptation of Brendan
Behan's autobiographical novel, *Borstal Boy* (10 October).
To some critics it seemed ironical that the theatre that Yeats
and the playwrights of the Irish dramatic movement had
founded in protest against stage Irishry should now open its
doors to one of its most flamboyant examples. But Boucicault's
superbly irreverent mixture of farce and melodrama, spectacle,
sentiment and suspense, his panache and totally shameless
exploitation of the most improbable coincidences, defy all
the high-flown tenets held by the purists, appealing directly
to the willing suspension of disbelief that lies at the heart of
all true theatre. Both Shaw and O'Casey acknowledged their
debt to Boucicault, and Synge's Christy Mahon owes not a
little to that glorious liar, Conn, the Shaughraun. If Dion
Lardner Boucicault cannot be claimed as the father of Irish
drama, this revival did at least suggest he might be its god-
father. The production was doubly blessed by the engagement of two guest artists, Cyril Cusack in the part of Conn, a
part that Boucicault created for himself, and Alan Barlow as
designer. Of Cusack's performance Seamus Kelly wrote in the
Irish Times: 'It was a great comeback by a great Abbey artist,
and the whole house rose to it.' The new Abbey stage that
seemed to have turned its back on realist illusion yielded itself sympathetically to Alan Barlow's visually enchanting
settings, capturing the essence of the romantic watercolours
of the nineteenth century. In the part of the English Captain
Molineux, baffled by the strange ways of the Irish and af-
flicted with an inability to pronounce the letter 'r', Donal
McCann gave a splendidly controlled comedy performance.
When in 1968 Peter Daubeny invited the Abbey to present
the play at the Aldwych Theatre, London (20 May) during
the World Theatre Season, Irving Wardle, the critic of *The
Times* wrote:

> I am told that many Dubliners oppose the transfer of
> *The Shaughraun* to London for fear that it would project
> the wrong image of the country. Let me assure them that
> no Dublin show I have ever seen has done more to put over
> the idea of a dynamic new Ireland than this, which at once

rescues a fine dramatist from oblivion and restores the Abbey to its old status as one of the jewels of the English-speaking theatre.

In a very different production style was Tomás Mac Anna's direction of *Borstal Boy* which became the greatest popular success of the new theatre to date with a record of 171 performances. On a bare stage, making full use of lighting, the story of the young Brendan Behan, touchingly played by the nineteen-year-old Frank Grimes, hitherto almost unknown to theatre audiences, was related by Niall Toibín in an uncanny representation of Behan's older self.

Other notable productions during the year 1967 were Brian Friel's *The Loves of Cass Maguire* (10 April) in which Siobhan McKenna returned to the Abbey to play the part Ruth Gordon had created in New York, the first Abbey production of *Red Roses for Me* (31 July), O'Casey's play of the General Strike of 1913, and a revival of *The Invincibles* (4 September) in which Patrick Laffan gave a notable performance as Joe Brady. During the latter part of the year an Irish-speaking section of the company toured the Gaeltacht with three plays in the Irish language, *An Cailín Bán* (The Colleen Bawn) a translation by Liam Ó Bríain of Boucicault's melodrama, Douglas Hyde's one act play, *An Pósadh,* and a translation of Synge's *Riders to the Sea.* Plays in the Irish language were also presented in the Peacock. The choice of Myles Na gCopaleen's fantasy *An Béal Bocht* (The Poor Mouth) as the opening production on 25 July was an earnest of the Board's intention to provide in the Peacock a permanent and separate home for plays in Irish, in support of which Blythe had arranged for the winding up of An Comhar Dramaíochta and the incorporation of its subsidy into the Abbey's annual grant. Unfortunately objections were raised to alterations in the text and the play had to be withdrawn. *An Choinneal* by Padraig Ó Giollagáin and *Faill ar an Bhfeart* by Séamus Ó Neill were two new plays presented on 22 August and 9 October respectively. The Peacock, too, paid an outstanding debt to the neglected playwright George Fitzmaurice. His play, *The King of the Barna Men* (18 Sept) received its first production, accompanied by *The Magic Glasses,* and both plays were directed by Sean Cotter, a new recruit to the production staff.

International theatre

The year 1968 opened with a new play in the Abbey, *The Last Eleven* (22 January) by Jack White and a notable adaptation by Mary Manning of Frank O'Connor's novel, *The Saint and Mary Kate* (18 March).

One of the most significant events of the year was an international seminar which took place from 30 September to 8 October. Organised by Carolyn Swift and sponsored by Arthur Guinness Limited, the seminar sought to explore the value of the National Theatre idea and its influence on the international scene. Among those taking part, other than leaders of the Irish theatre, were representatives from the national theatres of Iceland, the Soviet Union, Britain, the German Democratic Republic and West Germany. In calling together this distinguished gathering, the Abbey was extending its role to that of an international theatre. This new role was manifested in the following year, not only by partaking in the World Theatre Festival but by the official visit of the King and Queen of the Belgians on 16 May, and by one of the highlights of the theatre's long history, a production for the Dublin Theatre Festival of *The Cherry Orchard* (8 October) directed by Maria Knebel of the Red Army Theatre of the Soviet Union and the Moscow Art Theatre. For this superb production Siobhan McKenna returned to play Madame Ranyevskaia and Cyril Cusack to play 'Gayev. 'A supreme joy,' was how Desmond Rushe of the *Irish Independent* described it. 'The most eagerly awaited event of the Festival has exceeded our greatest expectations.' 'This production is the most beautifully staged, the best acted, and need I say, the best play we have seen,' was the comment of Maureen O'Farrell of the *Evening Press*.

The Abbey's international role was further marked by a visit to Italy in April of the same year where *In the Shadow of the Glen* and *The Shadow of the Gunman* were presented at the Teatro della Pergola, Florence, for the city's annual festival, and the first visit of an Abbey company to the

Edinburgh Festival in September where Tomás Mac Anna's production of *The Playboy of the Western World* was presented. After the theatre's appearance in Florence members of the company visited Rome to be received in audience by His Holiness Pope Paul. To mark this occasion Séamus Wilmot on behalf of the Directors of the National Theatre Society presented a specially bound edition of *The Playboy*. Needless to say, there were those who thought otherwise, as can be seen from this letter to the editor of the *Evening Herald* (24 April):

> Sir . . . The presentation of such a controversial play by our National Theatre must be regarded as in bad taste and an insult to our Catholic Nation. We must not forget that this is being presented to the Head of the Catholic Church by a Catholic country. Are we to presume that this is supposed to be an image of the Catholic Irish mind? Surely a more suitable volume would have been Padraig Pearse's plays? . . .

The Peacock, too, shared in the new international role by presenting plays by O'Neill, Genet and Strindberg, but the highlights of the little theatre's 1968 season were the first production of Thomas Murphy's *Famine* (18 March) and P. J. O'Connor's adaptation of Eric Cross's book, *The Tailor and Ansty*. Tom Murphy had, like Brian Friel, already made his mark as a playwright overseas before he became one of the most interesting of the new wave of Abbey playwrights. In 1961 his play *Whistle in the Dark* was produced at the Theatre Royal, Stratford East, later transferring to Shaftesbury Avenue. *Famine* drew full houses to the Peacock, but failed to have the same appeal when transferred to the larger stage of the Abbey. *The Tailor and Ansty* which brought to life the stories and anecdotes of the County Cork tailor and storyteller, Timothy Buckley, introduced a new recruit to the Abbey company, Eamon Kelly, whose brilliant gifts as a traditional story-teller have since proved a valuable addition to the repertoire of the theatre.

The policy of presenting plays in the Irish language in the Peacock was continued by the production of two new plays, *Breithiúntas* by Máiréad Ní Ghráda (5 February) for which the arena stage of this adaptable theatre was used for the first time, and *Is É Dúirt Polónius* by Criostóir Ó Floinn (16 May), as well as Brendan Behan's first draft of *The Hostage* (*An Giall*, 14 October) with additions from the London production by Joan Littlewood.

1969 saw a change in the direction of the theatre. In October 1968 Mac Anna retired to take up an appointment as visiting Professor and Director of Drama at Carleton College, Northfield, Minnesota. He was succeeded by Alan Simpson as from 1 December who, besides working as a freelance play director in Britain, had made a notable contribution to the Irish theatre by founding together with Carolyn Swift the little Pike Theatre in Dublin in which he was responsible for some notable productions, including the first performance in Ireland of Samuel Beckett's *Waiting for Godot*, and Brendan Behan's play of prison life, *The Quare Fellow*.

Simpson's first production for the Abbey was Oliver Goldsmith's *She Stoops to Conquer* (21 January 1969), transposed into an Irish setting. This production, together with *Borstal Boy*, was presented at the Théâtre National de L'Odéon for the Paris International Theatre Festival in the following March. The visit was described by an enthusiastic Irish critic as 'a blaze of glory'.

On 18 August Sir Tyrone Guthrie directed his first play for the Abbey, Eugene McCabe's *Swift*, dealing with the declining years of the Dean of St Patrick's. This production was made doubly important as it brought back Tanya Moiseiwitsch as a guest director after an absence of over thirty years, and the part of Swift was played by that great Irish artist, Micheál MacLiammóir.

A revival of Synge's *The Well of the Saints*, played in harness with George Fitzmaurice's fantasy, *The Dandy Dolls*, brilliantly designed by Alan Barlow, opened on 8 September. November saw the production of Thomas Murphy's most successful play to date, *A Crucial Week in the Life of a Grocer's Assistant* (10 November). 'His blend of sympathy and objective hatred have reached an almost incredible peak of perfection,' wrote the critic of the *Irish Independent*. In the Peacock there were new plays by Thomas Kilroy, *The O'Neill* (26 April), Liam Lynch, *Soldier* (26 July), Conor Farrington,

Aaron, thy Brother, (4 August) and Joe O'Donnell, *Let the Ravens Feed* (1 December), as well as Micheál Ó hAodha's adaptation of *The Weaver's Grave* by Seamus O'Kelly (6 October).

Financial problems

It might be thought that all was now well with the Abbey, but despite the vast tourist audiences that filled the theatre during the summer months, estimated at between 25,000 and 30,000 in 1968, the financial position was far from healthy. The trading loss during the year 1967/68 was £35,000, the Peacock showing a deficit of £10,000. In May 1968 the Peacock was closed except for lettings until 22 July, a tour of the Gaelteacht had to be abandoned and the future of plays in the Irish language looked decidedly dim. In August a twenty per cent cost of living increase in the salaries of players and staff forced the Board to go once again cap in hand to the Department of Finance for a supplementary grant, and, at the same time, to request a substantial increase in the annual subsidy. Its needs were partly met by a grant-in-aid to cover salary increases, but the subsidy for the following year fell far short of the Board's estimated requirement. By the end of 1969 it was evident that the current financial year would again show a substantial loss.

Artistic director

Financial worries apart, there were personnel problems to trouble the smooth running of the theatre. In September 1969 Alan Simpson, after a bare nine months in office, was informed that his contract, which expired on 30 November, would not be renewed. A brief press announcement stated that 'he did not see eye to eye with the Board'.

Simpson's departure brought to a head the question of the relationship between the Board and its artistic officer. In the Board's opinion there had been insufficient advance planning, but clearly the Directors could not have it both ways. If the members of the Board, meeting once a fortnight and some-times less frequently, wished to retain ultimate control of the

casting, choice, and scheduling of plays, it was hardly reasonable to expect their 'adviser' to make decisions that could be
thrown out at their next meeting. At the same time Simpson's
position was less influential than Mac Anna's, since he had
never worked in the Abbey prior to his appointment, and did
not enjoy the same confidence of the Directors, players and
staff as his predecessor.

His departure left a dangerous gap in the running of the
theatre with little time to advertise the post or interview candidates. On Blythe's advice Hugh Hunt was approached to fill
the vacancy.

> I consented to do so on condition that the title be changed
> to that of artistic director, since it was essential that the
> post carried with it the full duties of an executive officer
> rather than an adviser; also that I should only hold the
> post for an interim period, since I held strongly to the view
> that the leadership of the National Theatre must eventually
> be in the hands of an Irish citizen. As I was at that time
> Professor of Drama at Manchester University, the appoint-
> ment was made on a part-time basis for a two-year period,
> commencing on 1 December 1969.

At the same time the Board appointed Sean Cotter as
assistant artistic director with the responsibility to take decisions, in consultation with the manager, in matters that required immediate answers during Hunt's absence.

The first production of the new team was the Abbey's first
production of *Waiting for Godot* (1 December) with Peter
O'Toole in the part of Estragon making his first appearance
with the Abbey, teamed with Donal McCann as Vladimir.
The play was directed by Sean Cotter with designs by the distinguished artist Nora McGuinness. 'Historians may well mark
down Monday December the first as the night when the
"modern" Abbey Theatre became a truly National Theatre in
the widest sense of the word' wrote Gus Smith in the *Sunday
Independent* (7 December).

The year ended with what one critic mistakenly called 'the
first Irish musical', *Séadna* (26 December) adapted by Tomás
Mac Anna from the novel by An tAthair Peadar Ó Laoghaire,
in which members of Siamsóirí na Ríochta, a group of folk

dancers and singers from Tralee, County Kerry, under the direction of Father Pat Aherne, took a prominent part.

10

The Abbey in the Seventies

As Ireland entered the seventies two themes dominated the political scene like the scales of the blindfolded Justice that guards Dublin's law courts — Europe and the North of Ireland. In one scale lies the hope of future prosperity, in the other the fear of a future rent by civil strife.

The North

When the Abbey arose Phoenix-like from its ashes it seemed that after fifty years of partition between North and South a new dawn was breaking. In Terence O'Neill the Province of Northern Ireland possessed a Prime Minister intent on reconciling the Catholic and Protestant communities and bringing about economic co-operation with the Republic of Ireland. But centuries of conflict between the religious and politically opposed communities in the North could not speedily be ended. O'Neill's reforms, too late and too slow to win the confidence of the suppressed Catholic minority, inevitably incurred vitriolic attacks from the followers of the 'Pope-hating' Ian Paisley; more seriously O'Neill lost the support of his loyalist colleagues. His reforms coincided with a rise in unemployment and a severe housing shortage. Blatant preference given to Protestants in obtaining jobs and houses resulted in the formation of the Civil Rights Movement and later the left-wing People's Democracy of which Bernadette Devlin became a prominent member. In January 1969 a provocative march organised by the People's Democracy was savagely attacked at Burntollet by Paisley's followers. From then on, sectarian warfare escalated and by August the situation had reached a point where the Royal Ulster Constabulary – an almost entirely Protestant force – could no longer keep the peace. British troops were called in. It was now that the IRA, which up to 1970 had been rendered impotent by internal strife, began to emerge as a potent and sinister force. In December 1969–January 1970 most of the northern members of the organisation, together with a substantial number of southern traditionalists, broke away from the official body to form the Provisional Army Council. Thus were the 'Provos' born. They were supported by funds from the United States as well as, it seems, from another, more sensational source. Money voted from the Dublin government for the relief of distress in Northern Ireland appears to have been diverted, by means that are as yet obscure, to the purchase of arms. Now bullets took the place of stones and bottles.

Dawn raids in search of arms carried out by the army in Catholic areas, often with little regard for persons or property, changed the mood of the Catholic population from one of easy tolerance of the troops to one of bitter resentment. Rents and rates were withheld and the province stood on the verge of bankruptcy. From now on the IRA could count on the shelter and sympathy of many Catholic households. In the streets of Belfast and Londonderry, as well as in Dublin, Birmingham and London, bombs took the place of bullets. In August 1971 internment without trial was introduced. Meanwhile in the Republic, popular resentment against Britain rose as rumours spread of maltreatment of nationalist prisoners. On Sunday 30 January 1972 thirteen civilians were killed in Londonderry by British troops during a Civil Rights demonstration. In retaliation the British Embassy in Dublin was burnt down in the presence of an angry crowd. On 24 March the by now impotent Stormont government was suspended and direct rule from Westminster imposed. The death toll mounted against a background of political stalemate; by June 1978 1,837 civilians, soldiers and police had died in Ulster alone. Once again the ghost of Cuchulain, 'the Contorted One', stalked through the land carrying in his arms the son he had killed.

'My son, men of Ulster,' he said, 'Here you are.'
'Alas, alas!' said all Ulster.[1]

Plays of the North

As yet no playwright of the stature of O'Casey has arisen to
chronicle this decade of despair. The ever-changing situations
and sympathies as horror follows horror make dramatic comment of little more value than the glib solutions offered by
those who have neither experience nor understanding of the
age-old antagonisms in this unhappy province. Up to the time
of writing, however, eight productions have been staged in
the Abbey and Peacock bearing on the Ulster tragedy: seven
by the National Theatre and one by Belfast's Lyric Players
Theatre.

The earliest of these, *A State of Chassis,* took the form of
a satirical revue written by John D. Stewart, Eugene Waters
and Tomás Mac Anna in which personalities, political authorities and para-military organisations both north and south of
the border, not excluding the Pope himself, were duly lam-
pooned. On the opening night (Peacock Theatre, 16 September 1970) a group of guests from the North of Ireland rose in
protest following a sketch satirising Bernadette Devlin, then
serving a prison sentence. The stage was invaded and the pro-
testers addressed the audience. 'This display of the struggle
against British Imperialism in the North of Ireland is abysmally
ignorant,' shouted Eamonn McCann, Chairman of the Londonderry Labour Party. 'The caricature of Bernadette Devlin is a
disgrace . . . the people here are total hypocrites.' Looking
back in hindsight, and bearing in mind the tragedies that were
to come, the revue might seem a serious error of taste, but in
1970 the killing had not started.

On 2 April 1973 a polemic view of the Northern situation
was put forward in a one-act play, *King Herod Advises,* by
Conor Cruise O'Brien, at that time Minister for Posts and
Telegraphs. This was again presented in the Peacock with
Kevin McHugh and Ronnie Walsh in the leading parts. The
latter, in the character of a Jewish psychologist, Dr H. E.
Rodd, clearly expressed the views of the author himself.
David Nowlan in the *Irish Times* described it as 'a political
tract of considerable substance, wittily and entertainingly

written. But it is not by any stretch of the imagination a play'. Roland Jacquarello, a young recruit to the production staff, directed another play of the North presented in the Peacock, *The Night of the Rouser,* (22 August 1973) by Sean Walsh. In its portrayal of the agony of ordinary peace-loving citizens, Walsh's play, written in a rather clumsy documentary form, bears resemblance to the theme of *The Plough and the Stars.* In the leading part, 'Hughie', Bob Carlile, one of the new generation of talented Abbey actors, gave a moving performance.

In the same year two plays were presented in the Abbey both of which had London productions, Brian Friel's *The Freedom of the City* (20 February) and Wilson John Haire's *The Bloom on the Diamond Stone* (9 October). Friel's play came tantalisingly close to being a really important play about the North, combining both tragedy and humour and written with all this writer's brilliance of stage dialogue. Based on the fatal clash between troops and demonstrators in Londonderry on Sunday, 30 January 1972 ('Bloody Sunday'), the plot concerns an imaginary situation in which a group of innocent spectators take refuge in the city guildhall. Only gradually do they realise that they are being mistaken for terrorists. Instructed by loud-hailer to leave with their hands up, they do so. A burst of machine-gun shots ring out as the curtain falls. Less successful, however, is the intermingling with this essentially human story of a much condensed, impressionistic scene of the judicial enquiry into the causes of the Londonderry massacre. The play was presented two nights later at the Royal Court Theatre where it was directed by Albert Finney. In New York the play closed after nine performances, killed by the all-powerful critic of the *New York Times.* Richard Watts in the *New York Post* said the sudden collapse was 'outrageous' claiming that the play was 'a genuine masterpiece.'

John Haire's play, *The Bloom on the Diamond Stone* was also presented by arrangement with the Royal Court. Its author, a promising young dramatist from the North of Ireland, had previously won the London *Evening Standard* Drama Award for the Most Promising Playwright of the Year in 1972 with his play, *Within Two Shadows.*

Two years later Friel's second play of the North, *Volunteers* (5 March 1975) was presented at the Abbey. The plot revolves around a working party of political and civil prisoners on an archeological site in Dublin. The message of the play — Ireland's recurring agony of bloodshed — is somewhat blurred by Friel's delight in exuberant dialogue.

As guests of the Abbey the Lyric Theatre from Belfast presented Patrick Galvin's *We Do It For Love* on 15 June 1976. Making effective use of ballads to point up the tragedy and humour of the simple people of Belfast, Galvin's play, as Desmond Rushe indicated in the *Irish Independent,* has the same sort of appeal as Joan Littlewood's production of *Oh, What a Lovely War!* Ballads, too, and 'pop' music recurred in *Catchpenny Twist* (25 August 1977), 'A Charade with Music', by Stewart Parker in which the Northern situation is reflected in the story of a group of Belfast ex-school teachers trying to win fame in the music business. In their desire to take no sides in the North's conflict they write ballads for the IRA and, at the same time, comedy numbers for the loyalists. But for all their protests of non-involvement, nemesis catches up with them when, on the verge of success, a bomb explodes in a foreign airport. For some Dublin critics the play was disappointing after the acclaim the writer had won with his earlier play, *Spokesong,* first seen during the 1975 Dublin Theatre Festival. Nevertheless Stewart Parker, together with Tom MacIntyre and Wilson John Haire, is one of the small group of young writers from the North searching for new horizons in Irish drama, who hold out bright hopes for the future.

Apart from those plays that bear directly on the contemporary situation in the North, echoes of Ireland's tragedy resound in other plays that tell of the futility and waste of war, whether in Ireland or elsewhere.

A production of Brendan Behan's bawdy, compassionate vaudeville, *The Hostage* (28 April 1970), which centred on a young English soldier held as a hostage in a Dublin brothel for the life of an IRA prisoner sentenced to death in Belfast, assumed, in this its first production by the Abbey, a greater poignancy than in Joan Littlewood's 1958 production in London. A documentary play by G. P. Gallivan, *The Dáil Debate* (22 February 1971), which re-told in theatrical terms the debates on the Anglo-Irish Treaty of 1922, revived memories of the bitterly contested partition of Ireland. Above all, revivals of O'Casey's plays, more particularly *The Silver Tassie* (27 February 1972), took on a greater significance: an outcry, not only of the dead but of the mangled bodies of the living who face the future.

> Carry on, carry on to the place of pain,
> Where the surgeon spreads his aid, aid, aid,
> And we show man's wonderful work, well done,
> To the image God has made, made, made.
> And we show man's wonderful work, well done,
> To the image God has made.
> . . . .
> The power, the joy, the pull of life,
> The laugh, the blow, and the dear kiss,
> The pride and hope, the gain and loss
> Have been temper'd down to this, this, this,
> The pride and hope, the gain and loss
> Have been temper'd down to this.[2]

The Abbey and Europe

When O'Casey received the bitter news in 1928 that *The Silver Tassie* had been rejected by the Abbey, he could hardly have foreseen that forty-four years later his play would be Ireland's contribution to celebrate its entry into the European Economic Community. Perhaps, in the Elysian Fields, the sensitive soul of Brinsley Macnamara who, shaken by the accusations of blasphemy levelled against the play in 1935, had resigned from the Board, found eventual appeasement as the Catholic Archbishop of Dublin entered the Abbey to grace the first night of *The Silver Tassie* with his presence.

In the *Sunday Independent* (1 October 1972) Gus Smith wrote:

> Wherever you are, Sean — and I presume it's UP THERE — all is finally forgiven. You 'Silver Tassie', so flatly rejected by Yeats in 1928, but subsequently produced here, has now not only received the imprimatur of the Church but has been graced by the first night presence of the Arch-

bishop of Dublin. Ireland is rejoicing; your play set the Liffey alight, but more important, your theme of man's inhumanity to man and your revulsion of war is brilliantly, if tragically relevant to your darlin' country today.

On 25 May 1973 Hugh Hunt's production, with Alan Barlow's splendidly designed second act, was presented at the Théâtre Royal des Galeries in Brussels in the presence of the Irish Ambassador and representatives of the Common Market countries, having first been rapturously acclaimed at the Suomen Kansallisteattri (The Finnish National Theatre) in Helsinki (17—18 May).

Hunt's production of *The Hostage,* too, was to carry the Irish Theatre into Europe. In May 1970, under the management of Jan de Blieck, the Abbey production visited Antwerp, Zurich, Frankfurt, Cologne and the beautiful Theater an der Wien in Vienna, where Mozart's Magic Flute first appeared. In the leading parts were Angela Newman, Máire Ní Ghráinne, Brian Murray and Philip O'Flynn.

Internationalism and its effect

Not only has the Abbey extended its role through its visits to the Continent, but after an absence of over half a century it has renewed its contacts with America and has again been acclaimed in Britain.

In 1970 Tomás Mac Anna's production of *Borstal Boy* was presented in New York by an American management with Niall Toibín and Frank Grimes in the leading parts, winning the Tony Award for the Best Production Of The Year, and assuring Frank Grimes — named by twenty New York critics as the most promising actor of the year — a future career in films, television and theatre outside Ireland.

In 1976 the Abbey company was invited to take part in the American Bicentennial celebrations by presenting Mac Anna's Golden Jubilee production of *The Plough and the Stars* in New York (Brooklyn Academy, 17 November), Philadelphia (Annenburg Centre, 6 December), Washington (Hartke Theatre, 21 December), Boston (Shubert Theatre, 29 November).

A fine cast included Cyril Cusack as Fluther Good, Siobhan McKenna as Bessie Burgess, Angela Newman as Mrs Gogan, Bill Foley as Uncle Peter, John Kavanagh as The Covey, Sorcha Cusack as Nora Clitheroe, Maire O'Neill as Rosie Redmond, and Clive Geraghty as Jack Clitheroe: the sets were designed by Bronwen Casson. Clive Barnes wrote in the *New York Times:*

This anniversary, Bicentennial production, directed by Tomás Mac Anna, has been lovingly and beautifully staged. There is a sense of tradition here that enables the play to work with the conscious stylistic confidence of an opera. The actors move around one another with a friendly virtuosity, and voices blend in with one another like the cries of seagulls on Galway Bay.

Yes, the Abbey has had its bad times as well as its good times, and I have for my sins and for the pleasure of Dublin, had a few evenings that could, theatrically speaking, be better forgotten. But here they are putting their best foot forward and striding out like a national theatre.

Three performances stood out: Cyril Cusack's beautifully modulated Fluther, Angela Newman's deeply felt Mrs. Gogan, and, of course, the wonderful Siobhan Mc-Kenna, whom I have admired for 30 years now since her performance in Paul Vincent Carroll's "The White Steed", as the nobly petulant Bessie Burgess.

But all of them were fine in this bold genre study of Dublin on the eve — where so much of the action happens off stage, but the Irish rhetoric booms around a properly seedy stage so sensitively set by the designer Bronwen Casson. And so O'Casey and the Abbey (which rejected him, a decent touch of Irish irony and martyrdom) live again in Brooklyn.

Some critics, however, found the Dublin accent difficult to understand. The production was accompanied by Eamon Kelly in his evening of story-telling, *In my Father's Time,* of which Mel Gosson of the *New York Times* wrote,

With his hat sitting squarely on his head, his baggy suit looking freshly crumpled and wearing the bemused look of an ageing leprechaun, he begins to populate the stage with fathers and mothers, stone-masons and parish priests, beautiful young women and anxious young men. In the end, this is an enveloping evening. We are drawn into Mr. Kelly's world — folksy, amiably far-fetched and with a touch of vinegar.

In Britain an Abbey company was the guest of the British National Theatre at the Old Vic (3—8 August 1970) with the 1969 production of *The Well of the Saints* and *The Dandy Dolls*. Memorable performances were given by Eamon Kelly and Máire Ní Dhomhnaill as the blind couple of Synge's play, and Eamon Keane and Joan O'Hara in Fitzmaurice's fantasy. 'As weird and wondrous a double bill as anyone could wish,' wrote Eric Shorter in the *Daily Telegraph*. Michael Billington in *The Times*, while praising the performance of *The Well of the Saints*, found the rich Kerry dialect of *The Dandy Dolls* put 'a severe strain on both the understanding and the patience of the benighted English playgoer'.

Other productions seen in London of recent years were Alan Simpson's production of a posthumous play by Brendan Behan, *Richard's Cork Leg*, originally presented in the Peacock on 14 March 1972, and Patrick Mason's sensitive production of Thomas Kilroy's play *Talbot's Box* (Peacock Theatre, 13 December 1977). Both plays were presented at the Royal Court Theatre. The authorship of Behan's play needs qualification since he only completed the first act of this two-act play, the rest was stitched together, and the whole play edited, by Alan Simpson from notes left by the author with some additional material from his other writings. Its entertainment value was greatly enhanced by ballads and musical numbers supplied by The Dubliners. At the Peacock the play proved such a popular draw that it was transferred to Dublin's Olympia Theatre. When it appeared under Simpson's direction at the Royal Court, opening on 23 November 1972 with a strong contingent of Abbey players, Michael Billington in *The Times*, whilst praising the Dubliners as 'the backbone' of this 'rumbustious and joyous pub party', thought it 'perhaps unwise to translate it to the alien soil of Sloane Square'.

Kilroy's play, *Talbot's Box*, dealt in impressionist form with the secret life of one of Dublin's strangest characters, the working-class mystic Matt Talbot, chronic alcoholic turned Catholic zealot who when he died was found to have tied chains so tightly round his body that they had eaten into his flesh. The play and the production received universally good notices when it was produced at the Peacock on 13 October 1977, described by Kane Archer in the *Irish Times,* as '. . . a new play and a production that, by the highest standards, must be accounted a miracle of theatre'. Its transfer to the Royal Court in November proved less popular with Sloane Square audiences to whom this saintly masochist appeared to some as a candidate for an asylum than canonisation.

Patrick Mason, a young and valuable recruit to the production staff, also directed a revival of Shaw's *You Never can Tell* (14 April 1978). 'One of the best pieces of teamwork we've seen at the Abbey for a long time,' wrote Seamus Kelly in the *Irish Times.* This production in which Cyril Cusack appeared as 'the invaluable William' the waiter, was presented at the 1978 Malvern Festival (29 May).

Another festival production, this time for the September 1973 Edinburgh Festival, was *King Oedipus,* adapted by Yeats from Sophocles. Desmond Cave played Oedipus and Angela Newman played Jocasta in a production directed by the Greek film and stage director, Michael Cacoyannis. To those critics overseas who choose to believe that Abbey acting is a mixture of incomprehensible 'peasantry' and inarticulate Dublin 'guttery' this highly choreographed and articulated production with its stylistic and mesmeric ritual came as a revelation. Of its Dublin performance (4 April 1973) J. J. Finegan wrote in the *Evening Herald,* 'Nothing quite so stunning has been seen on the stage of the new Abbey.'

Besides being the guest of other nations the Abbey has acted as hosts to a number of overseas companies. For this, as for the engagement of many distinguished guest directors, the National Theatre Society owes a debt of gratitude to the financial assistance of the Cultural sections of several Embassies, as well as the Dublin Theatre Festival Committee. Among other overseas companies that have played in the Abbey and Peacock during the past ten years have been: The Royal Shakespeare Company, Le Tréteau de Paris, The Glasgow Citizens' Theatre, Tanz Forum from Cologne, Brücke

Theater Ensemble, the Schiller Theater from Berlin, The New London Ballet, Teatro Nacional Maria Guerrero De Madrid, The London Theatre Company, The 7.84 Company, Marcel Marceau, and the Joint Stock Company.

In addition to those guest directors from outside Ireland already mentioned, others have been Peter Luke (Hadrian VII), Colin George (*The Playboy of the Western World*), Barry Davis (*The Gathering*), Robert Gillespie (*Volunteers*), Jonathan Hales (*The Sanctuary Lamp, The Morning After Optimism* revival, *Wild Oats*), Voytek (*Desire under the Elms*), William Chappell (*The Rivals*), Max Stafford-Clark (*Tea and Sex and Shakespeare*), Eugene Lion (*Waiting for Godot* revival, *The Crucible*). Among designers from overseas have been Sean Kenny, Matias, Voytek, Christopher Baugh, Alan Barlow and Alistair Livingstone. Both Barlow and Livingstone were for a time members of the Abbey staff.

Further proof of the theatre's growing international role can be found in the considerable increase in the repertoire of plays written by non-Irish writers. This represents a major shift in the theatre's policy, although it is one that was consistently advocated by Yeats, though strongly opposed by Synge and Lady Gregory. The Abbey's international commitment does not imply the abandonment of the theatre's national character, nor that it has neglected plays by Irish writers, though plays in Irish appear less frequently on its stages. Nor has the employment of foreign artists prevented the Abbey from inviting Irish directors, designers and players from outside its organisation to partitipate in its work.

This extension of the theatre's policy has brought about a greater flexibility in the acting style; while the cross fertilisation of ideas and cultures has acted as a stimulant to the whole organisation. Confining the theatre's work to a narrow field of native drama has in the past tended to lead to a drying up of the actors' creative urge. More especially this was true once poetic drama, with its greater challenge to the actor, had effectively been killed by the demand for popular drama and 'real life' plays.

Plays and players of the seventies

Throughout the western world naturalistic drama has largely

been banished from the stage by the greater actuality of the television camera. When Irish playwrights turned from the poetic idealism of the Celtic revival to satisfy popular demand, plays about real life in settings as close to reality as the stage permits were necessary to engage the interest of an audience, the majority of whom had little desire to extend their perspective beyond their belief in a stable universe firmly guided by a powerful and all-knowing Church. Today, when doubts erode the old beliefs and truths are tangled in a confusion of conflicting ideologies, the playwright can find no certain formula to reach the hearts and minds of a rootless and fragmented society. During the Seventies the National Theatre's repertoire reflects this constant search for new forms in the plays by both foreign and native writers. Revivals from the repertoire of the Queen's and the old Abbey have, with the exception of the plays of O'Casey and Synge, seldom succeeded. *The Far Off Hills* (Peacock, 29 April 1970), *Grogan and the Ferret* (Peacock, 27 May 1970) in which Eileen Crowe made her last appearance on the stage, *The Moon in the Yellow River,* (Abbey, 30 March 1970), *The King of Friday's Men* (Abbey, 14 August 1973), *Katie Roche,* (Abbey, 2 June 1975), *The Whiteheaded Boy* (Abbey, 25 March 1974) all resulted in disappointing returns at the box-office. However, a musical, *Innish,* adapted from Robinson's *Drama at Inish* by Fergus Linehan and Jim Doherty, produced at the Abbey on 8 September 1975 under Alan Simpson's direction, proved a resounding success. Another revival, though not of an Abbey play, Boucicault's great old melodrama, *Arrah-na-Pogue or The Wicklow Wedding* (Abbey, 4 January 1972), proved almost as great a success as *The Shaughraun.* Once again drawing rounds of applause in its 'sensation scene' as the engaging rascal (but true-hearted patriot) Shaun the Post escaped from his prison cell, climbing the ivy-clad tower — that sank like the scarlet runners in the pantomime *Jack and the Beanstalk* — to rescue Arrah Meelish as she was about to be hurled from the summit by the villainous informer, Michael Feeny. The production owed much to Bronwen Casson's designs and to performances of great charm by Bob Carlile and Dearbhla Molloy.

Escapist drama has its rightful place in the theatre, but it is

upon new plays and new playwrights that a theatre's enduring importance must depend. Here the names of some dozen
or more contemporary playwrights stand out as an earnest of
the continuing health of Irish drama: Edna O'Brien, perhaps
more successful as a novelist, but whose play *The Gathering,*
despite a vicious press reception, grossed the highest week's
box-office receipts of any play in the new Abbey's history,
playing to 105 per cent of the theatre's normal capacity;
Wesley Burrowes, twice winner of the Irish Life play competition; Crióstoir Ó Floinn, Pádraig Ó Giollagáin and Eoghan
Ó Tuairisc, three of the sadly few writers searching for new
ways to give life to performances in the Irish language; Brian
Friel, Thomas Kilroy and Hugh Leonard, already established
as playwrights overseas; Thomas Murphy, now a member of
the Board of Directors and Eugene McCabe, one of the older
generation. To evaluate their plays is outside the function of
this history; nor is it proposed to describe all the plays, new
and old, presented during the past seven years; to do so would
weary the reader and do scant justice to the playwrights. No
more will be attempted than to dwell briefly on those plays
that proved to be highlights in the theatre's repertoire.

1970. This was a disappointing year for the Abbey; no new
plays opened on its main stage and revivals were generally
unsuccessful at the box-office. Peter Luke's adaptation of
Frederick Rolfe's story, *Hadrian VII* (20 January), a spectacular production directed by Luke himself, proved a *tour
de force* for Cyril Cusack but failed to live up to box-office
expectations, despite the success the play had achieved in
London and New York. After the unexpected failure of *The
Moon in the Yellow River, The Hostage* did something to
retrieve the Abbey's fortunes, but neither Eugene McCabe's
revised version of *The King of the Castle* (14 September), a
play that was originally performed at the Gaiety in 1964, nor
Chekhov's *The Seagull* (20 October) succeeded in filling the
theatre. The latter was directed by Hilton Edwards with costumes designed by Micheál Mac Liammóir, Angela Newman
giving a fine performance as Madame Arkardina. Even Shelah
Richard's authentic production of *The Plough and the Stars*
(1 December), set on a revolving stage by Patrick Scott, failed

to live up to the play's reputation for filling the theatre. In fact, it was the Peacock that took such public limelight as there was, opening the year with Wesley Burrowes's prize-winning play, *The Becauseway* (5 January), 'a weird and wonderful combination of Beckett, *Everyman* and Lewis Carroll,' as one critic described it. This was followed by the equally weird and wonderful *At Swim Two Birds* (12 February), a dramatisation of the novel by Flann Ó Brien, alias Myles na gCopaleen. Tomás Mac Anna, back from America, took over as the director of Peacock productions in August and after filling the theatre to capacity with the revue, *A State of Chassis* – there is of course nothing to equal a riot in drawing audiences to the National Theatre – he directed an Irish translation of Micheál Mac Liammóir's *The Mountains look Different* (*Tá Crut Nua Ar Na Sléibhte*) which opened on 21 October to be followed by a fine production of *The Plebians Rehearse the Uprising* (2 December), by Gunter Grass and Ralph Manheim.

1971. The highlight at the Abbey in 1971 was Thomas Murphy's play, *The Morning after Optimism* (15 March), presented for the Dublin Theatre Festival (held that year in the spring as opposed to the autumn), where it became a centre of controversy. Set in an imaginary forest – one of Bronwen Casson's most imaginative designs – this fascinating and, for some, puzzling enigma of dream and reality unfolds like the movements of a vast symphony as a fairy-tale Prince and a virginal nymph intertwine their lives with a ponce and a whore, the latter parts brilliantly played by Colin Blakely and Eithne Dunne. The year 1971 marked the centenary of Synge's birth. To celebrate the occasion the National Theatre presented *The Playboy of the Western World* (19 April), *Riders to the Sea* and *The Tinker's Wedding* (26 April) on the Abbey stage, and *Deirdre of the Sorrows* (30 March) on the stage of the Peacock. *The Playboy,* directed by Colin George and designed by Brian Collins, was set on a circular platform against a background of 'blown up' newspaper cuttings of the riots in Dublin and America that accompanied the original production. In *Riders to the Sea* Marie Kean played the part of the bereaved Maurya with an austere dignity drained of tears, deliberately abstaining from the sing-song that too often accompanies the final lament. Sean Cotter's production of *The Tinker's Wedding* marked the first appearance of the play on the Abbey stage. Completed at the end of 1907, both Synge and Yeats considered that after the *Playboy* riots — 'We think it too dangerous to put on in the Abbey.' Máire Ní Dhomnhaill, Aideen O'Kelly, Desmond Cave and Patrick Layde made up an impressive cast. On 26 September Shakespeare returned to the Abbey stage after an absence of more than thirty years. *Macbeth,* proverbially doomed to disaster, brought no worse catastrophe than an injured knee to Macduff. Ray MacAnally returned to the Abbey to give a stirring performance in the name part, accompanied by Angela Newman as a fine Lady Macbeth. Press opinions varied — a not unusual state of affairs in Dublin.

> Poor Mr Hunt, he must know it now, when he attempts to produce Shakespeare with the Abbey company he is like a potter who has handled peat instead of clay with which to mould his design. . . . This is not the worst Macbeth I've ever seen. No, that crime was emitted in the old Abbey in 1934 when the witches were trees and the rest of the cast tied up in sacking as if ready for loading at the North Wall.
>
> Mary Manning (*Hibernia*)

> The Abbey *Macbeth* is a triumph for all involved. Any lingering fears that the company generally might not be quite ready for high Shakespearian tragedy were dispelled within minutes of the rise of the curtain.
>
> J. J. Finegan (*Evening Herald*)

1972. Following *Arrah na Pogue* and a new play by two American dramatists, *The Prisoner of the Crown* (15 February), dealing with the trial of Roger Casement, finely played by John Kavanagh, Thomas Murphy's new play, *The White House,* with Dan O'Herlihy in the leading part, opened on 20 March directed by Vincent Dowling who succeeded Mac Anna as director of plays in the Peacock. Sean Cotter's production of *The Iceman Cometh* by Eugene O'Neill (3 May) had an appropriately sleazy set by the Polish designer, Voytek. In *The Silver Tassie* Patrick Laffan gave one of his finest performances as the crippled footballer Harry Heegan. O'Casey's play was followed by Brian Friel's most successful play, *Philadelphia Here I Come!* (30 October) originally produced at the Gaiety Theatre for the Dublin Theatre Festival by Hilton Edwards and subsequently a considerable success in the United States. In the Peacock after the success of *Richard's Cork Leg,* Heno Magee's first play *Hatchet* (2 May), set in the Dublin slums, received encouraging notices. Mary Manning in *Hibernia* wrote: '*Hatchet* is an exciting, disturbing, frightening play. The author has a keen ear for dialogue. He has wit and produces flesh and blood, mostly blood-stained characters.' Tom MacIntyre's *Eye Winker Tom Tinker* (8 August), directed by Leila Doolan, and Pádraig Ó Giollágain's *Fleadh* (25 September), directed by Eamon Kelly, were two plays by new playwrights of considerable promise.

1973. Following Michael Cacoyannis's production of *King Oedipus,* another guest director was T. P. McKenna who returned to the Abbey to direct Tom Kilroy's *The Death and Resurrection of Mr. Roche* (8 May). Sean Kenny who had been invited to direct and design a revival of M. J. Molloy's *The King of Friday's Men,* his first work for the Abbey, died a bare two months before the scheduled date of production — a sad loss to the stage of one of the finest contemporary designers. The production, which opened on 14 August, was taken over by Lelia Doolan using Kenny's impressive sets. A rollicking nouveau art production of *The Importance of Being Earnest* opened on 13 September — more Feydeau than Wilde — directed and designed by Alan Barlow who in the previous year had shown himself to be a sensitive director as well as a brilliant designer with his production of Harold Pinter's *Old Times* (6 December 1972). The year ended with a highly successful production by Alan Simpson of *The Scatterin'* (4 December) by James McKenna, a rock'n roll musical of the 1950s Teddy Boy period, originally presented at the Dublin Theatre Festival in 1964.

In the Peacock there was another musical — this time in Irish — *Johnny Orfeo* (27 April) by Pádraig Ó Giollágain, directed by Leila Doolan and Colm Ó Bríain. In Irish, too, was Criostóir Ó Floinn's *Mise Raifteirí An File* (22 October), a play about the blind poet Raftery.

1974. In the Abbey, Bertolt Brecht's satire on the ruthless rise of the Nazi party to power, *The Resistible Rise of Arturo Ui* in which Desmond Cave excelled as the Hitler figure, opened on 14 January. Edna O'Brien's play *The Gathering* (9 October) gave Geoffrey Golden, one of the most powerful Abbey actors, a leading part, and in Thomas Murphy's adaptation of Oliver Goldsmith's *The Vicar of Wakefield* Cyril Cusack returned to play Dr Primrose: 'A fully rounded, lovable and indeed credible character,' wrote Desmond Rushe in the *Irish Independent*. In the Peacock where Joe Dowling took over the direction of plays, there was a very full programme of lunch time and late night performances, including a number of foreign plays.

1975. Tomás Mac Anna who had returned as artistic director in 1974, had long cherished the hope that the time would come when O'Casey's later plays would find a receptive audience in Dublin. In 1975 he directed *Purple Dust* in the Abbey, opening on 30 January, and in the Peacock two short plays *Figuro in the Night* and *The Moon Shines on Kylenamoe* (14 August). In his review of *Purple Dust,* Desmond Rushe wrote, 'not a great play but great fun'. Certainly the audience found it so. This could hardly be said to apply to Thomas Murphy's play, *The Sanctuary Lamp* (6 October), the theatre's main contribution to the Dublin Theatre Festival, which in Gus Smith's words 'sparked off more heated controversy among Abbey audiences than I've seen for two decades', (*Sunday Independent,* 12 October). David Nowlan in the *Irish Times* considered it to be 'the most anti-clerical play ever staged by Ireland's National Theatre: which makes it politically important,' adding 'it is a fine – albeit exquisitely difficult – play'. Murphy's play is a powerful example of how far public opinion has changed in Ireland. Despite its outspoken, if not blasphemous, language the play did no more than cause a few members of the audience to leave the theatre, more often because they were unable to follow what the play was about than because of religious scruples. Among the play's powerful supporters was the President of the Republic, Cearbhall Ó Dalaigh, who in a debate on the play following the performance on 10 October declared it to be 'a play that ranks in the first three of this theatre'. There are some who would find it hard to accept that Murphy's play can claim equality with the plays of Synge and O'Casey, but it is certainly one of the most important plays produced in the new Abbey. *The Sanctuary Lamp* was directed by the English director Jonathan Hales, drawing out fine perform- ances from Geoffrey Golden, John Kavanagh and Bernadette Shortt. Particularly impressive was Bronwen Casson's setting of the church interior.

In the Peacock Clive Geraghty gave an impressive per- formance as Malvolio in *Twelfth Night* (10 March), Joe Dowling's first production of a Shakespeare play, and Sorcha Cusack, playing for the first time with an Abbey company, appeared in Patrick Laffan's production of *A Doll's House* (28 April), the theatre's gesture to International Women's Year. The summer programme included a one-man show by the master of story-telling, Eamon Kelly, *In my Father's Time* (23 June).

1976. Sorcha Cusack appeared again this time on the Abbey stage as Sister Jeanne of the Angels, the possessed nun, in a production of John Whiting's play *The Devils* (4 February), in which John Kavanagh played the condemned priest, Grandier. Directed by Mac Anna the play had a particularly impressive set designed by Wendy Shea. Among other pro- ductions were the Golden Jubilee production of *The Plough and the Stars,* destined for America, and two important new plays, Thomas Kilroy's *Tea and Sex and Shakespeare* (6 October) and Hugh Leonard's *Time Was* (17 December). Critics offered diametrically opposed views of Kilroy's play in which Donal McCann and Aideen O'Kelly played the lead- ing parts, but for John Barber of the *Daily Telegraph* 'it was the best play I have seen at the Festival'. The press was equally divided regarding the merits of Leonard's play, a witty saire on the effects of nostalgia in which the romanticised memories of favourite film stars brings a bevy of unwanted guests to a middle-class household when dreams become reality, and characters from old movies including a 'Beau Geste' Legion- naire, some shadowy Arabs, a 1949 street-walker and finally Laurel and Hardy invade their drawing-room. Godfrey Quigley and Kate Flynn appeared as the married couple and Raymond Hardie was an impressive Legionnaire, but it was May Cluskey as the ageing tart who won the critical acclaim.

In the Peacock Joe Dowling directed *Much Ado about Nothing* (24 March) with John Kavanagh as Benedick and Sorcha Cusack as Beatrice, before leaving to take up an appointment as artistic director of the recently formed Irish Theatre Company.[3] He was succeeded by Patrick Laffan as director of the Peacock plays. Kate Flynn gave a memorable performance as Hedda Gabler in Laffan's production of Ibsen's play which opened on 10 May. During the summer recess Eamon Kelly once again held audiences spell-bound with another one-man show of story telling, *Bless Me, Father . . .* (17 June). In August there were performances of the much neglected George Fitzmaurice's plays, *The Pie Dish* and *The Enchanted Land*.

1977. In the Abbey Brian Friel's play *Living Quarters* with Ray MacAnally as guest artist received rough treatment from the critics when it opened on 24 March, but its revival in October for the Theatre Festival brought at least one critic, David Nowlan, to question the earlier verdicts of his colleagues, finding it 'a brave experiment which offers a marginally new form to the theatre, for some at least the experiment proved successful. I am happy to number myself among those who found it so' (*Irish Times*, 4 October).

The Emperor of Ice-Cream by Bill Morrison, based on the novel by Brian Moore, both hailing from the North of Ireland, opened on 28 April. The play was first produced on radio in 1975. After a farcical beginning using the easy target of Home Guard practice during the Second World War, the play culminates in the bombing of Belfast and a horrific last scene in the city morgue, during the course of which a young man — the central pivot of the play — discovers a purpose in life. The part was played with considerable skill by a new young actor, Stephen Brennan.

Mac Anna was responsible for a second assault upon the last of O'Casey's full-length plays, *Cock-a-doodle Dandy*, which the playwright claimed to be his favourite. Most of the critics, though not all, failed to see any merits in this 'curious

concoction distilled by O'Casey from remote and slightly
suspect reports from an Ireland he had left many years before' (Seamus Kelly, *Irish Times*). 'In preaching his true faith
O'Casey is guilty of overkill. Much of the play is codswallop
– or is that cockswallop?' (Frances O'Rourke, *Sunday Press*).
In replying to the hostile review in the *Irish Times,* William
C. Ryan, aged 16 from New York, replied 'Nonsense! Sean
O'Casey's masterwork deserves the highest credit from both
the critic and the audience. I have no doubt that if the play
were run on Broadway with the same excellent cast it would
be a smashing success.' While David Krause, O'Casey's fore-
most biographer, filled two columns in his letter to the editor
of the *Irish Times* (13 August) expressing his concern about
'journalistic responsibility', 'critical prejudice and literary
fairness in both of which areas your reviewer's prejudice over-
comes his good sense'. He reminded his readers that O'Casey
was following

> the classic examples of Aristophanes, Molière and Swift
> in using laughter to attack the 'holy' puritanism and
> materialism of Ireland's not so distant past, a past that
> some would conveniently like to forget . . . The holy de
> Valeran Ireland of thou-shalt-nots is indeed one of O'Casey's
> satiric targets in this alternately merry and dark comedy,
> which is an imaginative attempt to laugh at all who wanted
> to turn the whole country into a monastery of strict ob-
> servance.

Later in the year came the Abbey's production of Edna
O'Brien's *A Pagan Place,* originally produced in London in
1972. The play opened on 17 November to be met with the
usual discordant and occasionally vitriolic notices that this
fine Irish novelist seems to attract from her compatriots;
though John Finegan in the *Evening Herald* found it 'a compassionate and, in the final moments particularly, a very
moving play'.

In the Peacock in addition to Stewart Parker's *Catchpenny
Twist* and Tom Kilroy's *Talbot's Box,* there were two produc-
tions written by Eoghan Ó Tuairisc, *Aisling Mhic Artain* (4
October), an extravaganza with music by Tom Cullivan, and
Oisín (29 December), a bilingual pantomime with lyrics by

Tomás Mac Anna. The *Irish Times* critic found the plot of the former — the wandering of a monk in a future Ireland where religion has been abolished, 'an ideal vehicle for Ó Tuairisc's pungent wit and provocative social comment'. Both Edward Golden's production and Maebh Browne's sets were particularly praised, as were the performances of some of the best of the National Theatre's Irish-speaking players, Micheál Ó Bríain, Peadar Lamb, Máire O'Neill and Máire Ní Ghráinne. Earlier in May Patrick Mason, who had directed Edna O'Brien's play on the Abbey stage, directed Tom MacIntyre's second play to be produced by the National Theatre, *Find The Lady*, (9 May). In his review in the *Irish Times* David Nowlan wrote,

> Of all Irish playwrights, Tom MacIntyre has probably done more to explore the new means of dramatic communication . . . In his latest, "Find The Lady", which received its first presentation last night in the Peacock Theatre, all forms are used: song, dance, mime, dialogue, wisecrack and even physical exposure, all in the cause of giving us the author's interpolation of the Salome story. It makes clear that Mr. Mac Intyre now has few equals in knowing how to say something in the theatre and that he can be very funny and entertaining in the process.

In the Peacock too, Patrick Mason directed Shaw's *Mrs. Warren's Profession* (27 July) in which Kate Flynn in the part of Mrs Warren repeated the success she had made in *Hedda Gabler*.

1978. The year brought an epic production of O'Casey's Communist drama, *The Star Turns Red* (27 January). In this example of the playwright's later work there could be no questions raised of critical prejudice. Ned Chaillet in *The Times* wrote:

> 'The Star Turns Red' is romantic and agitational, a theatrical work that is strengthened by its sense of conviction and refusal to give voice to the opposition. Respect for its art has spared the play the attacks one might have expected in Dublin, and confirmed the Abbey's decision to present all O'Casey's plays. Even James Agate once fell to praising the

play, and a major production in London would surprise many critics. . . . It is a masterwork of theatricality, remarkable in its ability to sustain surprise and impressive in its effective use of symbolism.

While John Finegan in the *Evening Herald* voiced the reaction of the majority of O'Casey's critics, 'The Star Turns Red emerged, to the astonishment of the critics, as one of the best of O'Casey's plays written in exile'. Tomás Mac Anna, whose last production this was as the theatre's artistic director, was finally justified in his hopes of reversing the general belief that O'Casey's later plays were of little dramatic value.

Arthur Miller's play *The Crucible,* portraying the seventeenth-century witch-hunt at Salem, New England, with its overtones of the hysterical accusations of un-American activities unleashed by Senator Joe McCarthy in the fifties — a past that some Americans would conveniently like to forget — opened on 10 March. Fine performances were given by Angela Newman and Patrick Laffan as Elizabeth and John Proctor, but the American director, Eugene Lion, came in for some rough criticism for what was felt to be a slow and ponderous production.

In the Peacock the year 1978 opened with yet another of Eamon Kelly's one-man entertainments of story-telling, *The Rub of a Relic* (30 January), which had first played to capacity houses at the Everyman Playhouse, Cork. It was followed on 12 March by a stylish production in the round of Tony Harrison's adaptation of Molière's *Le Misanthrope,* directed by Patrick Mason, with Clive Geraghty giving 'a brilliant and virile' interpretation of Alceste.

On 19 May *Stephen D,* Hugh Leonard's adaptation of Joyce's *A Portrait of the Artist as a Young Man* and *Stephen Hero,* opened in the Abbey, directed by the newly appointed artistic director, Joe Dowling. The leading part was played by one of the new generation of Irish actors, Barry McGovern. For most critics this revival did not live up to their memories of the excitement engendered by the original production at the Gate by Jim Fitzgerald in 1962, but time often blurs memories and today Joyce's defiant rejection of faith and fatherland can no longer shock an Ireland where nationalism is becoming a dirty word and faith has for many been replaced by indifference.

As part of its contribution to the 1978 Dublin Theatre Festival, the Abbey presented a play that neither time nor the dulling of our senses by violence and spiritual torpor can rob of its impact. Chekhov's *Uncle Vanya* (4 October) belongs to the universal theatre — the theatre of Sophocles, Shakespeare, Molière and Synge — that lifts us above the common realities into the higher reality of the human heart. Six weeks' rehearsal under the guidance of V. B. Monakhov, a guest director from the Maly Theatre, Moscow, drew forth some deeply felt performances, notably from Cyril Cusack as Vanya, Clive Geraghty as Astrov, and Bill Foley as Professor Serebriakhov; but it was as a team the players impressed: Peadar Lamb, Kathleen Barrington and May Cluskey bearing out Stanislavsky's dictum that 'there are no such things as small parts'. David Nowlan wrote in the *Irish Times:*

> Probably the most technically accomplished production seen at the Abbey for a decade. Sound, music and light are wed to the action and Bronwen Casson's sets of towering fretwork and her perfect costume designs are a total delight. As is the whole evening. Better, it is a triumph.

Less successful was the Japanese director, Hideo Kanze, in his production of two of Yeats's plays for dancers, *At the Hawk's Well* and *The Only Jealousy of Emer* (Peacock Theatre, 30 November). Kanze, himself honoured as 'a national treasure' whose family have been associated with the Noh theatre since its foundation in the fourteenth century, is a leading Noh actor as well as an experienced director of western plays. But the highly technical art of Noh acting cannot be mastered by western actors in some six weeks' rehearsal, and attempts to emphasise the Noh influence in Yeats's plays is of little more than academic interest. 'Entertainment — Noh! Worthwhile and admirable experiment — Yesh!' was the somewhat facetious comment of the *Irish Times* critic.

A revival of Heno Magee's *Hatchet* (23 November) reinforced earlier criticisms that the play is one of the best new plays of recent years in its exposure of violence in contemporary urban life, unhappily more relevant in 1978 than it was six years before. Once again John Kavanagh brought a quiet dynamism to his performance in the leading part that earned general praise; notable, too, were Maureen Toal as Mrs Bailey and Philip O'Flynn as Joey.

The year ended with *Táinbócú* (1 January 1979) a bilingual pantomime based on the ancient legend of the Táin by Tomás Mac Anna and Eoghan Ó Tuairisc, in the Peacock, and Carlo Goldoni's *A Servant of Two Masters* (21 December) in the Abbey. David Nowlan wrote in the *Irish Times:* 'Lever the children off their new bicycles, lift them from their roller skates, disengage them from the dolls, sweep them from under the Christmas tree, and take them forthwith to the Abbey Theatre.'

Literary editor

In 1974 the Board accepted a recommendation by a sub-committee of shareholders and Board members to appoint a literary editor. The holder of this post was to be a playwright of established reputation who would be able to advise and encourage new writers, and to seek new plays from those who had already had plays produced. As often happens at the Abbey when new appointments are made, good intentions become dissipated by half-hearted implementation. The new post was to be offered to established playwrights on a part-time basis, as a one year appointment, the occupant to have no voting power in the acceptance or rejection of scripts. In such circumstances the chances of an organic and developing policy were unlikely to ensue. The first literary editor to be appointed was the doyen of Irish playwrights, Denis Johnston. His appointment commenced on 1 August 1975. Unfortunately he left before the end of his year in office to take up a lecturing commitment in the United States. His successors, Hugh Leonard and Tom Kilroy, were unable to stay long enough to make any major contribution to what should inevitably be a long-term investment. In November 1978 the Board accepted the advice of Kilroy and others that the literary editor must be a full-time and adequately paid member of the theatre's staff, and that it was neither necessary nor perhaps desirable that this post should be occupied by a working dramatist.

Inflation

The decade had not reached its second half before a third theme entered upon the political scene that was to affect the development of the Abbey closely, no less than the country itself.

Despite the hopes that entry into the Common Market would bring greater prosperity, the Irish economy proved to be no exception to the mounting spiral of cost and wage increases that affected all countries in Western Europe and America during the seventies. The greater need for modernisation in agriculture and industry, and for improvement in social services and wage structures, caused inflation to rise more steeply in Ireland than in most other European countries. The overflow of violence from the North of Ireland, involving bomb scares (and sometimes bombs) in Dublin itself, put an additional strain on business houses in the city. Between 1973 and 1975 the Abbey in particular suffered from a number of false alarms that bombs had been placed in the auditorium or foyers, causing the evacuation of the building, and occasionally the abandonment of performances with heavy penalties to the box-office. Nor was the situation helped by the police precautions of restricting the parking of cars in the centre of the city.

Theatres are at a disadvantage compared with most other businesses in the speed in which they can adjust prices to meet rising costs. Between 1973 and 1974 with inflation averaging 20% (16.2% in 1973, 24.5% in 1975) no change was made in seat prices.[4] In May 1974 the Board, faced with an overdraft of £117,000, set about the painful process of cutting back expenditure. The international seasons and external tours were suspended, production costs cut back, the Young Abbey closed down, the construction of a new green-room for the actors and the adaptation of the existing green-room to provide improved box-office facilities for both theatres were deferred,[5] and the continuity of plays in the Peacock, including the production of plays in Irish, could no longer be guaranteed. To some extent the situation was alleviated by a substantial increase in the government's subsidy for the following year, though a proportion of this was ear-marked for the purpose of reducing the overdraft.[6] In

1976, however, the tide of the theatre's financial problems began to turn. Despite the poor output of new plays in the Abbey, there was an audience attendance of 170,000 (75% of capacity) while the Peacock achieved a record audience attendance of 33,395 (94% of capacity).

However, a further anxiety lay ahead. In October 1973 the Dáil approved a Bill channelling all future grants to theatrical enterprises through the Arts Council. This radical change in the Abbey's relationship with the government commenced on 1 January 1976. Until 1973 the Irish Arts Council, established in 1951, was a modestly endowed organisation distributing such grants as it received from the Department of Finance to literature, the visual arts, music and a few amateur organisations. Under its new constitution the Council was enlarged and its funds greatly increased to meet its considerably greater commitments. Apart from the Abbey, the Council's new theatrical commitments consisted of such already established organisations as the Gate Theatre, the Dublin Theatre Festival, the Irish Ballet Company and the Irish Theatre Company. Of these, the National Theatre was by far the largest recipient of public funds, its annual subsidy being roughly equal to the aggregate of the grants made to the other four companies. Although these grants were channelled through the Department of Finance, henceforth it was the Arts Council that was to be responsible for deciding how much money the Abbey was to receive within the context of its own budget and in relation to the requirements of other theatrical and artistic organisations for whose financial welfare its newly appointed members were responsible.

In 1977, the first year that the Council was in full command of budgetary allocations to its new clients, national wage awards and ever increasing inflationary trends were to threaten this relationship at the outset. The Council's offer of £426,000 for the financial year 1977—78 was considered to be a reduction in real terms of the grant for the previous year. Failing a satisfactory solution, the Board threatened to refuse to implement the national wage award increases. The Players' and Staff Councils not unnaturally resented being used as pawns in the struggle between the theatre and the Arts Council, and their Unions threatened industrial action if the Labour Court ruled that the increases must be paid. Fortunately, peace was restored by the Council's offer to cover the cost of the wage increases, but clearly time and tolerant understanding on both sides are required before fears can be allayed, and a satisfactory working liaison established.

Players' contracts

In many ways the Abbey's contractual arrangements with its players are unique in comparison with theatrical employment in Britain and America. Under the Andrews Award of 1964 the terms of employment allowed for written agreements covering permanent employment for players after a three-year probationary period. Permanency also applies to other categories of staff, including designers, and all members benefit from the annual wage awards linked to cost of living increases as well as a pension scheme.

Permanency for the actor can, however, have its disadvantages. Denied the stimulus of competition the actor can become complacent in his attitude to his work, losing the will to succeed that is a vital part of his creative process. Moreover, in a small country where opportunities are limited to observe and benefit from the work and ideas of others, permanency can lead to artistic stagnation.

In February 1974 a sub-committee of shareholders and Directors, set up to examine artistic policy and the role of the National Theatre in the community, recommended that in future permanent contracts should be discontinued; however the principle of permanency still remains and in special circumstances, long service for instance, permanent appointments are still available.[7]

Training the actor

In most countries in which theatre flourishes today it is generally accepted that at least three years full-time training are required before an actor enters the professional stage. Students of acting are normally eligible for grants to cover living costs and training fees on the same basis as for other educational establishments. These facilities are not as yet available in the Irish Republic. Consequently schools of acting have either to limit full-time training to those few who can support themselves or whose parents are able to do so, or to provide evening classes for a wider section of potential talent whose circumstances require them to earn their living during the daytime. A young actor whose training is limited in this way finds himself at a disadvantage compared with stage aspirants in Britain where a far more comprehensive form of training is provided.

The Abbey School of Acting, revived under Dermody's direction in 1967, laboured under these and other limitations. It had no premises of its own; classes had to take place wherever space was not required for more urgent purposes; the teaching staff was largely drawn from members of the company whose availability depended on their work in the theatre itself, while continuity of class work was often interrupted by the employment of students in crowd scenes in one or other of the two theatres. It can be argued that the Fays and others managed to train Irish actors in similar conditions. Time, however, and Actors Equity have wrought their changes. The old system by which an actor could gain experience as an unpaid apprentice no longer applies, and the gulf between the amateur and the professional has perceptibly widened.

In 1970 the School was closed down following a number of complaints at the irregularity of classes. Apprentice workshops were instituted, offering actors and a selected number of ex-students classes in improvisation, speech, movement, physical training and experience of plays in Irish. For these classes specialist teachers from Britain as well as Ireland were employed, no fees were charged, and no claim was made that the workshops could be regarded as a full training for a stage career. Like other activities, the workshops eventually had to close down in the general cut backs in expenditure.[8]

The Young Abbey

Among the casualties of the 1974 cutbacks was the Young Abbey, an experiment in theatre-in-education that evolved out of the apprentice workshops, largely through the enthusiasm of the younger actors. The following account of this short-lived but valuable contribution to the wider field of theatre is supplied by Joe Dowling who became its first director.

The birth of the Young Abbey, Ireland's first 'Theatre-in-Education' group, in 1970 came about because the then Artistic Director of the theatre, Hugh Hunt, wanted to involve the theatre more closely with the community. It happened that at that time there was a new generation of Abbey actors, many of whom were anxious to explore different methods and approaches to their art. The main information and research was done on a short visit to the Octagon Theatre, Bolton, and to the Liverpool Playhouse, where successful groups were already in operation.

Armed with the advice of the British groups, the Young Abbey set about developing a programme suitable for Irish children, involving both a formal theatre presentation and improvised drama with children as participants. This mixture of theatre and creative drama was to form the basis of most of the group's subsequent work. Each programme of about an hour's duration took place in the school hall or classroom and dealt with a specific subject with rehearsed pieces performed by the actors, intermingled with carefully chosen improvisations in which the children acted out aspects of the subject and gained further information from the actors before and after the improvisations. Among the early themes was the 1916 Rising, containing extracts from *The Plough and the Stars* and Denis Johnston's play, *The Scythe and the Sunset,* with improvisations by the children outlining the events of Easter Week 1916; another was based on Synge's visits to the Aran Islands and included a production of *Riders to the Sea.*

At first schools needed some persuasion to accept visits from the group, but as time went on the popularity of the programmes resulted in more bookings than this part-time group was able to accept. Between 1970 and 1972 the group consisted of members of the Abbey company or graduates of the School of Acting. As time went on it was clear it would be necessary to form a full-time group whose members would not have to fit in their work between rehearsing with the Abbey company in the morning and performing in the evening. To do this it was estimated that an annual subsidy of £15,000 would be required from the funds of the Abbey.

The new group of which John McArdle became the director was contracted in September 1972. The work of the Young Abbey was by this time divided between visits to the schools and children's plays presented annually in the Peacock, and continued successfully on this basis until 1974 when, in the face of general cut backs in expenditure, the Board of Directors decided that it could no longer continue its support. An appeal to the Department of Education for assistance proved of no avail and in May of that year the Young Abbey gave its last performance.

This attempt to widen the theatre's perspectives was not without its results so far as the cause of theatre-in-education was concerned. In October 1975 Senator Gemma Hussey, at that time a member of the Abbey Board, together with Kathleen Barrington and Joe Dowling, founded Team Educational Theatre Limited, initially supported by a £3,000 grant from the Irish Banks Standing Committee and later by grants from the Arts Council and Dublin Corporation.

The Board and its executive officers

When Blythe's reign as managing director ended in 1967 it was inevitable that it would take time to adjust the relations between the Board and its executive officers, and to define the relative duties and responsibilities between the officers themselves.

In the spring of 1970 signs of disagreement arose between the manager and secretary concerning the division of their functions. The Board's decision to take a tighter hold on the running of the theatre by instituting weekly Board Meetings produced a threatened resignation from the manager. In July the Board asked Hunt to prepare a memorandum setting forth his views on the responsibilities of the artistic director and the relationship between this office and that of the manager. Hunt's proposals contained two basic principles:

one, that while the Board was responsible for laying down the general policy of the theatre, the Artistic Director and the manager must be given full responsibility for its implementation; two, that the artistic director and the manager should have equal status as the Board's chief executive officers, and that, while their functions were separate, all decisions that affected their mutual spheres of responsibility should be arrived at jointly. These principles were accepted with the proviso that the Board retained the right to veto its officers' plans and proposals. The manager pointed out that equal status with the artistic director would not apply if in the future the Board reverted to the principle of appointing an artistic adviser.

However, to state a platitude, memoranda may lay down principles, but they cannot dictate personalities. In March of the following year it was clear that O'Kelly was finding it hard to operate within the existing framework. His request to be appointed as a member of the Board itself was not accepted and in April 1971 he resigned. In the following August the secretary, John Slemon, was appointed to succeed him, combining the offices of secretary and manager. Slemon, an extremely able accountant, had had little experience of dealing with the sometimes excitable artistic temperament, but his skill in handling the theatre's relations with government and other official bodies and his solid and fair-minded qualities as an administrator quickly won the confidence of the Board and the respect of the players.

In September 1970 Hunt attempted to provide the Peacock with a more clearly defined identity and a degree of administrative independence by appointing Tomás Mac Anna, now returned from the University of Minnesota, as director of Peacock productions with Joe Dowling as his administrative assistant. Mac Anna's adventurous season of documentary drama, including lunch-time and late-night performances, as well as 'pop' concerts, might well have built up a younger and progressively minded audience, but it takes time as well as policy to overcome youthful prejudice against establishment theatres, and for both liberal funds are needed. In the early seventies the Abbey lacked the funds for lengthy experiment.

In April 1971 Vincent Dowling, who as a leading player had shown his abilities as a director, succeeded Sean Cotter as assistant artistic director, a post he occupied until Hunt's two years of office ended in December of that year.

The appointment of Leila Doolan, whose disagreement with, and departure from, Radio Telefís Eireann had been the cause of considerable controversy in the past, as Hunt's successor created a stir among those critics who regarded the Abbey as an old-fashioned, bourgeois institution managed by a Board of Directors whose average age was well over seventy. Lelia approached her task with caution, well aware of her reputation as a critic of the Abbey's conservatism and of her lack of experience as a theatre director. At a press conference in December 1971 she expressed her desire to encourage actors to take a broader view of theatre, 'not merely confined to acting but taking into account the whole range of theatre, not just as business but as a social institution, as an expression of literature, scenic art, musical art and thought.'

In this she was clearly right. During the sixties there had grown up a far wider conception of the theatre's role in society than that of an entertainment business, cultural or otherwise. Theatre, more particularly in its subsidised form, was proving a valuable instrument of civic and national prestige, and a powerful adjunct to the tourist industry. In universities and schools the study of theatre had become recognised as an educational medium. In cellars and attics, in streets and parks, political theatre, community theatre, young people's theatre and children's theatre were breaking down the barriers between actors and audience. The concept of the actor, too, was changing. He was no longer regarded as standing aloof from society, as a glamorous figure whose way of life set him apart from his fellow citizens. The modern actor sees himself as a worker within the community, concerned with economic, political and social problems, willing to give his services to help causes in which he believes, be they nuclear disarmament or moral rearmament, colour prejudice or Amnesty International. He is aware that the qualities necessary for the best acting are those needed for the fullest experience of life. In his approach to his work he no longer sees himself as a pawn to be pushed around in rehearsal by an autocratic director, but as a collaborator in the democratic process of bringing the play to life.

Though not unaware of the climate of change, the Abbey actor, deprived of the stimulus of keen competition and isolated from the main stream of the theatre, was in danger of falling into a 'civil service' attitude to his job.

In her desire to broaden the theatre's perspective Leila organised the performances in Helsinki and Brussels, arranging for the company to spend a week as guests in Leningrad between the two playing dates. New directorial talent was introduced — Michael Cacoyannis, T. P. McKenna, Alan Barlow, Roland Jaquarello, and there was the tragically frustrated attempt to bring Sean Kenny back to his native land, while Vincent Dowling, although no newcomer to directing at the Abbey, showed particular talent in his productions of *The Iceman Cometh* and James Joyce's play, *Exiles* (Peacock Theatre, 21 February 1923). But to bring about the changed outlook Leila sought demanded the co-operation of all concerned. Regrettably this was not forthcoming.

Among the players and staff were those who resented her plans to reorganise their work, and her laudable attempts to infuse a greater sense of commitment and corporate spirit met with little response. In an unguarded moment Hugh Hunt was unwise enough to outline a policy for the Abbey in which he stated, 'It is the job of the artistic director . . . to encourage the desire to serve the theatre and the nation, to build an ensemble — a team. The theatre is not a job: it is a vocation.'[9] To which the pragmatic and cynical Denis Johnston replied:

> Here Hugh is either romancing or has forgotten our Irish habits during his long absence from these shores. The Irish actor is — in my opinion — potentially one of the best in the world, and is always a joy to direct, so long as you can keep on the right side of him. But whatever he is, he is seldom dedicated and is never a part of a team. . . . One of the delights — and headaches — of the Irish actor is that he is a law unto himself, and can be as wicked in his off moments, usually when he is bored, as he can be brilliant when he is playing on his nerves.[10]

Denis Johnston was right in that actors – whether Irish or not – are individualists and as such tend to be egocentric. This, however, does not prevent their working as a team, but most Abbey actors today would resist the kind of corporate dedication to an artistic creed, based on a commonly held social, political or nationalist view such as was briefly, and somewhat naïvely, found in the earliest days of the Fays' company and, in more sophisticated forms today in companies like the Berliner Ensemble, Grotowski's Laboratory Theatre and Peter Brook's International Centre for Theatre Creations.

Despite her intelligence and idealism, Leila Doolan failed to win the confidence of the players and Board. Her position was not helped by an unhappy production of Shaw's *Saint Joan* in December 1972. In view of the uneasy atmosphere in the theatre the Board decided in September of the following year that her duties as artistic director should be taken over by Tomás Mac Anna. Leila was offered a position as play consultant; an offer she proudly declined. Once again the Board parted with an executive officer in circumstances that appeared to the Abbey's critics as yet one more example of the conservatism of an ageing Board of Directors.

The old order changeth . . .'

In fact the directorate of the National Theatre was undergoing the process of self-renewal. The privately owned Society, with its control vested in what was virtually a self-perpetuating governing body, was giving way to a public institution with an open and democratic form of government.[11]

In 1972, in spite of Blythe's misgivings, the Board acceded to a request of the Players Council that a representative nominated by the players should be co-opted as a member of the Board. In the same year the Board agreed to co-opt a representative selected from a list supplied by the shareholders; this list to consist mainly of playwrights and artists not necessarily associated with the Abbey. In June, Kathleen Barrington became the first player to sit on the Board of Directors and in the same month Tomás Mac Anna was also co-opted.[12]

On 5 September, Ernest Blythe, now eighty-six years old, informed the Board that he wished to resign. In recognition

. The Abbey fire, 1951

26. Ria Mooney

27. The Queen's Theatre

28. Tomás Mac Anna

29. The Golden Jubilee — a benign
Ernest Blythe with a Gort
cake

DUBLIN OPINION

The National
Humorous
Journal of
Ireland

February, 1965

"They're getting a good house to-night, Willie."
"That's no house, Augusta, that's the new shareholders."

31. The ghosts of Yeats and Lady Gregory
watch the arrival of the new shareholders

30. President de Valera lays the Foundation stone of the new Abbey,
3 September 1963

32. The new Abbey

33. The new Peacock

Borstal Boy, 1967. The young Brendan Behan is interrogated by the police

The Silver Tassie, 1972. Act 2

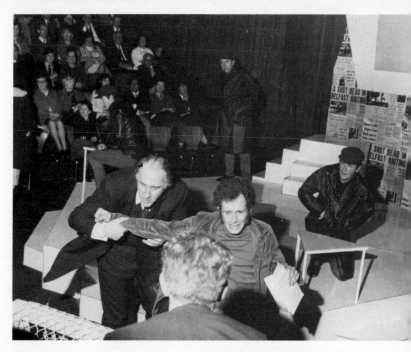

36. Riot in the Peacock, 6 Sept. 1970. Eamon McCann is conducted out of the theatre by Tomás Mac Anna

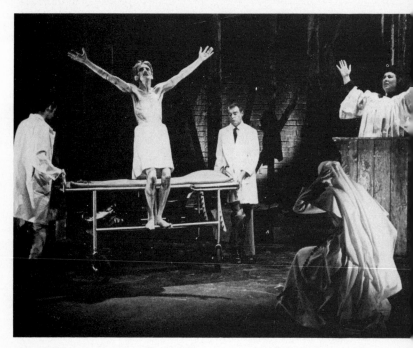

37. *Talbot's Box*, 1978: Stephen Brennan, John Molloy, Clive Geraghty, Ingrid Craigie, Eileen Colgan

39. Wendy Shea: costume design for Estragon, *Waiting for Godot*, Abbey 1976

38. Bronwen Casson: costume drawing for *Macbeth*, Abbey 1971

40. *The Plough and the Stars*, 1976: Angela Newman as Mrs Gogan, Siobhan McKenna as Bessie Burgess, John Kavanagh as the Young Covey, Cyril Cusack as Fluther Good

41. *Uncle Vanya*, 1978: Máire Ní Ghráinne as Sonia and Cyril Cusack as Vanya

of his thirty-seven years service as a member of the Board, he was made a life member of the Society, retaining ten shares, and an annual lectureship was instituted (The Ernest Blythe Lectures) in his honour. Whatever his faults, and harshly as contemporary critics have judged him, without his tenacity, financial astuteness and political cunning, the Abbey would not have survived the long agony of its exile, nor would the new Abbey have risen from the ashes of the old. When he died on 25 January 1975 the Taoiseach, Liam Cosgrave, said of him, 'Once he made a decision he allowed no public outcry to change his mind . . . Ireland is the poorer for his passing.'

Blythe's place on the Board was taken by Mac Anna who thus became an ordinary member inheriting the balance of Blythe's shares. In August the playwright, Thomas Murphy, was co-opted.

With Blythe's resignation one of the last links between the old and the new Abbey was broken. Yet another link with the past was severed in October 1973 when Roibeárd Ó Faracháin, standing for re-election, was surprisingly out-voted in favour of the highly active shareholder, Charles McCarthy. A bare three months later, in January 1974, Gabriel Fallon resigned after a lifelong and often tempestuous association with the Abbey, including fifteen years' service as a member of the Board. Shortly afterwards it was Séamus Wilmot's turn to leave; as a representative of the government his resignation was made to the Minister for Finance on 31 January. Murphy was now appointed to take Fallon's place as shareholding Director, and in July Gemma Hussey was appointed to fill the place of Wilmot as one of the two government representatives, the other being Micheál Ó hAodha who was duly re-appointed for a further four years. In July 1978 Gemma Hussey was replaced as government representative by Mrs Margaret Ó Dalaigh. Finally, to bring the directorate into line with the modern trends in industrial relations, Leslie Scott, the theatre's chief electrician and senior lighting designer, was co-opted in December 1974 as the first representative of the newly formed Staff Council. In little over a year the average age of the Abbey Board had dropped from over seventy to forty.

. . . giving place to new

At the same time new and younger blood was being injected into the theatre's staff. When Mac Anna was appointed to succeed Leila Doolan as artistic director, his place in the Peacock was taken by the twenty-five-year-old Joe Dowling, bringing with him some of the young players who had worked in the Young Abbey. Dowling made considerable progress in capturing the interest of a younger audience, aided by a young and talented public relations officer, Deirdre Mc Quillan, appointed in 1974. When in April 1975 Dowling was seconded from the Abbey to take over a two-year appointment as artistic director of the Irish Theatre Company, Patrick Laffan, who succeeded him in the Peacock, skilfully directed the repertoire to include new interpretations of classical plays: *Measure for Measure* (4 April 1977) and *The Misanthrope* (12 March 1978), and new drama: *Talbot's Box* and *Catchpenny Twist*.

In the design department new appointments and young talent were broadening the theatre's horizons. Bronwen Casson, a student of the National College of Art and the Sadlers Wells school of theatre design, joined the Abbey in 1970, quickly winning critical acclaim in a series of exciting designs. In 1973 she was joined by Wendy Shea, an Associate of the National College of Art and a designer of considerable experience in Britain. To the Design Department also came a promising young Arts graduate from University College, Dublin, Maebh Browne; while Brian Collins, himself a designer of considerable talent, was appointed as the theatre's production manager.

In the administrative and artistic offices equally radical changes were taking place. David Liddy from the Theatre Royal, Liverpool, who succeeded John Slemon as manager, was replaced by the thirty-year-old secretary, Martin Fahy, in January 1977. In July the Board announced that, when Mac Anna's contract as artistic director came to an end in March 1978, he would be succeeded by Joe Dowling. Meanwhile, Edward Golden was seconded from the company for one year to take over Dowling's job with the Irish Theatre Company. In spite of his youth Dowling had gained considerable experience as an actor, director and administrator. His five-year term of office is, as pointed out in *The Guardian* interview (31 March 1978), likely to be 'evolutionary rather than revolutionary . . . building a tradition of classical works, repeating past successes from home and abroad and encouraging new plays'.

To complete this evolutionary process from the old to the new, Douglas Kennedy, a twenty-three-year-old New Yorker living in Dublin, was appointed as administrator of the Peacock. Thus, Ireland's National Theatre goes forward into the eighties with youth at the helm.

The Irish Thing

However, the Abbey cannot escape its past. Though it be but a short time that those who have served it linger in our memories, yet, what they contributed to it — however small — lives on so long as this age-old country remains true to itself.

As the decade draws to its close, the theatre applauds the last exit from the great stage of life of many of its contributors.

Arthur Shields, actor, play director and Honorary Member of the company (April 1970),
Eric Gorman, actor and secretary (December 1971), May Craig, actress (February 1972),
Seaghan Barlow, head carpenter (July 1972),
Ria Mooney, actress and play director (January 1973),
Ernest Blythe, Managing Director and member of the Board (January 1975),
Séamus Wilmot, member of the Board (January 1976),
Harry Brogan, actor (May 1977),
Christine Hayden, actress (November 1977),
Micheál Mac Liammóir, actor, designer, playwright and honorary member of the company (March 1978),
Eileen Crowe, actress (May 1978),
Frank Dermody, play director (June 1978),
Denis O'Dea, actor (June 1978),
Angela Newman, actress (April 1979),
Séamus Kelly, drama critic (June 1979),

and many others before them who served as players and play-wrights, as members of the Board, managers, play directors and staff, as critics who praised and sometimes condemned, this ever-living 'Irish Thing' —

THE ABBEY THEATRE

Appendix:

Abbey Productions

PLAYS PRESENTED PRIOR TO 18 JULY 1966

The following list of plays only includes dates of first productions. Adaptations are shown by / placed between the original writer and the adaptor. Translators' names, when known, are only given in the case of translations into Irish and are indicated by a hyphen placed after the name of the original playwright.

THE IRISH LITERARY THEATRE
Antient Concert Rooms
1899
8 May
The Countess Cathleen
W. B. Yeats
9 May
The Heather Field
Edward Martyn

Gaiety Theatre
1900
19 February
The Bending of the Bough
George Moore
The Last Feast of the Fianna
Alice Mulligan
20 February
Maeve
Edward Martyn

Gaiety Theatre
1901
21 October

Diarmuid and Grania
Yeats and Moore
Casadh an tSúgáin
(The Twisting of the Rope)
Douglas Hyde

W. G. FAY'S IRISH NATIONAL DRAMATIC COMPANY
St Teresa's Hall
1902
2 April
Deirdre
G. W. Russell (AE)
Cathleen Ni Houlihan
W. B. Yeats

THE NATIONAL DRAMATIC COMPANY
Antient Concert Rooms
29 October
The Sleep of the King
James Cousins
The Laying of the Foundations
Fred Ryan
30 October

A Pot of Broth
W. B. Yeats
31 October
The Racing Lug
James Cousins
Eilís agus an Bhean Déirce
Peadar Mac Fhionnlaoich

THE IRISH NATIONAL
　　THEATRE SOCIETY
Molesworth Hall
1903
14 March
The Hour Glass
W. B. Yeats
Twenty-Five
Lady Gregory
8 October
The King's Threshold
W. B. Yeats
In the Shadow of the Glen
J. M. Synge
3 December
Broken Soil
Pádraic Colum

1904
14 January
The Shadowy Waters
W. B. Yeats
The Townland of Tamney
Seamus MacManus
25 January
Riders to the Sea
J. M. Synge

Abbey Theatre
27 December
On Baile's Strand
W. B. Yeats
Spreading the News
Lady Gregory

1905
4 February
The Well of the Saints
J. M. Synge
25 March

Kincora
Lady Gregory
25 April
The Building Fund
William Boyle
9 June
The Land
Pádraic Colum
9 December
The White Cockade
Lady Gregory

1906
20 January
The Eloquent Dempsey
William Boyle
19 February
Hyacinth Halvey
Lady Gregory
16 April
The Doctor in Spite of Himself
Molière-Gregory
20 October
The Gaol Gate
Lady Gregory
The Mineral Workers
William Boyle
24 November
Deirdre
W. B. Yeats
8 December
The Canavans
Lady Gregory
The Shadowy Waters
(revised)
W. B. Yeats

1907
26 January
The Playboy of the Western World
J. M. Synge
23 February
The Jackdaw
Lady Gregory
9 March
The Rising of the Moon
Lady Gregory
16 March

Interior
Maurice Maeterlinck
1 April
The Eyes of the Blind
W. M. Letts
3 April
The Poorhouse
Gregory-Hyde
27 April
Fand
Wilfred Scawen Blunt
3 October
The Country Dressmaker
George Fitzmaurice
31 October
Dervorgilla
Lady Gregory
21 November
The Unicorn from the Stars
Yeats-Gregory

1908
3 February
The Man who Missed the Tide
W. F. Casey
13 February
The Piper
Conal O'Riordan
10 March
The Pie-Dish
George Fitzmaurice
19 March
The Golden Helmet
W. B. Yeats
Teja
H. Sudermann-
Gregory
4 April
The Rogueries of Scapin
(Les Fourberies de Scapin)
Molière-
Gregory
20 April
The Workhouse Ward
Lady Gregory
29 May
The Scheming Lieutenant
R. B. Sheridan

1 October
The Suburban Groove
W. F. Casey
8 October
The Clancy Name
Lennox Robinson
15 October
When the Dawn is Come
Thomas MacDonagh

1909
21 January
The Miser
(L'Avare)
Molière-
Gregory
11 March
Stephen Gray
D. L. Kelleher
1 April
The Cross Roads
Lennox Robinson
Time
Conal O'Riordan
29 April
The Glittering Gate
Lord Dunsany
27 May
An Imaginary Conversation
Conal O'Riordan
25 August
The Shewing-up of Blanco Posnet
G. Bernard Shaw
16 September
The White Feather
R. J. Ray
14 October
The Challenge
W. M. Letts
11 November
The Image
Lady Gregory

1910
13 January
Deirdre of the Sorrows
J. M. Synge
10 February

The Green Helmet
W. B. Yeats
24 February
Mirandolina
Carlo Goldoni-
Gregory
2 March
The Travelling Man
Lady Gregory
12 May
Thomas Muskerry
Pádraic Colum
26 May
Harvest
Lennox Robinson
28 September
The Casting-out of Martin Whelan
R. J. Ray
27 October
Birthright
T. C. Murray
10 November
The Full Moon
Lady Gregory
24 November
The Shuiler's Child
Seamus O'Kelly
1 December
Coats
Lady Gregory

1911
5 January
The Nativity Play
Hyde-
Gregory
12 January
The Deliverer
Lady Gregory
26 January
*King Argimenes and the Unknown
    Warrior*
Lord Dunsany
The Land of Heart's Desire
W. B. Yeats
30 January
Mixed Marriage
St John G. Ervine

23 November
The Interlude of Youth
Anon
The Second Shepherd's Play
Anon
30 November
The Marriage
Douglas Hyde
7 December
Red Turf
Rutherford Mayne

1912
4 January
The Annunciation
Anon
The Flight into Egypt
Anon
11 January
Mac Donough's Wife
Lady Gregory
15 January
An Tincéar agus an tSídheóg
Douglas Hyde
29 January
The Worlde and the Chylde
Anon
28 March
Family Failing
William Boyle
11 April
Patriots
Lennox Robinson
15 April
Judgment
Joseph Campbell
20 June
(At the Court Theatre, London)
Maurice Harte
T. C. Murray
4 July
(At the Court Theatre, London)
The Bogie Man
Lady Gregory
26 September
The Countess Cathleen (revised)
W. B. Yeats
17 October

The Magnanimous Lover
St John G. Ervine
21 November
Damer's Gold
Lady Gregory
26 December
A Little Christmas Miracle
E. H. Moore

1913
13 January
The Cuckoo's Nest
John Guinan
23 January
The Dean of St. Patrick's
G. S. Paternoster
20 February
Hannele
Gerhardt Hauptmann
6 March
There are Crimes and Crimes
August Strindberg
10 April
The Homecoming
Gertrude Robins
17 April
The Stronger
August Strindberg
24 April
The Magic Glasses
George Fitzmaurice
Broken Faith
S. R. Day and
G. D. Cummins
17 May
The Post Office
Rabindranath Tagore
30 June
The Gombeen Man
R. J. Ray
11 September
Sovereign Love
T. C. Murray
2 October
The Mine Land
Joseph Connolly
16 October
My Lord

Mrs Bart Kennedy
20 November
The Critics
St John G. Ervine
16 December
Duty
Seamus O'Brien
18 December
The Bribe
Seamus O'Kelly

1914
29 January
David Mahony
Victor O'D. Power
13 March
The Orangemen
St John G. Ervine
The Lord Mayor
Edward McNulty
2 April
Kinship
J. Bernard MacCarthy
15 April
The Cobbler
A. Patrick Wilson
27 August
A Minute's Wait
Martin J. MacHugh
3 September
The Supplanter
J. Bernard MacCarthy
9 September
The Dark Hour
R. A. Christie
23 September
The Crossing
Con O'Leary
30 September
The Prodigal
Walter Riddall
13 October
The Cobweb
F. Jay
20 October
The Jug of Sorrow
W. P. Ryan
3 November

The Slough
A. Patrick Wilson
26 December
The Critic
R. B. Sheridan

1915
27 January
By Word of Mouth
F. C. Moore and
W. P. Flanagan
2 February
The Dreamers
Lennox Robinson
5 April
The Bargain
William Crone
The Philosopher
Martin J. MacHugh
8 April
Shanwalla
Lady Gregory
30 November
John Ferguson
St John G. Ervine

1916
4 January
Fraternity
Bernard Duffy
8 February
The Coiner
Bernard Duffy
28 March
The Plough Lifters
John Guinan
25 September
John Bull's Other Island
G. Bernard Shaw
9 October
Widower's Houses
G. Barnard Shaw
16 October
Arms and the Man
G. Bernard Shaw
25 October
Nic
William Boyle

15 November
Partition
D. C. Maher
11 December
The Counter Charm
Bernard Duffy
13 December
The Whiteheaded Boy
Lennox Robinson

1917
8 January
Tommy-Tom-Tom
Martin J. MacHugh
19 January
The Crusaders
J. Bernard MacCarthy
2 February
Fox and Geese
S. R. Day and
G. D. Cummins
26 February
Man and Superman
G. Bernard Shaw
12 March
The Inca of Perusalem
G. Bernard Shaw
25 April
The Strong Hand
R. J. Ray
26 May
The Doctor's Dilemma
G. Bernard Shaw
24 September
The Parnellite
Seamus O'Kelly
30 October
The Bacach
John Barnewell
13 November
The Spoiling of Wilson
R. J. Purcell
20 November
Friends
Herbert Farjeon
11 December
Blight
'Alpha and Omega'

1918
8 January
Spring
T. C. Murray
22 January
When Love came over the Hills
W. R. Fearon and
Roy Nesbitt
29 January
Hanrahan's Oath
Lady Gregory
12 March
Aliens
Rose McKenna
9 February
The Lost Leader
Lennox Robinson
28 May
A Little Bit of Youth
C. Callister
16 September
Sable and Gold
Maurice Dalton
12 November
The Grabber
E. F. Barrett
17 December
Atonement
Dorothy Macardle

1919
11 March
The Rebellion in Ballycullen
Brinsley Macnamara
21 April
The Dragon
Lady Gregory
4 August
Brady
Sadie Casey
19 August
The Fiddler's House
Pádraic Colum
A Serious Thing
Gideon Ousley
2 September
The Saint
Desmond Fitzgerald

A Night at an Inn
Lord Dunsany
30 September
The Labour Leader
Daniel Corkery
7 October
Meadowsweet
Seamus O'Kelly
14 October
Queer Ones
Con O'Leary
4 November
Androcles and the Lion
G. Bernard Shaw
25 November
The Enchanted Trousers
Gideon Ousley
9 December
The Player Queen
W. B. Yeats

1920
6 January
The Golden Apple
Lady Gregory
10 February
The Devil's Disciple
G. Bernard Shaw
17 February
The Daemon in the House
F. Barrington
27 April
The Good-natur'd Man
Oliver Goldsmith
4 May
The Yellow Bittern
Daniel Corkery
24 May
The Tents of the Arabs
Lord Dunsany
9 August
The Wooing of Julia Elizabeth
James Stephens
7 September
The Drifters
F. J. H. O'Donnell
21 September
A Royal Alliance

Fergus O'Nolan
5 October
The Serf
Stephen Morgan
12 October
The Island of Saints
St John G. Ervine
30 November
The Land for the People
Brinsley Macnamara
27 December
Candle and Crib
K. F. Purdo n

1921
6 January
Bedmates
George Shiels
24 February
The Revolutionist
Terence MacSwiney
17 March
Aristotle's Bellows
Lady Gregory
18 October
The Perfect Day
Emile Mazaud
A Merry Death
Nikolai Evreinov
8 November
The Courting of Mary Doyle
Edward McNulty
15 November
The Piper of Tavran
Bernard Duffy
13 December
Insurance Money
George Shiels

1922
10 January
Aftermath
T. C. Murray
31 January
The Round Table
Lennox Robinson
9 March
The Man of Destiny

G. Bernard Shaw
6 April
The Young Man from Rathmines
M. M. Brennan
Ann Kavanagh
Dorothy Macardle
29 August
The Moral Law
R. J. Ray
5 September
The Leprecaun in the Tenement
M. M. Brennan
3 October
Paul Twyning
George Shiels
24 October
The Grasshopper
Keyserling/
Colum and Washburn Freund
14 November
Crabbed Youth and Age
Lennox Robinson

1923
9 January
The Long Road to Garranbraher
J. Bernard MacCarthy
8 March
*'Twixt the Giltenans and the
    Carmodys*
George Fitzmaurice
22 March
A Doll's House
Henrik Ibsen
9 April
The Shadow of a Gunman
Sean O'Casey
22 April
She Stoops to Conquer
Oliver Goldsmith
3 September
Apartments
Fand O'Grady
1 October
Cathleen Listens-in
Sean O'Casey
27 November
The Glorious Uncertainty

Brinsley Macnamara
26 December
First Aid
George Shiels
31 December
The Old Woman Remembers
Lady Gregory

1924
12 February
The Two Shepherds
G. Martinez Sierra
3 March
Juno and the Paycock
Sean O'Casey
8 April
Never the Time and the Place
Lennox Robinson
14 April
The Story brought by Brigit
Lady Gregory
12 May
The Retrievers
George Shiels
8 September
Autumn Fire
T. C. Murray
29 September
Nannie's Night Out
Sean O'Casey
3 November
The Kingdom of God
G. Martinez Sierra
16 December
The Passing
Kenneth Sarr
22 December
Old Mag
Kenneth Sarr

1925
24 February
The Old Man
Dorothy Macardle
17 March
Anti-Christ
F. J. H. O'Donnell
31 March

Portrait
Lennox Robinson
21 April
Fanny's First Play
G. Bernard Shaw
28 April
The Proposal
Anton Chekhov
14 September
Professor Tim
George Shiels
12 October
The White Blackbird
Lennox Robinson

1926
4 January
The Would-be Gentleman
(Le Bourgeois Gentilhomme)
Molière-
Gregory
8 February
The Plough and the Stars
Sean O'Casey
16 February
Doctor Knock
Jules Romains
12 April
Look at the Heffernans!
Brinsley Macnamara
16 August
Mr. Murphy's Island
Elizabeth Harte
6 September
The Big House
Lennox Robinson
6 November
The Importance of being Earnest
Oscar Wilde
6 December
Oedipus the King
Sophocles-
Yeats

1927
24 January
The Emperor Jones

Eugene O'Neill
Trifles
Susan Glaspell
14 March
Sancho's Master
Lady Gregory
5 April
Parted
M. C. Madden
9 May
Dave
Lady Gregory
16 May
Black Oliver
John Guinan
8 July
The Round Table (revised)
Lennox Robinson
22 August
The Drapier Letters
Arthur Power
12 September
Oedipus at Colonnus
Sophocles-Yeats
3 October
The Pipe in the Fields
T. C. Murray
24 October
Caesar and Cleopatra
G. Bernard Shaw
29 November
Cartney and Kevney
George Shiels

1928
6 March
The Master
Brinsley Macnamara
3 April
John Gabriel Borkman
Henrik Ibsen
30 April
The Blind Wolf
T. C. Murray
16 July
Before Midnight
Gerald Brosnan
27 August

Full Measure
Cathleen M. O'Brennan
22 October
The Far-off Hills
Lennox Robinson
12 November
The Women have their Way
Quintero Brothers
26 November
King Lear
William Shakespeare

1929
5 March
Mountain Dew
George Shiels
13 August
Fighting the Waves
W. B. Yeats
10 September
The Woman
Margaret O'Leary
8 October
Ever the Twain
Lennox Robinson
29 October
The Gods of the Mountain
Lord Dunsany
31 December
Dark Isle
Gerald Brosnan

1930
28 January
Peter
Rutherford Mayne
18 March
The Reapers
Teresa Deevy
19 April
The New Gossoon
George Shiels
15 September
Let the Credit Go
Brian Cooper
17 November
The Words upon the Window Pane
W. B. Yeats

1931
6 January
The Critic
Sheridan-Robinson
9 February
The Rune of Healing
John Guinan
23 February
Peter the Liar
A. Leprovost
9 March
Money
Hugh P. Quinn
27 April
The Moon in the Yellow River
Denis Johnston
8 June
The Admirable Bashville
G. Bernard Shaw
7 July
Scrap
J. A. O'Brennan
24 August
A Disciple
Teresa Deevy
21 September
The Cat and the Moon
W. B. Yeats
6 December
The Dreaming of the Bones
W. B. Yeats

1932
27 June
Michaelmas Eve
T. C. Murray
25 July
All's Over Then
Lennox Robinson
15 August
Things that are Caesar's
Paul Vincent Carroll
12 September
Temporal Powers
Teresa Deevy
17 October
The Mating of Shan M'Ghie
G. H. Stafford

24 October
Vigil
A. P. Fanning
31 October
The Wild Duck
Henrik Ibsen
7 November
The Big Sweep
M. M. Brennan
14 November
Sheridan's Mills
Norman Webb
21 November
Wrack
Peadar O'Donnell

1933
6 February
Drama at Inish
Lennox Robinson
13 March
Men Crowd me Round
Francis Stuart
17 July
Margaret Gillan
Brinsley MacNamara
25 July
The Drinking Horn
Arthur Duff
21 August
The Jezebel
J. K. Montgomery
25 September
1920
F. X. O'Leary
13 November
Grogan and the Ferret
George Shiels
26 December
You never can Tell
G. Bernard Shaw

1934
5 February
The Marriage Packet
Arthur Power
16 April
Days without end

Eugene O'Neill
21 May
Church Street
Lennox Robinson
18 June
Bridgehead
Rutherford Mayne
9 July
On the Rocks
G. Bernard Shaw
30 July
The Resurrection
W. B. Yeats
*The King of the Great Clock
  Tower*
W. B. Yeats
1 October
Parnell of Avondale
W. R. Fearon
25 October
Macbeth
William Shakespeare
12 November
Gallant Cassian
Arthur Schnitzler
The School for Wives
J. P. Molière
3 December
*Six Characters in Search of an
  Author*
Luigi Pirandello
26 December
At Mrs. Beam's
G. K. Munroe

1935
29 April
The King of Spain's Daughter
Teresa Deevy
12 August
The Silver Tassie
Sean O'Casey
16 September
A Deuce o' Jacks
F R. Higgins
30 September
A Village Wooing
G. Bernard Shaw

Candida
G. Bernard Shaw
4 November
Noah
André Obey
2 December
A Saint in a Hurry
José Maria Penam
9 December
Summer's Day
Maura Molloy

1936
13 January
Coriolanus
William Shakespeare
3 February
The Grand House in the City
Brinsley Macnamara
24 February
Boyd's Shop
St. John G. Ervine
16 March
Katie Roche
Teresa Deevy
13 April
The Passing Day
George Shiels
1 June
Hassan
James Elroy Flecker
14 September
The Silver Jubilee
Cormac O'Daly
12 October
The Jailbird
George Shiels
9 November
The Wild Goose
Teresa Deevy
30 November
Wind from the West
Maeve O'Callaghan
26 December
Blind Man's Buff
Ernst Toller and
Denis Johnston

1937
25 January
Shadow and Substance
Paul Vincent Carroll
8 February
The End of the Beginning
Sean O'Casey
29 March
Quin's Secret
George Shiels
19 April
Killycreggs in Twilight
Lennox Robinson
17 May
Who will Remember . . . ?
Maura Molloy
31 May
In the Train
Frank O'Connor and
Hugh Hunt
5 August
The Patriot
Maeve O'Callaghan
27 September
The Man in the Cloak
Louis D'Alton
18 October
The Invincibles
Hugh Hunt and
Frank O'Connor
8 November
Cartney and Kevney (revised)
George Shiels
22 November
Coggerers
Paul Vincent Carroll
27 December
She had to do Something
Sean O'Faolain

1938
17 January
Neal Maquade
George Shiels
14 February
A Spot in the Sun
T. C. Murray
28 February

Moses' Rock
Hugh Hunt and
Frank O'Connor
4 April
The Dear Queen
Andrew Ganly
10 August
Purgatory
W. B. Yeats
12 September
Bird's Nest
Lennox Robinson
19 September
The Great Adventure
Charles I. Foley
10 October
Pilgrims
Mary Rynne
12 December
Baintighearna an Ghorta
Séamus Wilmot
26 December
Time's Pocket
Frank O'Connor

1939
6 February
Caesar's Image
E. F. Carey
13 March
Tomorrow never comes
Louis D'Alton
8 April
The Heritage
J. K. Montgomery
15 May
Donnchadh Ruadh
Séamus Ó hAodha
31 July
Illumination
T. C. Murray
28 August
Fonham the Sculptor
Daniel Corkery
25 September
Kindred
Paul Vincent Carroll
30 October

Give him a House
George Shiels
4 December
They went by the Bus
Frank Carney

1940
29 January
The Spanish Soldier
Louis D'Alton
23 March
William John Mawhinney
St John G. Ervine
22 April
Mount Prospect
Elizabeth Connor
13 May
The Birth of a Giant
Nora MacAdam
15 July
Today and Yesterday
W. D. Hepenstall
5 August
The Rugged Path
4 November
George Shiels
4 November
Three to go
Olga Fielden
25 November
Peeping Tom
Frank Carney
9 December
Strange Guest
Francis Stuart

1941
6 January
Trial at Green Street Court House
Roger McHugh
10 February
The Summit
George Shiels
10 March
The Money Doesn't Matter
Louis D'Alton
19 May
The Lady in the Twilight
Mervyn Wall

30 June
Friends and Relations
St John G. Ervine
18 August
Remembered for ever
Bernard McGinn
1 September
The Fire Burns Late
P. J. Fitzgibbon
22 September
Swans and Geese
Elizabeth Connor
20 October
Lovers' Meeting
Louis D'Alton
24 November
The Three Thimbles
Brinsley Macnamara
26 December
Forget me not
Lennox Robinson
28 December
Black Fast
Austin Clarke

1942
22 February
Gloine an Impire
Traolach Ó Raithbheartaigh
Cách
(Everyman)
Anon/Earnán de Blaghd
(Ernest Blythe)
9 March
The Cursing Fields
Andrew Ganly
6 April
The Singer
Pádraic Pearse
13 April
The Fort Field
George Shiels
3 May
La La Noo
Jack B. Yeats
6 July
The Whip Hand
B. G. MacCarthy

7 September
An Apple a Day
Elizabeth Connor
29 November
An Stoirm
Alexander Ostrovsky-
Aodh Mac Dubháin

1943
25 January
Faustus Kelly
Myles na gCopaleen
31 January
An Bhean Chródha
Piaras Béaslaoi
21 February
Ar an mBóthar Mór
J. J. Bernard-
Liam O Briáin
8 March
The O'Cuddy
Anthony Wharton
21 March
Assembly at Druim Ceat
Roibeárd Ó Faracháin
4 April
An Coimisinéar
Tomás Ó Súilleabháin
24 April
Old Road
Michael J. Molloy
26 April
Lost Light
Roibeárd Ó Faracháin
30 May
An Traona sa Mhoinfhear
Séamus de Faoite-
Fachtna O hAnnracháin
9 August
Thy Dear Father
Gerald Healy
24 October
Ordóg an Bháis
Micheál Ó hAodha
27 December
Poor Man's Miracle
F. B. Czarnomski-
Marian Hemar

1944
30 January
Laistiar de 'n Eadan
Eibhlín Ní Shúileabháin
7 February
The Wise have not Spoken
Paul Vincent Carroll
6 March
The New Regime
George Shiels
26 March
Stiana
Peadar O hAnnracháin
8 May
The Coloured Balloon
Margaret O'Leary
21 May
Sodar i nDiaidh na nUasal
(Le Bourgeois Gentilhomme)
J. P. Molière
28 August
The End House
Joseph Tomelty
20 November
Railway House
Ralph Kennedy
22 October
Borumha Laighean
Seán Ó Conchobhair

1945
7 January
An t-Ubhall Oir
(The Golden Apple)
Gregory Ó Briain
18 March
Giolla an tSoluis
Máiréad Ní Ghráda
31 March
Rossa
Roger McHugh
13 May
An t-Udar i nGleic
Labhrás Mac Brádaigh
6 August
Marks and Mabel
Brinsley Macnamara
10 September

Tenants at Will
George Shiels
20 September
Nuair a bhionn Fear Marbh
(Prenez Garde à la Peinture)
René Fauchois-
Ó Briain
20 December
Muireann agus an Prionnsa
Micheál Ó hAodha

1946
11 February
Mungo's Mansion
Walter Macken
25 March
The Old Broom
George Shiels
20 April
Cáitlin Ní Uallacháin
(Cathleen Ni Houlihan)
Yeats-
Tomás Luibhéid
29 July
The Righteous are Bold
Frank Carney
18 November
The Visiting House
Michael J. Molloy
29 December
Fernando agus an Dragan
Pantomime

1947
18 February
They got what they wanted
Louis D'Alton
12 May
The Dark Road
Elizabeth Connor
19 May
Caitriona Parr
(Catherine Parr)
Maurice Baring-
Liam Ó Laoghaire
*Oíche Mhaith agat, a Mhic
    Uí Dhomhnaill*
(Good Night Mr O'Donnell)

Roibeárd Ó Braonáin-
Liam Ó Briain
25 August
The Great Pacificator
Sigerson Clifford
16 September
Cursaí Cleamhnais
(The Proposal)
Anton Chekhov-
Muiris Ó Cathain
3 November
Diarmuid agus Gráinne
Micheál MacLiammóir

1948
1 January
Réalt Dhiarmuda
Pantomime
16 February
The Caretakers
George Shiels
16 March
Máire Rós
(Mary Rose)
James Barrie-
Siobhán Nic Chionnaith
5 April
Moill na Mithidi
(A Minute's Wait)
Martin J. McHugh-
Gobnait Ní Loinsigh
12 July
The Drums are out
John Coulter
18 August
Arís
(La Joyeuse Farce des "Encore")
Ghéon-Ó Briain
23 August
The Lucky Finger
Lennox Robinson
11 October
Na Cloigíní
(Le Juif Polonais)
Erckmann-Chatrian-
Maighread Nic Mhaicín
18 October
The King of Friday's Men

M. J. Molloy
27 December
Brian agus an Claidheamh Soluis
Pantomime

1949
14 March
The Bugle in the Blood
Bryan MacMahon
Oíche Bhealtaine
Micheál MacLiammóir
16 April
All Souls' Night
Joseph Tomelty
23 May
An Béar
(The Bear)
Anton Chekhov
3 October
Ask for me Tomorrow
Ralph Kennedy
15 October
An Pósadh
Douglas Hyde
31 October
Bean an Mhi-ghra
(La Malquerida)
Jacinte Benavente-
Padraigin Ní Neill
26 December
Nial agus Carmelita
Pantomime

1950
8 April
Design for a Headstone
Séamus Byrne
22 May
Tristan agus Isialt
(Tristan et Iseult)
Joseph Bédier and
Louis Artus Don Piatt
10 August
Mountain Flood
Jack P. Cunningham
2 October
The Goldfish in the Sun
Donal Giltinan

15 October
Clocha na Coigheríce
Aindreas Ó Gallchobhair
26 December
Una agus Jimín
Pantomime

1951
5 February
House under Green Shadows
Maurice G. Meldon
19 February
Na Cruiteacháin
(Le Farce des Bossus)
Pierre Jalabert-
Liam Ó Briain
30 April
Geamaireacht Droichid an Diabhail
(La Parade du Pont au Diable)
Henri Ghéon
20 May
Na Ciste Tógála
(The Building Fund)
William Boyle-
Piaras Mac Lochlain
Aís na nDéithe
Eamon Guallí

THE QUEEN'S THEATRE
10 September
The Devil a Saint would be
Louis D'Alton
22 October
Window on the Square
Ann Daly
19 November
Innocent Bystander
Seamus Byrne
26 December
Réamonn agus Niamh Óg
Pantomime

1952
24 May
The Gentle Maiden
Donal Giltinan
26 May
An Crann Ubhall

(The Apple Tree)
Harold Brighouse-
Seamus O Tuama
28 July
Home is the Hero
Walter Macken
11 October
Eirí na Gealaí
(The Rising of the Moon)
Lady Gregory
19 October
Ag Baint lae as
(The Passing Day)
George Shiels-
Seán Toibin
26 December
Setanta agus an Chú
Pantomime

1953
26 January
The Wood of the Whispering
M. J. Molloy
2 March
An Duais-Bheidhlín
(The Prize Winning Violin)
Francois Coppée-
Risteard Ó Foghlu and
Ernest Blythe
6 April
An Fear a phós Balbhán
(The Man who Married a Dumb
Wife)
Gearóid Mac An Bhuaidh and
Tomás Mac Anna
1 June
This Other Eden
Louis D'Alton
5 September
The Paddy Pedlar
M. J. Molloy
1 November
Lá Buí Bealtaine
Máiréad Ní Ghráda
26 December
Blíthín agus an Mac Rí
Pantomime

1954
25 January
The Half Millionaire
John O'Donovan
22 February
John Courtney
John Malone
29 March
Twenty Years A-Wooing
John McCann
19 July
Knocknavain
J. M. Doody
26 July
A Riverside Charade
Bryan Guinness
16 October
Diarmuid agus Gráinne
Micheál MacLiammóir
8 November
Is the Priest at Home?
(First Abbey Production)
Joseph Tomelty
21 December
Sonia agus an Bodach
Pantomime

1955
25 July
Blood is Thicker than Water
John McCann
5 September
The Will and the Way
M. J. Molloy
24 October
The Last Move
Pauline Maguire
27 October
An Murlán Práis
(The Brass Doorknob)
Mathew Bolton
5 November
Saoirse
Rísteárd de Paor
Úll Glas Oíche Shamhna
Máiréad Ní Ghráda
21 November
Twilight of a Warrior

Walter Macken
26 December
Úlyssés agus Penelopé
Pantomime

1956
23 January
The Big Birthday
(First Abbey Production)
Hugh Leonard
20 February
Judgement on James O'Neill
Francis MacManus
16 July
Early and Often
John McCann
13 August
Iomrall Aithne
John O'Donovan
20 August
Strange Occurrence on Ireland's Eye
Denis Johnston
8 October
The Quare Fella
(First Abbey Production)
Brendan Behan
21 October
Gunna Camh agus Sliabhra Óir
Seán Ó Tuama
26 November
Winter Wedding
Tomás Mac Anna
26 December
An Cruiscin Lan
Pantomime

1957
21 January
A Leap in the Dark
Hugh Leonard
25 February
Waiting Night
P. S. Laughlin
18 March
Céad Feadha Síos
Labhrás Mac Brádaigh

22 April
The Flying Wheel
Donal Giltinan
22 July
The less we are together
John O'Donovan
21 October
The Wanton Tide
Niall Carroll
25 November
Give me a Bed of Roses
John McCann
26 December
Muireann agus an Prionnsa
Pantomime

1958
11 February
Pota an Anraith
(A Pot of Broth)
W. B. Yeats-
Breandan Ó hEithir
10 March
Look in the Looking Glass
Walter Macken
17 March
An Oighreacht
Risteard de Paor
7 April
Iosagán
Pádraig Mac Piarais
14 April
Cafflin Johnny
(First Abbey Production)
Louis D'Alton
28 April
Seven Men and a Dog
Niall Sheridan
19 May
The Scythe and the Sunset
Denis Johnston
15 July
Ar Buille a hOcht
(A Knock at Eight)
Marjorie Watson
4 August
A Change of Mind
John O'Donovan

23 September
The Risen People
James PLunkett
27 October
The Right Rose Tree
M. J. Molloy
17 November
An Briob
Séamus Ó Ceallaigh
An Strainsear
An Seabhac
26 December
Oisín i dTír-na-nÓg
Pantomime

1959
26 January
I Know where I'm going
John McCann
28 April
Long Day's Journey into Night
Eugene O'Neill
11 May
The Country Boy
John Murphy
17 August
Stranger, Beware
Tomás Coffey
14 September
Leave it to the Doctor
Anne Daly
29 September
Sugan Sneachta
Máiréad Ní Ghráda
19 October
Danger, Men Working
(First Abbey Production)
John D. Stewart
9 November
No Man is an Island
Peter Hutchinson
30 November
In Dublin's Fair City
Criostóir Ó Floinn
26 December
Gráinne na Long
Pantomime

1960
31 January
It can't go on for ever
John McCann
28 March
The Bird in the Net
Sean Dowling
19 April
Mac Uí Rudaí
Máiréad Ní Ghráda
25 April
The Shaws of Synge Street
John O'Donovan
19 July
An Doctúir Bréige
(Le Médecin Malgré Lui)
J. P. Molière
1 August
Anyone can Rob a Bank
Tomás Coffey
12 September
The Song of the Anvil
Bryan MacMahon
19 September
Chun na Fairrge Síos
(Riders to the Sea)
Synge-
Tomás Ó Muircheartaigh and
Séamus Ó Sé
31 October
The Lady of Belmont
(First Abbey Production)
St John Ervine
14 November
The Deputy's Daughter
Anthony Butler
26 December
An Sciath Draíochta
Pantomime

1961
10 January
The Evidence I shall give
Richard Johnson
20 March
All the King's Horses
John McDonnell
10 April

Put a Beggar on Horseback
John McCann
22 May
The Honey Spike
Bryan MacMahon
19 September
The Long Sorrow
Tomas Coffey
13 November
An Fear Og Umhal Malda
(The Good and Obedient Young
  Man)
Betty Barr and
Gould Stevens-
Eoin Ó Súilleabháin
4 December
Brave Banner
Eamon Cassidy
26 December
Diarmuid agus Balor
Pantomime

1962
27 February
A Light in the Sky
Donal Giltinan
19 March
The Living and the Lost
Kevin Casey
Thompson in Tir na nOg
Gerald Macnamara
8 May
Do Thrushes Sing in Birmingham?
Liam Lynch
6 August
The Enemy within
Brian Friel
27 August
A Jew called Sammy
John McCann
5 November
Liúdaí Óg na Lairge Móire
(The Lad from Largymore)
Séamus Mac Manus
12 November
Hut 42
John B. Keane
12 December

Ah, Wilderness
Eugene O'Neill
26 December
An Claíomh Soluis
Pantomime

1963
25 February
Copperfaced Jack
John O'Donovan
5 August
The Man from Clare
John B. Keane
30 September
The Successor
ReinhardtRaffalt-
Steven Vas
11 November
A Sunset Touch
Michael Mullvihill
26 December
Flann agus Clemintín
Pantomime

1964
21 September
The Wooing of Duvesa
Michael J. Molloy
6 October
A Matter of Practice
Cyril Daly
30 October
The Big Long Bender
(First Abbey Production)
Stewart Love
23 November
A Page of History
Eilis Dillon
26 December
Aisling as Tír na nÓg
Pantomime

1965
15 March
The Face of Treason
Eoin Neeson and
Colm McNeill
26 April

The Best of Motives
Sean Dowling
5 July
Coiriu na Leapan
Liam Mac Uistin
12 July
The Pilgrim's Mother
Arnold Hill
20 September
The Life of Galileo
Bertolt Brecht
28 December
Emer agus an Laoch
Pantomime

1966
2 February
The Conspiracy
Kenneth Deale
14 March
The Call
Tomas Coffey
25 April
The Hall of Healing
(First Abbey Production)
Sean O'Casey
16 May
The Irishwoman of the Year
John Power
23 May
Geata an Phríosúin
(The Gaol Gate)
Lady Gregory

PLAYS PRESENTED FROM 18 JULY 1966 to 31 DECEMBER 1978

The following list of plays includes new productions of revivals both of Irish and foreign plays, as well as new plays. The latter are indicated by * placed before the title.

THE ABBEY THEATRE
1966
18 July
*Recall the years
Walter Macken
15 August
The Plough and the Stars
Sean O'Casey
3 October
*One for the Grave
Louis MacNeice
7 November
*Death is for Heroes
Michael Judge
22 November
*Tarry Flynn
Patrick Kavanagh/
P. J. O'Connor
26 December
*Fernando agus an Ríonn Óg
Pantomime

1967
31 January
The Shaughraun
Dion Boucicault
10 April
The Loves of Cass Maguire
(First Abbey Production)
Brian Friel
26 April
*Dearly Beloved Roger
John O'Donovan
5 June
Long Day's Journey into Night
Eugene O'Neill
31 July
Red Roses for me
Sean O'Casey
4 September
The Invincibles
Hugh Hunt and
Frank O'Connor

10 October
Borstal Boy
Brendan Behan/
Frank McMahon
26 December
An Cailín Bán
(The Coleen Bawn)
Dion Boucicault-
Liam Ó Briaín

1968
22 January
The Last Eleven
Jack White
18 March
The Saint and Mary Kate
Frank O'Connor/
Mary Manning
6 May
The Shadow of a Gunman
Sean O'Casey
In the Shadow of the Glen
J. M. Synge
24 July
Happy as Larry
(First Abbey Production)
Donagh Mac Donagh
19 August
The Playboy of the Western World
J. M. Synge
The General's Watch
M. D. Power
7 October
The Cherry Orchard
Anton Chekhov
16 December
The Subject was Roses
(First Abbey Production)
Frank D. Gilroy
16 December
An Baile seo Gainne
An Seabhac/Michael Judge
20 December
She Stoops to Conquer
Oliver Goldsmith

1969
10 March

John Bull's Other Island
Bernard Shaw
31 March
The Wakefield Mystery Plays
Anon
23 June
The Quare Fellow
Brendan Behan
18 August
Swift
Eugene McCabe
8 September
The Well of the Saints
J. M. Synge
The Dandy Dolls
George Fitzmaurice
6 October
Juno and the Paycock
Sean O'Casey
10 November
*A Crucial Week in the Life of a
    Grocer's Assistant*
Thomas Murphy
1 December
Waiting for Godot
Samuel Beckett
26 December
Seadna
Peadar Ó Laoghaire and
Tomás Mac Anna

1970
20 January
Hadrian VII
Peter Luke
30 March
The Moon in the Yellow River
Denis Johnston
28 April
The Hostage
(First Abbey Production)
Brendan Behan
14 September
The King of the Castle
(First Abbey Production)
Eugene McCabe
20 October
The Seagull

Anton Chekhov
1 December
The Plough and the Stars
Sean O'Casey

1971
11 January
The Homecoming
Harold Pinter
1 February
A Loud Bang on June 1st
Wesley Burrowes
1 March
The Devil at Work
Constantine Fitzgibbon
15 March
The Mornings after Optimism
Thomas Murphy
19 April
The Playboy of the Western World
J. M. Synge
26 April
Riders to the Sea
J. M. Synge
The Tinker's Wedding
(First Abbey Production)
J. M. Synge
23 August
Today the Bullfinch
Jack White
28 September
Macbeth
William Shakespeare
8 November
The Shadow of a Gunman
Sean O'Casey
The Gaol Gate
Lady Gregory
29 November
Sweet Love till Morn
Padraic Fallon

1972
4 January
Arrah na Pogue
Dion Boucicault
15 February
Prisoner of the Crown
Richard F. Stockton and

Richard Herd
20 March
The White House
Thomas Murphy
3 May
The Iceman Cometh
Eugene O'Neill
27 September
The Silver Tassie
Sean O'Casey
30 October
Philadelphia Here I Come!
(First Abbey Production)
Brian Friel
5 December
Saint Joan
Bernard Shaw

1973
17 January
The School for Scandal
R. B. Sheridan
20 February
The Freedom of the City
Brian Friel
4 April
King Oedipus
Sophocles/
Yeats
8 May
*The Death and Resurrection of
    Mr. Roche*
(First Abbey Production)
Thomas Kilroy
14 August
The King of Friday's Men
M. J. Molloy
13 September
The Importance of being Earnest
Oscar Wilde
9 October
*The Bloom of the Diamond
    Stone*
Wilson John Haire
4 December
The Scatterin'
(First Abbey Production)
James McKenna

1974
14 January
The Resistible Rise of Arturo Ui
Bertolt Brecht
19 February
Three Sisters
Anton Chekhov
25 March
The Whiteheaded Boy
Lennox Robinson
6 May
Blood Wedding
F. Garcia Lorca
15 July
Ulysses in Nighttown
(First Abbey Production)
James Joyce/
Marjorie Barkentin
27 August
The Devil a Saint would be
Louis D'Alton
9 October
*The Gathering
Edna O'Brien
13 November
*The Life and Times of
    Benvenuto Cellini
Hugh Carr
16 December
*The Vicar of Wakefield
Oliver Goldsmith/
Thomas Murphy

1975
30 January
Purple Dust
(First Abbey Production)
Sean O'Casey
5 March
*Volunteers
Brian Friel
8 May
Tarry Flynn
Kavanagh/
O'Connor
2 June
Katie Roche
Teresa Deevy

8 September
*Innish
Lennox Robinson/
Fergus Linehan and
Jim Doherty
6 October
*The Sanctuary Lamp
Thomas Murphy
22 December
The Shaughraun
Dion Boucicault

1976
14 February
The Devils
John Whiting
4 March
Lovers
(First Abbey Production)
Brian Friel
8 April
Desire under the Elms
Eugene O'Neill
14 May
The Plough and the Stars
Sean O'Casey
2 September
The Rivals
R. B. Sheridan
6 October
*Tea and Sex and Shakespeare
Thomas Kilroy
18 November
Waiting for Godot
Samuel Beckett
17 December
*Time was
Hugh Leonard

1977
17 February
The Old Lady says No
(First Abbey Production)
Denis Johnston
24 March
*Living Quarters
Brian Friel
28 April
*The Emperor of Ice Cream

Brian Moore/
Bill Morrison
7 June
The Morning after Optimism
Thomas Murphy
11 August
Cock-a-Doodle Dandy
(First Abbey Production)
Sean O'Casey
12 October
Travesties
Tom Stoppard
17 November
A Pagan Place
(First Abbey Production)
Edna O'Brien
21 December
Wild Oats
John O'Keefe

1978
27 January
The Star turns red
(First Abbey Production)
Sean O'Casey
10 March
The Crucible
Arthur Miller
14 April
You never can tell
G. Bernard Shaw
18 May
Stephen D
(First Abbey Production)
Hugh Leonard
7 September
The Loves of Cass McGuire
(First Abbey Production)
Brian Friel
4 October
Uncle Vanya
Anton Chekhov
23 November
Hatchet
Henno Magee
21 December
The Servant of two Masters
Carlo Goldoni-
Kenneth Richards

THE PEACOCK THEATRE
1967
26 July
*An Béal Bocht
Myles na gCopaleen/
Seán Ó Briain
22 August
*At Bantry
James McKenna
*An Choinneal
Pádraig Ó Giollagáin
18 September
*King of the Barna Men
George Fitzmaurice
The Magic Glasses
(First Abbey Production)
George Fitzmaurice
9 October
*Faill an Bhfeart
Séamus O'Neill
6 November
Film and *Play*
Samuel Beckett
27 December
The Doctor in Spite of Himself
Molière-
Gregory
Spreading the News
Lady Gregory

1968
5 February
*Breithiúnas
Máiréad Ní Ghráda
26 February
Come and Go
Samuel Beckett
The Maids
Jean Genêt
Before Breakfast
Eugene O'Neill
18 March
*Famine
Thomas Murphy
15 April
The Rising of the Moon
Lady Gregory
The Workhouse Ward

Lady Gregory
Hyacinth Halvey
Lady Gregory
16 May
Is É Dúirt Polónius
Criostóir Ó Floinn
22 July
The Sound of the Gong
Fergus Linehan and
Tomás Mac Anna
3 October
The Stronger
August Strindberg
The Tailor and Ansty
Eric Cross/
P. J. O'Connor
14 October
An Gaill
(The Hostage)
(First Abbey Production)
Brendan Behan

1969
3 February
The Countess Cathleen
W. B. Yeats
The Second Kiss
(First Abbey Production)
Austin Clarke
1 May
An Deisceart Domhain
Diarmuid Ó Súilleabháin
26 May
The O'Neill
Thomas Kilroy
11 July
Soldier
Liam Lynch
4 August
Aaron thy Brother
Conor Farrington
22 September
Is Glas iad na Cnuic
(the Far-Off Hills)
Lennox Robinson
6 October
The Weaver's Grave

Séamus O'Kelly/
Micheál Ó hAodha
Meadowsweet
Séamus O'Kelly
1 December
Let the Ravens Feed
Joe O'Donnell

1970
5 January
The Becauseway
Wesley Burrowes
12 February
At Swim two Birds
Flann O'Brien/
Audrey Welsh
29 April
The Far-off Hills
Lennox Robinson
27 May
Grogan and the Ferret
George Shiels
27 June
The Director
Sydney Cheatle
Retreat
Sydney Cheatle
18 July
The Lover
Harold Pinter
The Dumb Waiter
Harold Pinter
25 August
The Rising of the Moon
Lady Gregory
Purgatory
W. B. Yeats
In the Train
Frank O'Connor/
H. Hunt
Krapp's Last Tape
Samuel Beckett
16 September
A State of Chassis
John D. Stewart and
Tomás Mac Anna
21 October
Tá Crut nua ar na Sléibhte

(The Mountains Look Different)
(First Abbey Production)
Micheál Mac Liammóir-
Liam Ó Briain
2 December
*The Plebians Rehearse the
    Uprising*
Gunter Grass and
Ralph Manheim

1971
1 January
*Dragan
Seán Ó Briain
and Tomás Mac Anna
4 January
The Serpent Prince
Lyn Ford
22 February
*The Dáil Debate
G. P. Gallivan
22 March
*Pocléim
Liam Mac Uistin
30 March
Deirdre of the Sorrows
J. M. Synge
20 May
The Land of Heart's Desire
W. B. Yeats
The Player Queen
W. B. Yeats
24 May
*The Rose in the Fisted Glove
Tom Tessier
22 June
The Hall of Healing
Sean O'Casey
The Shadow of a Gunman
Sean O'Casey
6 September
Ulysses in Nighttown
James Joyce/
Marjorie Barkentin
5 October
Fairy Tales of New York
J. P. Donleavy
Fando and Lis

Fernando Arrabal
15 December
The Blue Demon
Lyn Ford

1972
6 January
Scéal Scéalaí
Eamon Kelly and
Tomás Mac Anna
11 February
Easter
August Strindberg
14 March
*Richard's Cork Leg
Brendan Behan
2 May
*Hatchet
Henno Magee
24 May
*Splinters from a glass
Edward Rowe
Bedtime Story
Sean O'Casey
The End of the Beginning
Sean O'Casey
12 July
An Evening in
Paul Shephard
8 August
*Eye Winker Tom Tinker
Tom MacIntyre
21 August
Pull Down a Horseman
(First Abbey Production)
Eugene McCabe
18 September
**They Feed Christians to Lions
    here, don't they?*
Frank Harvey
25 September
*Fleadh
Pádraig Ó Giollagáin
8 November
Picnic on the Battlefield
Fernando Arrabal
6 December
Old Times

Harold Pinter
19 December
The Golden Apple
Lady Gregory

1973
1 January
Scéal Scéalaí Eile
Tomás Mac Anna and
Eamon Kelly
21 February
Exiles
James Joyce
The Briery Gap
T. C. Murray
26 February
The Doll in the Gap
Helen Cahill
19 March
Death Watch
Jean Genet
Rites
Maureen Duffy
2 April
King Herod advises
Conor Cruise O'Brien
9 April
Happy Days
Samuel Beckett
27 April
Johnny Orfeo
Pádraig Ó Giollagáin
24 May
Dear Edward
Tomás Mac Anna
18 June
Red Biddy
Henno Magee
30 July
In the Shadow of the Glen
J. M. Synge
Coats
Lady Gregory
22 August
The Night of the Rouser
Sean Walsh
18 September
Purgatory

W. B. Yeats
The Herne's Egg
(First Abbey Production)
W. B. Yeats
1 October
Escurial
Michel De Ghelderode
22 October
Mise Raifteirí an File
Criostóir Ó Floinn
22 November
Laom Luisne Fomhair
(Autumn Fire)
T. C. Murray
Ar Leitheidi
Pádraig Ó Maoleoin
19 December
The Golden Horseman
Patrick Duggan

1974
14 January
Seo Scéalaí Eile
Eamon Kelly and
Tomás Mac Anna
13 February
One is One and All Alone
Henry Comerford
27 February
*The Man with the Flower in his
    Mouth*
Luigi Pirandello
1 May
Them
Edward Manet
4 March
The Glass Menagerie
Tennessee Williams
20 March
The Illumination of Mr Shannon
Don Howarth
29 March
*The Architect and the Emperor
    of Assyria*
Fernando Arrabal
3 April
The Food of Love
Peadar MacGiolla Cearr

15 April
Home
David Storey
1 May
The Missing Link
John Antrobus
13 May
*Sarah
James Ballantyne
20 May
*The Truth in the News
Wesley Burrowes
8 August
*Struensee
John McKendrick
5 September
*The Happy-go-likeable Man
(Les Fourberiès de Scapin)
Molière/
Jim Sheridan
25 September
Motherlove
August Strindberg
16 October
*Earwig
Sean Walsh
16 December
Witche's Brew
Lyn Ford

1975
An Béal Bocht
Myles na gCopaleen/
Seán Ó Briain
10 March
Twelfth Night
William Shakespeare
16 April
The Two Executioners
Fernando Arrabal
18 April
A Doll's House
Henrik Ibsen
25 June
*In my Father's Time
Eamon Kelly
18 August
*Figuro in the Night

Sean O'Casey
The Moon Shines on Kylenamoe
(First Abbey Production)
Sean O'Casey
8 October
*Rhyming Couplets
Kevin Grattan
9 October
Dreaming (or am I?)
Luigi Pirandello
The Old Tune
Robert Pinget
Architruc
Robert Pinget
20 October
*A Short Walk to the Sea
Desmond Egan
24 November
*A Cry for Help
Ernest Gebler

1976
1 January
*Mise le Meas
Revue
12 January
And They used to Star in Movies
Campbell Black
29 January
*Mothers
May Cluskey
(one-woman show)
9 February
The Birthday Party
Harold Pinter
24 March
Much ado about Nothing
William Shakespeare
5 April
*The Whipping
Seán Walsh
10 May
Hedda Gabler
Henrik Ibsen
17 June
*'Bless me Father . . .'
Eamon Kelly
28 July

Friends
Kevin O'Connor
5 August
The Pie Dish
George Fitzmaurice
The Enchanted Land
George Fitzmaurice
10 August
Jack be Nimble
Tom MacIntyre
31 August
Our Town
Thornton Wilder
7 October
The Hard Life
Flann O'Brien/
Pat Layde
15 November
All You Need is Love
John Lynch
9 December
End of Term
Maeve Binchy
Sanctified Distances
Desmond Hogan

1977
3 January
Manus and the Mighty Dragon
Gregory/
Sean Walsh
18 February
Little Murders
Jules Feiffer
29 March
Measure for Measure
William Shakespeare
9 May
Find the Lady
Tom McIntyre
27 July
Mrs Warren's Profession
G. Bernard Shaw
25 August
Catchpenny Twist
Stewart Parker
21 September
The Actress and the Bishop

Stewart Parker
4 October
Aisling mhic Artain
Eoghan Ó Tuairisc
13 October
Talbot's Box
Thomas Kilroy
21 December
*Conn and the Conquerors of
   Space*
Bill Morrison
26 December
Oisin
Eoghan Ó Tuairisc

1978
30 January
The Rub of the Relic
Eamon Kelly
12 March
The Misanthrope
Molière-Harrison
15 March
An Gabha go Raibh
Pádraig Ó Giollagáin
17 April
Ivanov
Anton Chekhov
19 April
Hisself
Pat Ingoldsby
25 April
Act without Words
Samuel Beckett
Come and Go
Samuel Beckett
That Time
Samuel Beckett
19 May
Faustus Kelly
Myles na gCopaleen
19 June
Patrick Gulliver
Eamonn Morrisey
2 October
Diarmuid agus Ghráinne
Micheál MacLiammóir

11 October   *At the Hawk's Well*
Catappletits   W. B. Yeats
Pascal Petit   *The only Jealousy of Emer*
17 October   W. B. Yeats
When am I getting me Clothes?   25 December
Pat Ingoldsby   *Rhymin' Simon*
30 November   Pat Ingoldsby

Notes

PROLOGUE (pp. 1-17)

1 George Bernard Shaw, Preface to *John Bull's Other Island*, London 1907, 15—16.
2 Sean O'Casey, *The Plough and the Stars*, Act One.
3 'Literature in Modern Ireland' in *Conor Cruise O'Brien Introduces Ireland*, ed. Owen Dudley Edwards, London 1969, 137.
4 Shaw, *John Bull's Other Island*, Act One.
5 Joseph Holloway, *Impressions of a Dublin Playgoer*, National Library of Ireland (N.L.I.), MS. 1803.
6 Gabriel Fallon, *The Abbey and the Actor*, Dublin 1969, 34.
7 For a fuller account of Yeats's relation to the Symbolists see James W. Flannery, *W. B. Yeats and the Idea of a Theatre*, Toronto 1976, 101—27.
8 *Beltaine*, May 1899, 6. The name of this occasional magazine was chosen to reflect the timing of the Literary Theatre's seasons; 'Beltaine' being an ancient Irish spring festival. Three numbers were published between May 1899 and April 1900. This publication was succeeded by *Samhain*, this being the name of an Autumn festival. Seven numbers of *Samhain* appeared between October 1901 and November 1908. Both magazines were edited by Yeats.
9 Quoted by T. F. O'Sullivan in *The Young Irelanders*, Tralee 1944, 32—3.
10 AE (George Russell), 'The Dramatic Treatment of Legend' in *Imaginations and Reveries*, London 1915, 22.

11 Yeats, 'The Man and the Echo', *Collected Poems,* London, 1961, 393.

12 Peter Costello, *The Heart Grown Brutal,* Dublin 1977, 90.

13 John Synge, I and Augusta Gregory, thought
    All that we did, all that we said and sang
    Must come fróm contact with the soil, from that
    Contact everything Anteus-like grew strong.
    We three alone in modern times had brought
    Every thing down to that sole test again,
    Dream of the noble and the beggar-man.
    W. B. Yeats, 'The Municipal Gallery Revisited' in *Collected Poems,* 368.

14 Padraig Pearse, *Collected Works: Political Writings and Speeches,* Dublin 1934, 38.

15 W. B. Yeats, 'The Statues' in *Collected Poems,* 375.

16 W. B. Yeats, *Autobiographies,* London 1955, 396.

17 Miss Horniman to National Players Society, 2 December 1908, N.L.I., MS. 10, 1952.

18 *Beltaine,* February 1900, 4.

19 Máire Nic Shiubhlaigh (Mary Walker) was the first Irish player to use the Irish form of her name for stage purposes.

CHAPTER 1 (pp. 18—31)

1 In compiling this chapter and chapters 2 and 3 I am indebted to Robert Hogan and James Kilroy's valuable publications, *The Irish Literary Theatre 1899—1901,* Dublin 1975, *Laying the Foundations,* Dublin 1976, and *The Abbey Theatre: The Years of Synge 1905—1909,* Dublin 1978.

2 Quoted in Lady Gregory, *Our Irish Theatre,* London 1913, 20.

3 Ibid, 20.

4 *Beltaine,* May 1899, 7.

5 W. B. Yeats in *Samhain,* October 1901, 3.

6 W. B. Yeats, 'The Theatre' in *Beltaine,* May 1899, 20—21.

7 Elizabeth Coxhead, *Lady Gregory,* London 1961, 44.

8 Denis Gwynn, *Edward Martyn and the Irish Revival,* London 1930, 15.

9 George Moore, *Hail and Farewell,* London 3 vols. *Ave* 1911, *Salve* 1912, *Vale* 1913.

10 Quoted in Gwynn, 142.

11 *The Letters of W. B. Yeats,* ed. Allan Wade, London 1954, 211.

12 Coxhead, *Lady Gregory,* 18.

13 Moore, *Ave,* Ebury edition, London 1937, 29—33.

14 Ibid, 52—9, 68—70.

15 Margaret Webster, *The Same Only Different, Five Generations of a Great Theatre Family,* London 1969, 205—6.

16 Ibid.

17 W. B. Yeats, 'The Countess Cathleen' in *Collected Plays,* London 1934, 50.

18 *Beltaine,* February 1900, 5.

19 *Ave,* 127.

20 *Our Irish Theatre,* 29.

21 *United Irishman,* 26 October 1901.

22 Quoted in J. C. Trewin, *Benson and the Bensonians,* London 1960, 129.

23 Joseph Holloway, *Impressions of a Dublin Playgoer,* ed. Robert Hogan and Michael J. O'Neill, Illinois 1967, 13.

CHAPTER 2 (pp. 32—56)

1 *United Irishman,* 4 May 1901.

2 W. G. Fay and C. Carswell, *The Fays of the Abbey Theatre,* London 1935, 114.

3 Frank Fay to Yeats, dated 21 February 1903, N.L.I., MS. 13068.

4 Holloway, *Impressions,* ed. Hogan/O'Neill, 16.

5 Frank Fay to Yeats, dated 15 December 1902, N.L.I., MS. 13068.

6 Máire Nic Shiubhlaigh and Edward Kenny, *The Splendid Years,* Dublin 1955, 17.

7 *Letters from AE,* ed. A. Denson, London 1961.

8 Gerard Fay, *The Abbey Theatre, Cradle of Genius,* Dublin 1958, 44.

9 N.L.I., MS. 13068.

10 Frank Fay to Yeats, dated 26 September 1902, quoted in Lennox Robinson, *Ireland's Abbey Theatre,* London 1951, 28—9.

11 Gerard Fay, in *The Abbey Theatre, Cradle of Genius,* 48, erroneously states the first performance was given in the Camden Street Theatre in December 1902.

12 *The Fays of the Abbey Theatre,* 125.

13 Holloway, *Impressions,* ed. Hogan/O'Neill, 20.

14 Rules of the Irish National Theatre Society, N.L.I., MS. 13068 (1).

15 Rule 6 was modified in June 1905 when power to reject plays was given to The Reading Committee which at that time consisted of Yeats, Russell, Pádraic Colum, Synge and the two Fays. Acceptance of plays, however, still rested in the hands of the members themselves.

16 The title 'producer' was substituted for 'stage manager' in 1910 when, for the first time, credit was given to the production in the Abbey programmes. Today the person responsible for the production is known as the 'director'. I have used this title, or that of 'play director' throughout without a capital letter to distinguish it from 'Director', being a member of the Board of Directors of the theatre.

17 Holloway, *Impressions,* ed. Hogan/O'Neill, 23.

18 Katherine Worth, *The Irish Drama of Europe from Yeats to Beckett,* London 1978, 48.

19 Ibid, 59.

20 *Samhain,* October 1903, 9-10.

21 John Masefield, John M. Synge: *A Few Personal Recollections,* Letchworth 1916, 14.

22 Seán Ó Tuama, 'Synge and the Idea of a National Literature' in *J. M. Synge Centenary Papers,* ed. Maurice Harmon, Dublin 1971, 9.

23 *The Splendid Years,* 42—3.

24 Micheál Ó hAodha, *Theatre in Ireland,* Oxford 1974, 38—9.

25 Miss Horniman also financed, designed and made the costumes for *The Shadowy Waters* and *On Baile's Strand.*

26 Lennox Robinson, 'The Man and the Dramatist' in *Scattering Bromelies, Tributes to the Memory of W. B. Yeats,* ed. Stephen Gwynn, London 1940, 76.

27 Quoted in Gerard Fay, 42—3.

28 *The Fays of the Abbey Theatre,* 132.

29 In addition to *The Saxon Shillin'* withdrawn during rehearsal.

CHAPTER 3 (pp. 57—83)

1 Miss Horniman to Yeats, letter quoted in *Ireland's Abbey Theatre*, 44—5.
2 Ibid, 44—5.
3 *Samhain,* December 1904, 53.
4 Miss Horniman to Yeats, quoted in Gerard Fay, 109.
5 *The Splendid Years,* 58.
6 Gerard Fay, 92.
7 *Impressions,* ed. Hogan/O'Neill, 53.
8 Quoted in Gerard Fay, 94.
9 *Impressions,* ed. Hogan/O'Neill, 54.
10 *Impressions,* N.L.I., MS. 1803, 570—1.
11 *The Letters of W. B. Yeats,* 461.
12 *The Splendid Years,* 72.
13 Miss Horniman to Synge, letter dated 7 January 1906, N.L.I microfilm 5381.
14 *Ireland's Abbey Theatre,* 66.
15 *Impressions,* ed. Hogan/O'Neill, 74—5.
16 *The Fays of the Abbey Theatre,* 208.
17 Miss Horniman to Yeats, letter dated 11 February 1907, N.L.I., MS. 13068.
18 *The Fays of the Abbey Theatre,* 211.
19 Ibid, 211—13.
20 Mary Colum, *Life and the Dream,* Dublin 1966, 119.
21 Pádraic Colum, *The Road Round Ireland,* New York 1926, 368.
22 *The Splendid Years,* 81.
23 *Under the Receding Wave,* 107—8.
24 *Impressions,* ed. Hogan/O'Neill, 129.
25 Boyle to Yeats, letter dated 31 January 1907, quoted in above, 87.
26 Mary Colum, 'Memories of Yeats' in *The Saturday Review of Literature,* XIX, 25 February 1939, 4.
27 *Impressions,* ed. Hogan/O'Neill, 95.
28 *Letters of W. B. Yeats,* 495—6.
29 *Impressions,* ed. Hogan/O'Neill, 107.
30 *The Plays of George Fitzmaurice,* 3 vols. Dublin 1967, 1969, 1970.
31 *Impressions,* ed. Hogan/O'Neill, 96.

32 N.L.I., MS. 10, 952.

33 W. G. Fay to Yeats, letter dated 17 December 1908, N.L.I., MS. 13068.

34 Yeats to Synge, letter dated 18 December 1908, N.L.I., microfilm 5380.

35 N.L.I., MS. 10, 952.

36 W. G. Fay to Yeats, letter dated 13 January 1909, N.L.I., MS. 1731.

37 *Samhain* No. 7, November 1908, 3.

38 *Impressions*, ed. Hogan/O'Neill, 98.

39 Gerard Fay, 137.

CHAPTER 4 (pp. 84—102)

1 Synge, 'Deirdre of the Sorrows' in *Collected Plays*, London 1910, 343—4.

2 Lennox Robinson, *Curtain Up*, London 1942, 18—19.

3 *Our Irish Theatre*, 96.

4 Robinson to Yeats, letter quoted in *Ireland's Abbey Theatre*, 86.

5 *Impressions*, ed. Hogan/O'Neill, 144.

6 *Ireland's Abbey Theatre*, 95—6.

7 *Our Irish Theatre*, 102.

8 Ibid, 112.

9 Ibid, 118.

10 Ibid, 120.

11 Arthur and Barbara Gelb, *O'Neill*, New York 1962, 172.

12 *The Letters of W. B. Yeats*, 587.

13 *Impressions*, ed. Hogan/O'Neill, 154.

CHAPTER 5 (pp. 103—18)

1 Gogarty's claim to the sole authorship of *Blight*, previously attributed to himself and Joseph O'Connor, has now been established. See Michael Hewson, 'Gogarty's Authorship in *Blight*', in *Irish Book* I, 1959, 19—20.

2 W. B. Yeats, *Essays*, London 1924.

3 Yeats to Mr Bailey (solicitor), letter dated 20 July 1915, N.L.I., MS. 13068.

4 *Impressions*, ed. Hogan/O'Neill, 199—200.

5 Lady Gregory, *Journals,* ed. Lennox Robinson, London 1946, 54—5.
6 *Impressions,* ed. Hogan/O'Neill, 203.
7 Quoted in Joseph Hone, *W. B. Yeats,* New York 1943, 320.
8 *Journals,* 55.
9 Michael J. O'Neill, *Lennox Robinson,* New York 1964, 55.
10 Quoted in Lennox Robinson, *Curtain Up,* London 1942, 119—20.
11 Radio Eireann interview, Abbey archives, undated.
12 The play was presented during the Abbey's closed season by an independent group of players.
13 *The Abbey and the Actor,* 36.

CHAPTER 6 (pp. 119—44)

1 Sean McCann, 'Introduction' in *The World of Sean O'Casey,* ed. Sean McCann, 9.
2 Quoted in David Krause, *Sean O'Casey and His World,* London 1976, 45.
3 *Curtain Up,* 13.
4 *Journals,* 73.
5 Quoted in Coxhead, *Lady Gregory,* 192.
6 *Journals,* 74—5.
7 *Impressions,* Hogan/O'Neill, 236.
8 During the Abbey's closure period, normally June to mid-July, players were free to accept outside engagements.
9 Gabriel Fallon, *Sean O'Casey, The Man I Knew,* London 1965, 29.
10 *Journals,* 87.
11 Ria Mooney, *The Days Before Yesterday,* an unpublished autobiography, 48.
12 *Impressions,* Hogan/O'Neill, 251.
13 *The Days Before Yesterday,* 51—2; Sean O'Casey, *Inishfallen Fare Thee Well,* London 1949, 175—7; *The Irish Times,* 12 February 1926; Shelah Richards, an unpublished autobiography; *Impressions,* ed. Hogan/O'Neill 254; *Sean O'Casey, The Man I Knew,* 92—3.
14 *Inishfallen Fare Thee Well,* 181.

15 *Journals,* 104.
16 Ibid, 106.
17 Sean O'Casey, *Rose and Crown,* London 1952, 34.
18 Correspondence relating to the rejection of *The Silver Tassie* is published in *The Letters of Sean O'Casey, 1910—41,* ed. David Krause, London, 1975, 225—326.
19 Journals 106—11, 123—4.
20 Quoted in Micheál Ó hAodha, *The Abbey Theatre — Then and Now,* Dublin 1969, 61.
21 W. B. Yeats, 'A People's Theatre, A Letter to Lady Gregory' in *The Irish Statesman,* 29 November and 6 December 191.
22 *Journals,* 70.
23 In *Ireland's Abbey Theatre,* 149, Lennox Robinson states: 'I had become a Director in 1923'. The minutes of the Board of Directors, however, record that his appointment dated from 15 April 1924. In the same year he succeeded St. John Ervine as dramatic critic of *The Observer* but continued to be resident in Ireland. M. J. Dolan succeeded him as manager and director of plays until the end of his newspaper assignment in August 1925.
24 *Journals,* 81—2.
25 Ibid, 90—1.
26 *Inishfallen Fare Thee Well,* 270.
27 Liam Miller, *The Noble Drama of W. B. Yeats,* Dublin 1977, 231.
28 *Joseph Holloway's Irish Theatre,* Vol. 1, 1926—1931, ed. Robert Hogan and Michael J. O'Neill, California 1968, 51.
29 Ibid, 78.
30 Flannery, *W. B. Yeats and the Idea of a Theatre,* 366—77.
31 W. B. Yeats, *Essays and Introductions,* London 1911, 165—6.
32 *Journals,* 117.
33 W. B. Yeats, 'Coole Park' in *Collected Poems,* 274—5.

CHAPTER 7 (pp. 145—75)

1 From a letter written by Yeats to an English friend, quoted in Hone, *W. B. Yeats,* 426.
2 *Holloway's Irish Theatre,* Vol. 2, 19 and Vol. 3, 14.

3 *Irish Times,* 28 August 1935.
4 Ibid.
5 Ibid.
6 Frank O'Connor, *My Father's Son,* London 1968, 145—99.
7 *Holloway's Irish Theatre,* Vol. 2, 1932—7, 52.
8 Ibid. O'Connor was mistaken in stating that 'after Mac Liammoir left, (so) Hunt took on the part himself'. This was in fact suggested but turned down by the Board.
9 *Holloway's Irish Theatre,* Vol. 2, 1932—7, 52.
10 T. C. Murray also contributed a two-act play, *Illumination* (31 July 1939).
11 W. B. Yeats, 'Under Ben Bulben', *Collected Poems,* 397.
12 His appointment dated from 1 September 1938.
13 *My Father's Son,* 197.
14 *Ireland Since the Famine,* 557—8.
15 Anonymous (Ernest Blythe), 'Ruthless Warfare' in An tOglach, quoted in P. Béaslaí, *Michael Collins and the Making of a New Ireland,* London 1926, 211—12.
16 *Holloway's Irish Theatre,* Vol. 3, 1938—44, 89.
17 Quoted in *The Story of the Abbey Theatre,* Ed. Sean McCann, London 1967, 156.
18 *The Days Before Yesterday,* 171—2.

CHAPTER 8 (pp. 176—93)

1 Interview with Sean O'Casey in the *Irish Times,* 30 June 1964.
2 O'Casey had already sold the amateur rights of his plays to Samuel French and Company.
3 Tomás Mac Anna, 'New Abbeys for Old' in the *Irish Times,* 4 September 1969.
4 Mrs Lennox Robinson (Dorothy Travers Smith) was for a time a designer of Abbey productions. She died in 1978.
5 Peter Daubeny, *My World of Theatre,* London 1971, 287—8.
6 Interviews and statements in the *Irish Press, Evening Herald, Irish Times* and other papers, dated 30 June, 1 July, 3 July, 5 July 1964.
7 The following were appointed as shareholders in accordance with the Articles of Association of the National

Theatre Society Limited as amended in 1966: Shelah Richards, Mairéad Ni Ghráda, Christine Countess of Longford, Ria Mooney, Mary O'Malley, Tarlach Ó Raifeartaigh, Liam Ó Bríain, Maurice McGonigal, Micheál Mac Liammóir, Bryan MacMahon, Brian Friel, Cyril Cusack, Seán Ó Tuama, Cearbhall Ó Dálaigh, Micheál Ó hAodha, Arland Usher, Tomás Luibhéad, Jeremiah Murphy, Richard J. Hayes, Theodore W. Moody, Charles McCarthy, David Thornley, Denis Donoghue, Louis Marcus, Denis O'Dea.

CHAPTER 9 (pp. 194—208)

1 *Irish Times,* 28 July 1969.
2 Roibeárd Ó Faracháin in Abbey commemorative programme, 18 July 1966.

CHAPTER 10 (pp. 209—46)

1 *The Táin,* trs. Thomas Kinsella, Dublin 1969, 45.
2 Sean O'Casey, 'Song of the Stretcher Bearers' in *The Silver Tassie,* Act Two.
3 The Irish Theatre Company was founded in 1972 with the support of the Minister for Finance, Charles Haughey. The company is based in Dublin but owns no theatre of its own. Its primary task is to tour its plays in Ireland, though short seasons of plays are presented from time to time in Dublin theatres.
4 The capacity value of the Abbey auditorium in 1973—74 was £533; by 1978 price increases for seats had raised this total to £1,214.
5 The new green-room, located in adjacent premises (5—6 Old Abbey Street) was formally opened by Cyril Cusack in September 1977. The new box-office was opened in 1978.
6 The grant-in-aid rose from £240,000 in 1974—75 to £355,000 in 1975—6, of which £35,000 was earmarked for reduction of the theatre's overdraft. For the year 1978—79 the grant-in-aid rose to £470,000 with an addi-

tional guarantee to cover wage increases estimated at £30,000.

7 In December 1978 there were 40 players on the Abbey strength, of whom 18 were on permanent contract and the remainder on contracts varying between one and three years.

8 Other dramatic schools are the Brendan Smith Academy and the Irish Institute of Drama and the Allied Arts. The latter, founded in 1978, offers courses in Dublin as well as weekend workshops in regional centres.

9 Hugh Hunt, 'The Abbey — A Policy?' in *Hibernia*, 15 May 1970, 20.

10 Denis Johnston, 'Policy in Theatre' in *Hibernia*, 29 May 1970, 16.

11 Members of the Board are elected by the shareholders and required to retire after three years service. They can, however, submit themselves for re-election. Since the Board itself holds the majority of the shares, it can in fact re-elect its own members. However, in every fourth year the election of a retiring director is by show of hands.

12 Players representatives were at first co-opted for one year. Since March 1975 both Players Council, and later Staff Council, representatives have been co-opted for two years service.

Index

INDEX OF PLAYS

GENERAL INDEX

The Abbey Theatre is acknowledged a.
the world's outstanding dramatic centres,
having contributed a unique style of acting a.
many plays of permanent value to the theatrica.
canon.

The history of the Abbey is intimately
associated with Ireland's literary renaissance
and also with the political movement which
ultimately lead to independence. Indeed, the
history of Ireland from the early years of the
present century finds a total reflection in the
story of the Abbey.

The last authorised history of the theatre, by
Lennox Robinson, was published in 1951.
The present volume provides an up to date
history of the oldest State-subsidised theatre
in the English speaking world from its inception
as the Irish Literary Theatre in 1899. Hugh
Hunt traces the development of the theatre
from an amateur organisation to a highly
professional theatre of international reputation
and sets it against the social and political
background of Ireland itself together with the
many distinguished poets and playwrights,
directors and actors in its long and frequently
tempestuous history.

The book was undertaken at the invitation of
the Board of Directors of the Abbey to
coincide with the Diamond Jubilee of the
foundation of the theatre in 1904. The author
has been given privileged access to the minute
books and other classified documents in the
keeping of the theatre, as well as letters,
programmes and press cuttings housed in the
National Library of Ireland.

The book is illustrated, and contains a check
list of all new production in the Abbey and
Peacock theatres from 1904 to the present day.